Critical Analysis of Organizations

Theory, Practice, Revitalization

CATHERINE CASEY

SAGE Publications
London • Thousand Oaks • New Delhi

© Catherine Casey 2002

First published 2002

Apart from any fair dealing for the purposes of research or
private study, or criticism or review, as permitted under the
Copyright, Designs and Patents Act, 1988, this publication may be
reproduced, stored or transmitted in any form, or by any means,
only with the prior permission in writing of the publishers, or in
the case of reprographic reproduction, in accordance with the
terms of licences issued by the Copyright Licensing Agency.
Inquiries concerning reproduction outside those terms should be
sent to the publishers.

 SAGE Publications Ltd
6 Bonhill Street
London EC2A 4PU

SAGE Publications Inc
2455 Teller Road
Thousand Oaks, California 91320

SAGE Publications India Pvt Ltd
32, M-Block Market
Greater Kailash - I
New Delhi 110 048

British Library Cataloguing in Publication data

A catalogue record for this book is available from
the British Library

ISBN 0 7619 5905 X
ISBN 0 7619 5906 8 (pbk)

Library of Congress Control Number available

Typeset by SIVA Math Setters, Chennai, India
Printed and bound in Great Britain by Athenaeum Press, Gateshead

In Memoriam

Christopher Lasch

Vivit etiamnunc ingenii afflatus.

Contents

Acknowledgements

I extend my heartfelt thanks to Philip Wexler for his personal and intellectual inspiration and encouragement, and for his friendship. The book is greatly indebted to his critical and generous discussion of ideas over the years. I thank, with much love, Judy Robson for her support and understanding throughout the writing of this book, and much else.

My graduate students at the University of Auckland, especially Joe Beer and Tricia Alach, contributed much through their lively interest in discussing many of the ideas in this book. I thank them and others I haven't mentioned by name. To Margaret Tibbles, librarian *par excellence*, I extend many thanks for her careful reading of the draft manuscript, and to Chris Rojek my thanks for his quiet support of the project. My thanks to Brett Warburton, Nicola Gavey, Maeve Landman and Gill Denny, especially for their encouragement at timely moments.

I acknowledge my research grants from the University of Auckland which enabled the empirical part of this research, and I thank all the people who kindly shared their stories.

And I remember, with love, Christopher Lasch, critic of modernity, and my teacher at the University of Rochester.

Introduction

As the crisis in modernity deepens, a network of markets ascends in the place of modern society and institutions. Among the social fragments of a liberal marketization, two conflicting tendencies are clear – one of a heightened individualism of the rationally choosing consumer, and the other of a cultural current of identity and communalism. Both are antithetical to the idea of society. Now, in weakened confidence, after classical sociology, critical theory, and postmodernism, sociology turns, more than ever, to a profound reflexivity. Amid the myriad uncertainties, there is little question that the privileged place given to rationality in classical social theory is rescinded. It is also clear that social theorists are struggling with far more questions raised by their reflexivity, and by a fragmenting modernity, than they have answers for. The grand project of modernity is now thoroughly epistemologically undone, and its social practices found gravely lacking, even as it delivers a measure of what people want. Many theorists declare their ambivalence as though a final word on the matter. Some sociologists, it appears, now shy away altogether from theorizing society and seeking its revitalization. They avoid, too, many of the central problematics of modern sociology, including institutions and organizations. But organizations, as social relationships, are immensely affected by, and constituent of, these vast changes in modernity.

For many, the cultural turn to the postmodern takes centre stage in intellectual debate and analysis in the West. As social analysts discern patterns of technological, economic and political change manifesting a condition of late or postmodernity, many theorists welcome the disruption and affirmation of difference enabled by postmodern fracture and epistemological alternatives to modernist formalism and reified instrumental rationality. Postmodern theories in their various ways express our experience of the decomposition of the world. They have widened the negative space in which regenerative criticism might be sought. But their alternatives to rationalizing modernity ultimately deliver little more than quietism or fetishized identity pursuits. Indeed, postmodernism's inability to pose a regenerative imagination for transformation of social practices which continue to produce social, and personal, consequences of disparate value or irrefutable repugnance bespeaks its failure as critical theory.

Even as the earlier popular, celebratory embrace of the postmodern has passed, so too have the critical possibilities portended by postmodern theorizing quite typically found accommodation with long-standing powerful interests in the utilization of knowledge products. Now a preference for cultural theory shaped by prevalent notions of the postmodern as ironic, deconstructive and indeterminate displaces social theory. Social theory as critical, socially transformative practice is relegated – as though it is ineluctably culpable with the imperatives and outcomes of a monological rationalizing modernity – to a relative isolation.

Postmodern problematics have generated important questions and challenges to conventional sociological and organizational theories and modes of analysis, as well as a plethora of interpretations of contemporary organization practices. But a more serious concern with the limits of modern reason and the rationalized, economistic culture of commodity capitalism as the context of organizational practice scarcely appears in postmodern analyses of organizations. Moreover, sober and serious engagement with its implications and the moral and practical dilemmas to which postmodernism has given rise are systematically ignored by most advocates of postmodern ideas in organization studies. Indeed, these very notions are rejected by some postmodern analysts as modernist illusions which, in the words of one, 'the postmodern analyst refuses to take seriously' (Rouleau and Clegg 1992: 18).

Many invoke postmodernism as affirmation and legitimation of quite diverse new organizational practices. For the more pragmatic, postmodern ideas and approaches provide access to dimensions of organizational life not yet fully utilized by instrumentally rational approaches, and which are arearable to strategic managerial interventions. In the everyday world of organizations, it is difficult to discern signs of structural and political alteration, beyond expected neorationalist restructurings and realignments of dominant power relations in changing social conditions, inspired by postmodern organizational analyses. Discursive undecidability, as the abstract antidote to subjectification and governmentality, evidently has more appeal in the academy than it does among strategic rationalists in organizational practice who are quick to decide their preferences and to assert foundations where there are none.

Of course, many organizational analysts, especially economic and management science analysts, have disdainfully rejected or avoided postmodernism, as they did earlier forms of criticism. But conventional organizational analysis barely conceals its deepening inadequacy to the task of socially analysing organizational practices in manifestly altering postindustrial conditions. A heightened focus on micro, fragmented and socially abstracted issues of organization and economy, typical of positivist and functionalist social science, is an impoverished, ideological response. The privileging of the most utilitarian forms of knowledge refuses reflection on the ends to which such knowledge is put. The perdurability of functionalism and its many derivatives, despite considerable empirical sociological evidence since the mid-20th century disconfirming its practical operation, now aligns with the moral eclipse effected by a dominant instrumental reason. Even though many critics endeavour to describe the limitations and immense risks posed in modern technical rationalities, the imperatives of instrumental rationality continue to feed an assumption of inexhaustible planetary resources fuelling economic production and growth in conventional terms. Consequently, much modern organizational analysis provides little answer to the postmodern theoretical disruption, other than more of the same grossly distorted and unreflective rationalizing modernity.

Critical analysis of society and of organizations in contemporary conditions confronts complex, multilayered problems and dynamics. Many social theorists feel isolated in their attempts to think about contemporary society. They feel caught between those who reject modernity, and those who are completely immersed in it. How might we move on from this weakened state ? Reflexivity, which has always been a great strength of sociological thought but which lately has aroused a stifling ambivalence and hesitancy, needs new inspiration. Looking around at the signs of action and struggle going on in the world inspires new consideration of both our conventional notions of modernity and our current forms of criticism. These myriad activities inspire a revitalized sociological imagination, as C. Wright Mills once famously advocated.

A principal task now confronting analysts of organization, and practitioners, is one that refuses a salvage and repair enterprise – a renovation and restoration of the same modern agenda and criticism. It refuses too, a routinized postmodern deconstruction which results only in observation, or denial, of the politically coercive response to extreme uncertainty and multiple contestation in neo-conservative restoration under the guise of liberal globalization. On the contrary, the task upon us is, out of painstaking reflexivity, one of recomposition and revitalization of sociological organizational analysis. It is one that requires the recognition of new signs of action – action which is endeavouring to generate a surpassing response to the intensified instrumentality of late modernity which reduces social, cultural and planetary life to market commodification.

This is, of course, a grand task and it is, necessarily, a collective task. Yet in cultural conditions in which collective social practices are viewed – at least in the academy – with deep scepticism in fear of a restoration of normative, totalizing political programmes or communalist fundamentalism, possibilities for transformative organizational and social change are scarcely imagined. The apparent divorce of social and cultural theory, and the often denigrating views of exponents of one group of theorists for the other, has exaggerated the demise of collective interests and practices in contemporary society. The denial or bracketing of questions of political economy and social structures by cultural theorists and activists interested in the politics of difference, identity and recognition ignores the everyday effects of social institutions in producing injustice, unfreedom, and destruction. The deep intrication of the social practices of organizations constructed for the purposes of production, distribution and consumption in these social outcomes is seldom addressed. Moreover, the uses (some would say abuses) of postmodern ideas and approaches in analyses of organizations has turned deconstruction and indeterminacy to ends probably unanticipated by their founding critical theorists. These applications silence criticism that is neither playful nor dispersed through abstraction and that insistently attends to the social processes and outcomes of production and organization.

Critical Analysis of Organizations – Theory, Practice, Revitalization offers a new critical approach to contemporary organizational analysis. It emerges first out of a long tradition of critical theory, especially that of the Frankfurt School. But in order to avoid the scholastic tendencies in Frankfurt School critical theory and excessive focus on intra-philosophical components, I restore both a historical and an empirical dimension to the critical social analysis I offer here. Critical theory's neglect in recent years of substantive social, and sociological, research has weakened its capacity to elaborate new critical social theory in contemporary social conditions. Rather than abstract philosophical conceptualizations, the grounding for a renewed and revitalized critical theory may be found in a new sociology – a sociology which focuses on existing and emerging social tendencies, contestations and struggles.

The new sociology I practise in this book follows the sociology of Alain Touraine (1988, 1995, 1996). It is a sociology in which the modern idea of the social – of society conceived as rationally organized around a central system of institutional and behavioural regulation – is abandoned. I take this view of the social into my conception of organization and analysis of organizational practices. A conception of *social movement* displaces classical notions of society and of organization. But this break does not accept a social dissolution portended by most non- or anti-modern social theories as the alternative. Working with an idea of the social conceived as an ensemble of conflictual relations between social forces – which are both determinant and non-determinant – departs from classical notions, but does not regard the contesting social forces as asystemic, multiple currents. Rather, the social forces making up the social ensemble comprise actions between people and institutions which contest cultural modes of life. This contest is, as Weber saw it, over the setting of the rules of social life – over the means by which societies and organizations constitute themselves. The various features of cultural life, which include linguistic, religious, aesthetic and identity styles, are, like struggles over accumulation, class relations and institutions of power, fundamental matters of historical contestation.

A critical sociology of social action crafts a new social analytic, one appropriate to our postindustrial social conditions. The critical analysis of organizations I develop in this book begins with an excavation of the historical discourses of sociology and organizational analysis through 20th century industrial modernity. The classical antecedents and the industrial institutions of formal organizational analysis still cast the prevailing light on the contemporary terrain of organizational analysis. In this light, new forms of organizational analysis and new tendencies in social practice are often occluded. Similarly, a reflexive assessment of the postmodern turn in organization studies leads to a focus on new forms of critical organizational analysis emergent among people working in organizations. In hyper-industrial society, large organizations assert their dominance over nearly all aspects of social life. Their practices have immense social consequences, not least in their shaping of the working lives of most people in the West. Seeking among these hyper-industrial organizational practices signs of counter-practice or alternative actions reveals signs of postindustrial actors contesting the cultural stakes and raising new demands. The latter chapters of the book explore some of the ways in which these counter-practices are emerging and the ways in which new demands are articulated.

Against expert knowledge, new forms of critical organizational analysis, drawing in many cases on what are popularly called 'New Age' alternatives to modern social and cultural values, are being expressed among organizational employees. The active invocation of counter-modern rationalities and explorations of religious and spiritual interests among organizational employees in their workplaces requires serious analytic attention. These practices, which may at first glance be dismissed as postmodern idiosyncrasies and romantic flirtations, are exerting an influence in contemporary organizational life that may signify social action in a wider contest over the prevailing modes of life. They are, perhaps, signs of a breaking, as Foucault advocated, with 'the old categories of the negative' and a seeking of emancipation from congealed instrumental tyrannies in relentless production and consumption fuelled by myths of lack and need – at least in conventional forms. New Age seekers at work in organizations may indicate a generative social movement beyond a weariness with monological capitalist society and remnant asceticism.

Yet most of our current theoretical disputations and diversions, and the inadequate sociological formation of many current organizational analysts, render these events either unimportant and passing mystifications, or simply inaccessible to the prevailing impoverished condition of organizational analysis. Over recent decades a number of analysts have called for more historical and contextual awareness among theorists and practitioners in organization studies (e.g. Hassard 1993, Mouzelis 1965, Reed 1985, 1992). There has been much criticism of the myopic empiricism of organizational analysis since the mid-20th century and the succumbing of critical and social scientific inquiry of organizations to a dominant, ideological, managerialist agenda. The sociology of organizations has given way to applied, practitioner-useful, organization studies with scant interest in, or awareness of, the social world in which organizations practise, let alone the reflexive imperatives of sociology. This book offers some redress.

Chapter 1 traverses the current field of organization analysis and outlines a critique of modernity underlying the themes of this book. It considers the possibilities and requisites of a renewed sociological analysis of organizations. Chapter 2 explores the modern heritage of philosophy and sociology from which classical theories of organization and bureaucracy, discussed in Chapter 3, have arisen. The high modern search for a general theory of organizations and the expansion of organization science in the mid-20th century development of the field are examined. Chapter 4 discusses critical counter-movements to the consequences of a scientific organization sociology and to an expanding managerial orientation in organizational analysis. The turn of postmodernism, after the apparent failure of modern criticism, and the rise of new theoretical approaches to organizational analysis are discussed in Chapter 5.

A return to practice is explored in Chapter 6. In this chapter empirical research among organizational employees presents new expressions of subjective interests at work in organizations. Among these 'New Age' explorations and counter-modern rationalities practised at work, the chapter traces the 'return of the subject-actor' Touraine (1988, 1995), and its struggle for creative cultural and social action. Chapter 7 analyses and interprets these developments and reflects on possibilities for organizational and social revitalization.

1   Organizational Analysis Now

The analysis of production has been dominated by the idea of rationalization. Modern organizational analysis assumes that organizations, as sets of general principles operating in systems, are manifest agents of societal modernization. Critical views of organizations which emanated initially from workers' movements implicitly protested against this view, seeing production organizations as sites of capitalist social relations and of class struggle – and not as inevitable, irrefutable, agents of a universal modernization. But these views were themselves rationalized – as much by intellectuals aligned with leftist political struggles as by the spread of management science notions in the workplace. Critical organizational analysts by and large came to share the view of modern industrialists, intellectuals and management scientists that rationalization characterized modernization. Most accepted a view that only reasoned disputation over its methods and distribution of material goods, rather than over substantive sociocultural ends, was possible. Rationalizing modernity, therefore, defines the context in which our discussion of organizational analysis is set.

The antecedents and the unfolding of the story of modern organizational analysis – a story which remains powerfully in effect today – are discussed in the following chapters. In this chapter I wish to overview the present state of the field and sketch out the main contours of the debates that follow. Scrutiny of the present and excavation of the past are necessary tasks in reflecting on a modernity reduced to rationalization, and in the imagination of a different future after that modernity.

The Social Practices of Organization

The social and cultural practices of organization include the discourses of organization which are most typically found in disciplines of sociology, and in fields of management and organization studies which draw on behavioural psychologies, and economics of the firm. All of these modern discourses share the rationalization thesis of modernity, even if there are many other differences and divisions between them. Very often analysts favouring one set of disciplinary orientations seldom take notice of the contributions from the others. Sociology, which for many non-sociologists is too grand, unyielding to economic models, and disruptive of the contexts economists and psychologists assume as given, is reduced, when it can be, to empiricism and functionalism, or otherwise disqualified and rejected. Sociologists view their task as seeking to understand the relationships between social institutions and social historical action. Therefore, the ideas and practices of the institutions of economics and management come under the sociological gaze, as much as does the phenomenon of people gathering themselves into formal, purposeful organizations to produce things.

Conceiving organization, as Weber did, as social relationship is a long-standing, though not prominent, view among theorists of organization. Another sociological view of organizations, one in which organizations are more usefully described, as for Durkheim, as social systems – as entities in which people and production are organized – has attracted wide adherence and established considerable practical appeal among organization theorists throughout most of the 20th century. It is the source of an enduringly appealing organization science and of a functionalist approach to organizations which underpins, notwithstanding protestation, much organizational analysis today. For very many organization analysts a practical analytical concern assuming a systems framework and focused on solving functional systems and management problems prevails. Some analysts invoke elements of a Weberian social action approach, and others pursue a neo-rational, strategic management approach to analysing organizations. Yet among these various approaches, a shared commitment to a singularly privileged managerialist gaze is readily apparent. A socially critical interest in analysing organizations practised as societal relations is for many organization academics and practitioners beyond the business of organization studies.

The managerial view in organizational analysis has a long history, and many institutions of knowledge established in its service. It clearly accords with, and asserts as legitimate, an intensified economic and instrumental rationality characteristic of modernity – even as limits to that rationality and its always partial achievement present heightened risk, unmanageable complexity and contradiction. But this point of view, and the imperatives of rationalizing modernity, dominant as they are, compete, increasingly, with others.

Critical approaches to analysing and understanding organizations refuse the singular legitimacy of the managerial mainstream and its imbrication with instrumental rationality. Even as critical analysis largely displays the hallmarks of rationalization, many critics raise concerns with the limits of technological and instrumental rationality, and defend social and cultural aspirations of organizational practice which differ from those of positive, or conventional, organizational analysis. Critical approaches are more generally concerned with the sociocultural interests of humans working in, or affected by, organizational activities in societies and communities, and with the planetary environment. They are interested in organizations as social practices which reflect dominant agendas as well as cultural contests occurring in society. Some of these concerns are acknowledged, even strongly valued, by some analysts and practitioners aligned with the managerial mainstream. But ultimately involved in intensifying instrumental rationalities and efficiency in the search for the highest possible profit, these sociocultural ends are subordinated and contradicted. A utilitarian and fragmented knowledge displaces those sociocultural and moral concerns in everyday practice. Among managers and employees the compartmentalization and dissociation of values is more or less rationally accepted, and privately or organizationally managed.

Despite the differences among the two streams, a number of assumptions, analytical methods and interpretations are widely shared. The extensive influence of both a systems framework and a managerial dominance of the discourses has embedded a raft of assumptions. Many organization analysts, whether they align with a mainstream or a critical counter-stream, and whether they stem from sociological, psychological, economic or management science traditions, receive these assumptions as discursive givens now setting the terms of debate. Importantly, the spectre of system theories and functionalism, which shadows all forms of contemporary organizational analysis, continues to shape assumptions. Even among critical social approaches and neo-rational managerial approaches which reject modern systems notions, there is a mix of theoretical assumptions and analytical methods derived from an inadequate scrutiny of this immensely influential heritage. The hybridization and strategic utilization of competing assumptions is a primary source of dissent in the critical stream of organizational analysis, even as a managerial mainstream adeptly incorporates or expels, according to their utility, the knowledge products of critical discourse.

Throughout most of the 20th century, under rationalizing modern conditions of functional utility, an expanding academy favoured a professional division of labour and differentiation of subject matter and privileged forms of knowledge which focus on discrete problems and their treatment. The institutionalization of policy-useful social science marginalized socially and politically critical approaches to social problems. Of course, critical and competing perspectives continued, but as occurred in other social science fields, critical approaches to organizational analysis were abstracted from a dominant managerial mainstream of inquiry. Over the years critical approaches to the practices of organization, production and work more generally found expression in sociologies of work, industrial relations and some social psychologies, in which sociocultural questions were more often retained. But, notwithstanding the immense social presence and effects of formal organizations, societal levels of analysis and sociological interpretations of these social practices declined.

Organization studies as an academic field increasingly formed a managerial protectorate insulating itself from the interrogations of grand sociological inquiry, as well as from the sociocultural demands of a wider public. The effort characteristic of what we now call classical sociological and social theory toward more comprehensive analytical approaches to social practices and against ideological and functionalist tendencies to differentiate and to incorporate, decidedly lost favour. Organization theorists and analysts became, as in C. Wright Mills' (1959) view, 'servants of power'. If not entirely forgotten, grand sociological theory has become narrowly appropriated to legitimize particular notions in organization theory and to obscure ideological interests. For some contemporary organization theorists (e.g. Donaldson 1995) this is entirely as it should be; but still, organization theory's vulnerability to 'anti-management' theories of organization demands reform of academic institutions to shore up a beleaguered tradition.

But recent developments in modernity more generally, and in philosophy and cultural and social theory in the academy, have brought about an irrevocable decline in modernity's Promethean confidence in scientific and technical rationality, in progress, and in universal reasoned notions of social order and the good society. Among the waves of change are challenges to modern disciplinary differentiation and the relative stability of modern social science fields – including those of organization and management science. As stability gives way to greater fragmentation and diffusion, a plethora of interests and schools drawing unevenly from the sources of modern foundational disciplines now substitutes for former establishments of orthodoxy and legitimacy. Loosened from classical foundations, organization studies (like most of the social sciences) is now a highly contested arena, displaying the uncertainties, ambivalences and defences readily observable in modern social institutions more broadly.

At the same time many organizational analysts try to ignore the disruptive theoretical debates occurring more vigorously elsewhere in the academy. They continue to assert that the assumptions of business and management as applications of economic and technical rationality are unproblematically legitimate, and their rational goals achievable. But there are many cracks in that armour of assertions. Notwithstanding the prevalence in organization studies of an ideological managerialism pursuing particular sectoral interests at the expense of others, a disruption to modern knowledge practices, to classical notions of rationality, system, order and institutional legitimacy gains momentum. For many analysts, organization studies is in a state of unmanageable disarray and paradigm incommensurability. For some, the disarray, which simply presents in the diverse and conflicting advice organization analysts give to managers, is serious and chronic (e.g. Donaldson 1995, 1998, McKinley and Mone 1998, Scherer 1998). For others it is a creative condition encouraging new thinking about organizations in postindustrial conditions (e.g. Czarniawska 1998). For some analysts, paradigm incommensurability legitimizes an exclusive domain of task and value in which cross-domain criticism is invalidated. This view usefully defends an exclusive domain for managerial interests which, despite theoretical and methodological variations in approaches to those interests, excludes criticism from any other domain.

But a close look at the literature across the field of organization studies – which does show signs of an implicit recognition of the crisis in modernity, and plural solutions to the same practical problems – reveals a more effortful intent to recover and reinvigorate modern forms and legitimations of organizational practice and analysis. As well, there are some efforts to communicate across historically different orientations, from behavioural science to economic modelling of organizations. For most, discussions on paradigm incommensurability in the field rarely mean anything more than methodological differences in relation to implicitly agreed upon problems in the managerial mainstream. Even the range of cultural criticism which many claim indicates interests incommensurable with those of social analysis or management science and economic modelling of organizations finds publication in management journals. See, for example, the cultural theory intent in a 'post-humanist feminism' (Knights 2000, *Journal of Management Inquiry*) in which no traces of organizational or management analysis are found. While this is illustrative of much cultural criticism in organizational analysis which struggles to articulate its ends beyond a little reformism, it illustrates, too, the manner in which cultural criticism may be liberally, harmlessly published in management journals intent on eventual managerial utility. Alleged paradigm incommensurability poses no barrier to a liberal pluralist market ever ready to commodify new, potentially useful, critical knowledge. But on the other hand, despite the controversial ends to which cultural theory is put, the debate over paradigms indicates the contested terrain of organization and management studies. Divergent interests compete for attention and persuasion in a field which, in practice, is rife with uncertainty and always only tenuously monologically rational.

For critical analysts the terrain of organization studies is always a highly contested one. For critics, privileging sociocultural value ends of a substantive rationality (in Weber's term) over those of a reduced instrumental rationality does not indicate incommensurability. Conversely, it indicates demands intended to counter and surpass the absurd singular privileging of modern instrumental rationality. Some critics, however, have accepted defeat in the contest with apparently pervasive, intractable rationalization. They believe that incorporation by agents of modern rationalization is inevitable. The intensification of now hyper-capitalist management agendas in organizational practice and analysis forecloses debate with the managerial stream. This stream, now entirely unable to raise questions over the ends of technological and economic rationalization, manifests a normalization of culturally non-correspondent rationality. In order to protect a 'negative space' – in which oppositional criticism may be at least articulated (and alternative sociocultural agendas might be formulated) – paradigm closure is defensively asserted. For some critics, exhausted with the incorporation of critical theory into managerial paradigms, there is little expectation of critical, practical difference (e.g. Burrell 1997).

The crisis of modernity shows up more and more as purely instrumental rationality intensifies. Without sociocultural ends to this form of reason, social systems, including organizations, become only technical apparatuses. This condition of postmodernity ultimately weakens instrumental rationality and action, even as it first intensifies it. We see this in the rise of various counter-rational movements now raising new demands of the sociocultural sphere. Critical theorists, therefore, simultaneously pose a critique of rationalizing modernity with their critique of rationalizing managerial organizational analysis. They seek signs of critical action and demand setting which contest, and strive to alter and reconstitute, the dominant rule-setting agendas of modern institutions and actors.

A critical social analysis of organizations rejects arguments for paradigm incommensurability. Against the desocialization and depoliticization of most current organizational analysis and the prevailing normativity of the managerialist gaze, a revitalized critical analysis restores a vision of reflexive social thought. A wider, historical vision enables sources of knowledge recently excluded from organization studies (and other social sciences) to be reconsidered. These knowledge sources contribute anew to our efforts to understand the relationship between social institutions and social-historical action. Organization analysis at the present time pays scant attention to these tasks, and much contemporary sociology is weakened by the rise of views of society as an agent-less system of total domination, or conversely, as a non-social realm of strategic behavioural interactions abstracted from social system altogether. The sociological task of retrieval and revitalization is immense. Let us briefly review the main currents of ideas in organizational analysis at the present time.

Complex Organizations

Approaching the practices of organized relationships with the assumption that they are matters of fact of complex systems is a now classic modern view. The sociology of organizations, even more so than many other branches of sociology, established its primary and dominant categories from the largely North American successors of Weber and Durkheim. The mid-20th century theories, analytic frameworks and methods of Parsons and Merton and others (discussed more fully in Chapter 3) by and large instituted the normative practice of organizational sociology. A Marxist interest in institutions and organizations produced, in particular, substantive critiques of bureaucracy, state and corporate power, as well as criticism of the institutionalization of particular professional interests in academic practices. This school of thought developed both macro-social criticisms of the role of organizations in capitalist society, and explanations of the relations of capitalism through the labour process, and organization and employment practices on the shop floor. Economists, too, addressed the meso level of organizational practice and contributed, for instance, theories of institutional economics, transaction cost analysis and legal-rational constraints in organizational practice. This work continues in the 'new institutionalism' (e.g. Eggertsson 1990, Powell and DiMaggio 1991, Rowlinson 1997) and extensive empirical investigations and modelling theories are favoured and framed toward policy and problem-solving recommendations.

Within this diversity and comprehensiveness of interest in the practices of complex organizations in modern society, a mid-20th century organizational sociology cast a definitive influence over all subsequent developments in the field. Modern sociology of organizations, whether oriented toward managerialism or Marxist-influenced critique, implicitly took its operational definition of organization from Parsons (1960) as referring to 'social units devoted primarily to attainment of specific goals'. In this line of thought, organization stands, more or less, for 'complex bureaucratic organization'. While recognizing the rational characteristics that Weber identified, Parsonian structural-functionalism ultimately privileged organic systems features of organization, assuming an overall evolutionary rationalization. Weber's rational actors are seen as behaving within a greater societal complex of functional organization system processes.

Although structural functionalism has been well criticized in sociology generally, and in some organizational sociologies (as I discuss in Chapter 2), many of its categories, methods and imperatives toward order and stability remain more generally operative though unrecognized in organization studies than current cultural critics would admit. It comprises the substantive orientation of the academic tradition of 'organization theory' which, for some commentators, is an entirely separate field from sociology of organizations. Organization theory historically developed in schools of business and management studies in order to diminish the scientific abstraction and social and psychological criticism incumbent in more classical sociological approaches to social practices. Insistent on domain specificity and refusing meta-social and cultural criticism, organization theory seeks to enhance application to practical problems of organizational structure, design, efficiency and productivity. The traditions of organization theory variously retain functionalist views of complex system, structure, role, order and integration, while also emphasizing the role of management as decision-making actor, especially in regard to managing change and innovation.

Functionalist sociology of organizations described organizations, whether pursuing economic, administrative or social goals, as applications of instrumental rationality. Functional imperatives and rules could establish a correspondence, as Parsons and Merton elaborately argued, between organic system needs and individual and collective roles and behaviour – thus erecting a grand edifice of evolutionary rationalization. But in a disruption to that widely held view the work of theorists such as Herbert Simon, James March and Michel Crozier in the mid-20th century revealed, respectively, that any organization, far from exhibiting a central principle of rationality, which both functionalism and classical sociology assume, is really a fragile, unstable, weakly coherent ensemble of social relations. The organization is an ensemble of conflicts and adjustments between constantly challenging pressures and constraints. An efficient organization is not one in which stability and ordered functioning prevails, as functionalism holds, but one in which complexity, conflict, constant change and uncertainty are more or less managed or compromise reached. Simon's notion of 'bounded rationality', and Crozier's emphasis on power as the new central problem of organization analysis, launched a new emphasis on the management of uncertainty. These notions, which later became associated with 'contingency theory' in organization theory, emphasize the strategic movement between competing forces. No longer does an imagined central, unified and total governing rationality prevail, and no longer are worker-actors seen as cogs in a machine. The logic of domination unfolding through mechanisms of repression and exploitation which Marxist criticism of bureaucratic organizations emphasized is, or might be, thoroughly interrupted.

The idea of modernity as progressive rationalization is considerably challenged by these views. These views open up possibilities for organized relationships to be practised according to different value stakes and toward different ends. Organizations can now be seen as relationships produced and challenged by human actors in the relations of production. Yet, ironically, despite the considerable disruption to system theories and classical notions underpinning management theory posed by these theories, stronger views, whether those of Parsonian-influenced functionalism or Marxist-influenced structuralism, prevailed. Although functionalism has been theoretically surpassed, its normative appeal endures. More common now is a preference for a less troubling hybrid view in which functional systems are upheld as desirable and achievable, and managers play an agentic role in determining and maintaining the structures, roles and goals of organizations. Neo-rationalist theory in organization and management studies and practice emphasizes, above all, the notion of strategy. This approach endeavours to strategically integrate functionalist imperatives toward rational order and behaviour, and simultaneously manage innovation and change while being firmly directed toward the accomplishment of rational goals. Neo-rational strategic organization theory and management practice recognize that instability, uncertainty and disintegration threaten at any moment, but the rational, organizational, managerial actor must prevail.

Various strands of interest in organization and management theory, from socio-technical systems to so-called human resource management, serve these underlying imperatives. As a consequence, and necessity, of this viewpoint the only forms of organizational criticism that are admissible to the managerial gaze are those that amount to 'critical thinking' which enables managers and employees to strategically improve organization production methods and procedures for ends preferred by some and asserted by dominant others as unquestioned organizational imperatives and rationale. Criticism in this way of thinking refers, for instance, to calls for improved employee performance and involvement, for management attention to family life and flexible hours of work, for organizational cultures that promote belonging, identification and warm interpersonal relations in team and family-style work groups. A liberal reformist orientation in organizational studies, advocated widely as the best response to diverse organization expressions of disaffection and dissent, routinely appropriates and incorporates elements of theory produced by diverse critics including those claiming a radical or postmodernist cultural criticism. In this way a strategically rational, and neo-functional, academic division of labour facilitates the practical tasks of organizational management in changing environments of economy and culture.

For many critical analysts of organizations, the rise of strategic organizational management theory after the potentially transformative disruption to the classical sociological notion of a central principle of rationality regulating institutions and human action, and the disruption to functionalism, posed an even greater challenged than that of class domination and struggle. Strategic organizational theory is a flexible, liberal, incorporative response that weakens classical Marxist sociocultural criticism. It poses an ever more total system domination through strategic controls, *or* a dispersion of the forces of domination and exploitation. It becomes a decentred current of power maintaining a normalized governmentality over organizational participants and members of the public. Many of these critics had recourse in the turn to postmodernism.

Postmodernism in Organizational Analysis

Initially ideas from postmodern cultural theories were brought to organizational analysis by critical theorists exhausted with the apparent failure of modern criticism and oppositional social movements. The new wave of oppositional criticism, drawn significantly from philosophies of language and culture, undercut the modern project at its very foundations. It revealed the indeterminacy of language and the absence of metaphysical meaning obscured by the propositions of Enlightenment reason and science. Postmodern thinkers exposed the arbitrariness and particularity of truth claims and of technical rationalities privileged in modern social and production organizations. Yet while doing so, the postmodern cultural turn nonetheless largely retained the structuralist and poststructuralist view, via Foucault, that discursive systems exert a totalizing domination over human being and doing. Poststructuralism displaced a centralized, hegemonic source of power, but dispersed forms of power retain a totalitarian dynamic in normalization and governmentality. The idea of the human subject, which acts in pursuit of myriad goals and according to diverse imperatives within and against modern social and organizational systems, is dismissed as an illusion of modern humanism. Modern humanism, for Foucault, upheld a notion of subject selfhood in order to obscure the actual *subjectification* of the subject-self. Criticism of social and cultural practice, including organization, could offer only partial, particular, and for Foucault, always incorporated, opposition. Social structural changes toward the emancipatory goals of modernity are precluded by modernity's intractable, totalizing incursion of rationalization. These ideas encouraged a turn away from social system and structural analysis. Many postmodern theorists accepted a systemic dissolution of the subject, and posed an air of playfulness and ironic exuberance in linguistic indeterminacy in its place. The shift in focus to postmodern analyses of organizations emphasizes discursive practices of organization and their narrative theorization, as well as poststructural identity and expressivist movements (e.g. Clegg 1990, Rouleau and Clegg 1992, Cooper and Burrell 1988, Gergen 1992). Longstanding problematics of organizational analysis and of political economy are, for many postmodern organization analysts, relegated to disfavoured, though scarcely retreated, modernist organizational analysis – of both mainstream and critical inclinations.

Among the consequences of this turn is an apparent isolationism of some strands of organizational analysis. Many organizational analysts, especially those working in North America, pursue their work on the problematics of structure, systems, hierarchy, organizational forms and networks, technology, and macro-social relations of economy, capital and markets, with scant attention to the debates exciting their counterparts in organizational analysis circles elsewhere. (Evidence for these perduring foci is readily available. See, for example, recent issues of *Organization Science*, *Administrative Science Quarterly*, *Academy of Management Journal*, *Journal of Organization Change Management*). But there are also a number of efforts to bring postmodern notions and approaches to these core problematics of organizational analysis. To the chagrin of many organization scientists and neo-functionalists, as well as social theorists, postmodern approaches invoke poststructuralist literary and cultural theories, and neglect or deny social structures, in their analyses and interpretations of organizations. These narrative approaches privilege the discursivity of social life and in so doing render institutional and organizational structures as forms of narratives. Organizations are constituted by and produce discursive practices which are uncertainly alterable by alternative 'conversations'.

Postmodernist approaches have gained sufficient legitimacy to appear in teaching textbooks as well as in major conferences of organization and management academics. But in the majority of cases, the uses to which these approaches are put are, remarkably, not those of serious deconstruction, radical critique and new compositions, but those of strategic management and neo-rationalist organization analysis. Their application to standard organizational problems of cohesion, organizational environment, productivity, performance, strategy, leadership, power and personnel management, reveals intent and outcomes which are strikingly conventional. Economic success in the competitive marketplace is the end-game of postmodernism in organizational analysis. The postmodern turn in organization analysis has encouraged both a favouring of entrepreneurial models of organizing, for instance in the notion of self-organizing 'jazz bands' (a spontaneous organic system) and flexible, ad hoc teams as models of corporate organization, and a plethora of narrative analyses of sense-making, emotionality and cultural change in organization (e.g. Boje 1995, Czarniawska-Joerges 1996, Grant et al. 1998, Weick 1995). For many, these postmodern approaches now constitute critical organizational inquiry. Of course, workers in the everyday world of organizations very often view the pragmatic products of these highbrow activities when they are brought – usually by organizational consultants – to the shop floor in the form of advocacy of 'new conversations', 'flexible and adaptable employees', 'boundaryless organizations', 'fluid and undecidable meanings', and the like, as academic language games of dubious relevance – other than as mystification and legitimation – to the world of economy, labour and financial exchange in postindustrial capitalist conditions. New problematics brought by the postmodern turn, such as identity, culture, diversity, image and story, overlay the former terms of compliance and cohesion more familiar to students of Parsons and Etzioni, but do not supplant them.

While the adoption of selected postmodernist and poststructuralist frameworks by organizational analysis may offer emancipatory potential for both organizational practice and analysis, actual uses of these approaches have produced disparate results. There have been a number of welcome developments and improvements in organizational practices inspired by a popular critical commentary, which some claim as postmodern, that promotes workplace empowerment and belongingness through greater attention to issues of identity and diversity in everyday organizational life. But these developments more likely represent a revival of Durkheimian humanism – in its 1930s form of the Human Relations school – in the reform of organizations through recognition and legitimation of affective relations and human needs in the workplace. Anomie and alienation, mobilized into revolution or regeneration for Marx and Weber, are thereby, allegedly, resolved or at least managed without dysfunction. The organization, with the apparent resolution or repression of 'dysfunctional' conflicts and irrational demands, is better able to continue the pursuit of traditional goals. A reconsideration of what are regarded in modern organization theory as rational, normative goals, such as growth and market maximization, while preserving organizational order and stability, is notably absent in postmodernist organization analysis. Moreover, the use of the term 'human resources' which in its commonplace, unexamined acceptance by workers and academics alike, at the very time when postmodernism is cheerfully invoked by 'human resource' academics, represents an everyday triumph of instrumental rationality (that persons can be treated solely as the object of another's rational calculation and utility). It readily manifests the continued hold of a neo-rationalist functionalism in organization and management studies – including that claiming to be postmodern.

The dominant form of postmodern organizational analysis appears to have missed the profound tasks advocated by its invoked champions Foucault, Derrida and Lyotard of unceasing resistance to all forms of established thought and relations of power – including that which establishes organization as a social practice, and its representation in analytic inquiry. On the contrary, most ahistorical and naive postmodern organizational analyses and expository narratives ultimately direct their attention to the traditional tasks of organizational problem-solving for established power elites. The few more historically aware and defeated intellectual critics opt, it seems, for idiosyncratic textual abstractions and self-absorption abstracted from any kind of materiality at all (e.g. Burrell 1997).

Of course, I do not wish to argue that all current efforts invoking the postmodern in organizations are flagrantly, or unwittingly, managerialist or quietist. There are important, exemplary exceptions, among them Alvesson and Willmott (1992), Reed (1992), Hassard and Parker (1993).

Many others too, including textual analysts most interested in symbol and story, are endeavouring to understand organizations and in particular to attend to culture and psyche long neglected in conventional and critical organizational analysis (Alvesson 1990, Calas and Smircich 1996, Fineman and Gabriel 1996, Gergen 1992). A number of postmodern analysts also try to invoke postmodernism for leftist criticism and political projects. But there are many other postmodern organizational analysts, apparently convinced of the failure of modern criticism, or unaware of it altogether, and disillusioned with all prospects for emancipatory change, who find in postmodernism a retreat from the contested social relations of everyday workplaces and corporate organizations. Yet within these sites and relationships of production, people and institutions enact and refuse processes of exploitation and repression, and struggle for new demands over the cultural stakes of social life. Analysing these complex relations and movements requires efforts and imaginative insights beyond those of conventional, and postmodern, organizational analysis.

Some cultural critics defended by proclamations of paradigm incommensurability, readily abdicate to an ascendant generation of commentators (as epitomized by the postmodern sections at the American Academy of Management) ideologically established as setting the legitimizing gaze and agenda of popular, ahistorical postmodern organization studies. Conceding the personally and intellectually difficult task of serious reflexive criticism allows organizational policy academics, in their appropriation and dilution of the language and intent of an oppositional postmodernism, to privilege reformist criticisms of conventional modern practices of organizational structure and management engaged in business as usual. Correspondingly, the meta-social arrangements of late modern and postmodern (global) capitalism remain barely recognized and faintly challenged by organizational analysis. In this sense then, contemporary postmodern organization studies continues or facilitates the long-established orientation of modern organization theory: the analysis and resolution of management problems for capitalist corporations. A postmodern organization studies that does not include a deep interrogation of either its social and intellectual antecedents in the academy, or of postmodernism's implosion of sociality, denial of institutional structure, and elision of agency in cultural discourse, is readily and effectively absorbed into both neo-rationalist organization and management theory and liberal humanist reformism.

Strategic Neo-rationality

The dominant forms of organizational analysis and practice, including the incorporation of postmodernism, display an intensification of measures designed to counter the 'radical doubt' (Beck 1992) and routinized uncertainty which now permeate Western culture. Postmodernism represents not only a movement in cultural theory influential in the academy but a description of cultural conditions of postmodernity, in which an intensified, globalizing capitalism fragments modern society. Postmodernism, as the 'cultural logic of late capitalism' (Jameson 1984b), both describes and normalizes the deepening doubt and distrust people experience toward modern and traditional authority systems. It describes, too, the turn of heightened individualism, self-expressivism and consumption manifesting in hyper-modern capitalism. In implicit recognition and response to this, as Bell predicted in the 1970s (1976), neo-rational organizational analysis and management practice intensify their efforts to manage the contradictions of capitalism in contemporary conditions of 'risk society' (in Beck's 1992 term). Organizational analysis now, most analysts concur, must address more emphatically the tasks of strategically managing precarious organizational practice. Organizations, with their manifestly limited and challenged rationality, confront diverse contestational practices.

Currently influential theoretical and practical texts in organization and management studies readily display an institutionalized modernist response to these needs in the face of a widening legitimation crisis. Texts on new organizational forms, complexity systems, adaptations and restructuring; on network configurations; on chaos in organizations, on organizational leadership, strategy, decision-making; on organizational development and culture; on strategic human resource management (including for example, the 'management of cynicism'); on family-friendly, even spiritual, workplaces, and the like, abound in the business and management sections of bookstores and libraries, and in MBA curricula, around the Western world. All of these endeavours strive to develop ever more strategic organization and management practices for organizational adaptation in contemporary, some would say disorganized, hyper- or postmodern capitalism. Against a culture of radical doubt in cultural institutions and volatile uncertainty in economy and market, are posed a restoration of manager as guru-leader and a championing of the libertarian *laissez-faire* as the ironic guides through a condition of irresolvable ambivalence and uncertainty. The intent of these writings and advocacy seminars is the design and encouragement of a sophisticated management strategy for 21st century capitalism. The unleashed forces of diversity, pluralism, indeterminacy and chaos, with their effervescent, or nihilistic, energy are channelled into the production, organization and profitability goals of a very familiar modern capitalist agenda.

The incorporation and commodification of postmodern theory in these conditions raises little surprise among critical sociologists and social theorists. It represents a strategic postmodern knowledge practice; one espousing a neo-liberal postmodernism of methodological individualism, yet which ironically intensifies the instrumental utilization of persons in production organization in a flexible, uncertain global capitalism. Most of this form of organizational analysis – its intent, agenda and methods – takes place with little sociological analysis of either the academic practice, or of the practitioner sites of analysis in contemporary organizations. There is an irony here in that these practitioner commentators and organization theorists are indeed correct to continue to focus analytical attention – albeit with little extra-institutional contextual awareness – on the practices of production and the goings on of formal organization which are enduringly important in contemporary society, and mistakenly neglected in a culturally turned sociology. At the moment, what Touraine (1988) calls a non-social sociology tends to diminish or eclipse the importance of economic and political practices not only in structuring institutions and organizations but in generating new movements of contestation and historicity.

A reflexive sociological consideration of organizations as social and cultural practices co-constituting contemporary societies is now rare. Many commentators regard these considerations as denoting a modernist radicalism, which is of little relevance to organization management. For others, these sociological reflections represent modern humanist criticism which postmodernism has effectively deconstructed and discarded. Of course, notwithstanding modern critical interventions, there were ideological and political interests driving much of that older modern social science. There is no doubt that modern sociology in general and the sociology of organizations in particular warrant much and trenchant criticism. And a growing number of no longer grand, self-consciously modest criticisms are now emerging (e.g. Bauman 1991, Lash 1994, Lemert 1995, Smart 1999). Modern sociology and its methods, while delimited by the constraints of modern social science generally, has given way to many new forms of discursive representations, and to a thorough reflexivity. Much is welcome and significantly contributive to a regenerated sociological inquiry. But much more discussion is required, including foremost a serious reconsideration of the state of subjects and actors in a social world which continues to demonstrate their presence.

The crisis in sociology has contributed to the current state of affairs in organization studies of a deregulated market of undisciplined, often idiosyncratic ideas and approaches validated by an experimental, neo-liberal organization studies culture. But even as the increased complexity and global expanse of hyper-modern capitalism vitally affects the everyday world of organizational practices, the field of organization studies favours work in which historical and meta-theoretical approaches are disregarded and political and social questions remain unexamined.

Indeed, in much of the literature in organization studies even a spectre of sociological endeavour, other than its systems and functionalist forms, is absent. The reflective contextualization of critical sociology, as some analysts, notably Reed (1992) and Hassard (1993) have pointed out, is ignored. In sociology, analyses of institutional social practices, a central domain and task of modern sociology, are eschewed in a current preference for cultural practices of difference, identity, recognition and performativity. Among other sociocultural practices, such as religion, economy and polity, the study of organizational institutions has fallen from prominence on the sociological agenda. As the social apparently recedes (or is imploded by some theorists), and 'society' falls into disfavour, cultural studies in the academy and communalist differences in worldly practice assume more prominent status. As classical sociology, as Touraine (1988) suggests, has fallen into unavoidable decline, a new sociological orientation toward social practices is required.

A Critical Organizational Analysis

For many theorists affected by the crisis in modernity, all forms of modern categories and values are implicated in modernity's rationalization: its one-sided tendency toward totalitarian repression and mechanical petrification. They recognize the precariousness of any vantage point from which we endeavour to assert critique and preferred social practices. With this awareness, a number of theorists seek to retrieve modernity from its reduction to rationalization and totalitarianism. They pose a reflexive reconsideration of modernity (e.g. Beck et al. 1994, Habermas 1987, Touraine 1995, Lash 1999) and argue for renewed effort toward modernity's 'unfinished project' (Habermas 1987) and a 'radicalization of rationalized modernity', a 'new modernity' (Beck 1992, 1997). For Giddens (1996) greater possibilities for self and social emancipation might be found in a 'dialogic democracy'. Similarly, others argue for a 'second modernity' (Lash 1999) in which modernity's democratic aspirations allow for greater political contestations among diverse interests and cultural pluralism in contemporary social contexts. Furthermore, for Touraine (1995) and Toulmin (1990) the accepted conceptions of modernity, against which postmodernism is set, represent a distorted, one-sided view of the creatively dualistic vision of the Renaissance thinkers. The idea of modernity as no more than instrumental rationality is, for Touraine (1995), an error of judgement. Modernity contains and requires both rationalization and subjectivation in a society conceived as social movement of contest and negotiation (points to which I return in Chapter 7).

At the present moment, though, few organization analysts are drawing on these currents in social theory even though organizational analysis – much criticized for its ahistorical, narrow applications – has readily admitted more fashionable postmodern cultural theory. Although there are repeated calls for such attention, notably by Ulrich Beck (1992, 1997) and Alain Touraine (1988, 1995), there remains at present little effort to analyse and interpret organizational practices in relation to broader social relations of which they are constituent, and to seek their cultural, political and ecological transformation. The task of a critical, social, organizational analysis begins with a simultaneous recognition of our positioning by and within the epistemic knowledge schema and rules of our time, and a self-reflective refusal to concede their hegemonic delimitation. I invoke here Brown's 'mastered irony' (Brown 1995) – the ability to encounter the problematics presenting in postmodern and counter or non-modern conditions that manifest concurrently in the dominant discourses and social practices of modernity, and to act upon them. Modern theory and values, especially those of freedom and justice, far from requiring whole-sale abandonment as mystifications masking systemic domination, or degradation into communalist fragmentation, require excavation, reflection and recomposition, even as we grapple with the current acceleration of hyper, global capitalism.

Working through the contradictions and paradoxes of this multifarious, disparate condition reveals signs of the subject-actor acting in an always contestable and precarious social ensemble. Classical sociology's depiction of society as revolving round a central rational system, and its version under structural-functionalism, made it difficult to recognize effective social actors. Marxist-inspired sociology largely succumbed to a logic of domination and (post)structuralism's dissolution of subject-actors continues that view. But the Frankfurt School critical theorists (with the exception, perhaps, of Adorno), nonetheless maintained that utopian thought opens up 'alternatives for action and margins of possibility that push beyond historical continuities' (Habermas 1987: 49). A new sociology, as Touraine (1988, 1995) argues, seeks signs and sites of socially transformative movements and new social actors.

A new sociology, one appropriate to the postindustrial social formation in which we now live, requires a new iteration of some central ideas of modern sociology. Importantly, the concept of historicity which used to refer to the historical nature of social phenomena and which encouraged historically situated social research is now better understood as referring to 'the set of cultural, cognitive, economic, and ethical models by which a collectivity sets up relations with its environment' (Touraine 1988: 40). The important emphasis here is on society's capacity to produce itself.

This view rejects both the Parsonian idea of a society organized around a set of core values and functioning as a self-equilibrating system and the Marxist-inspired notion of society divided into irreconcilable separate classes maintained by ideological apparatuses of dominant class interests. It rejects too a poststructural notion of non-society in which rationally choosing role-playing consumers substitute for the subject-actor and interact with one another for instrumental ends in an unstructured current of forces.

For Touraine, the central social dynamic is indeed one of conflict, but one in which the unequal relations are not prefixed, nor free-floating. Rather, 'a field of historicity, a set of cultural models, is transformed into a system of social relations' (1988: 41). Hence, a notion of social classes as historical conditions shifts to a notion of classes as actors contesting, and oriented toward, values and stakes. In this context of *social movement*, actors create the social conditions in which they contest.

As we now recognize modernity's always only partial accomplishments, and the manifest limits to its rationalization, a pressing task for social theorists is to redevelop an intellectual endeavour and scholarship that both recognizes these limits and acts creatively with them. Organization itself is achieved within and against the forces of disorganization, indeterminate meaning, and always imperfect communication. In recognizing this affirmative and transformative possibility, analysts, like other organizational practitioners, may carefully retrieve many values and accomplishments of modernity as they reject and discard others. Organizational practices are among those crucially requiring transformed relations as we endeavour to craft civil society after modernity's crisis.

Social institutions, especially under complex late or postmodern conditions, require a new critical attention. At the moment there seems to be among many sociologists and social theorists a coy avoidance of the agenda associated with modernist radicalism – the sites and relations of production. But these sites and relations, once again, generate new social dynamics and problems. Postmodern intensification of instrumental rationalities and market economics effects an alteration in conditions and relations of work. Among the new practices of work and organization, patterns of structural unemployment, flexible and sporadic employment relations, and new demands for cultural and identity interests are evident. These patterns reveal new signs of human actors struggling, in unusual ways, to make their lives and contest the dominant cultural forms in which they live. Their incontrovertible appearance demands our sociological attention. In seeking to develop a revitalized sociological approach to contemporary societal events and activities, a new look at the everyday practices of social action among everyday people, especially of people at work in organizations, is richly illuminating.

Possibilities for renewal, regeneration and the creation of new forms of organizational and other social practices may be found among a range of new explorations evident in contemporary organizational life. Counter-modern, romantic, traditional discourses are as much in revival as in decline – as we can observe in everyday social life in much of the world. Tribal, ethnic and fundamentalist religious groupings, apparently untroubled by modern ambivalence are, for instance, significant forces in modern Western societies as they are in the East. The postmodern theoretical attention to the counter-modern, as well as to the contingency of knowledge and language, enables our analysis to include sources of knowledge formerly excluded by modern social science.

As social theorists we need little reminding that we need to reflect on and reconsider our current practices of knowledge as postmodernism exacerbates the crisis in modernity, and communalism returns. As Smart (1999: 39) puts it, it is not enough in contemporary social and cultural conditions to simply recycle or refurbish 'cherished and time-honoured' conceptions. In place of a capitalist-favoured rejection of the old and a championing of the new as commodities for purchase, we can excavate, rehabilitate and revitalize selections of our collective histories and cultural repositories. In so doing, possibilities and conditions for a more emancipatory social and cultural life may be imagined, and enacted. As the latter chapters of this book describe, many people working in contemporary organizations are, in post or counter-modern vein, already constructing from the fragments and opportunities of disjuncture made possible by informated capitalism alternatives to truncating and hyper-rationalized organization practice.

The first task of this book is a historical one. To move toward a new sociology we need to know well the analytical traditions of modernity shaping our task. The following chapters critically reflect upon the traditions of modern sociology of organization and postmodern theory. These traditions of knowledge provide the context and the resources for the discussion of the second task of the book. That task is a critical exploration of forms of organizational criticism, and social action, emergent in organizations of work around the Western world.

2   The Modern Heritage

Philosophy and Sociology

Modernity

Philosophical debates over the origins of modernity typically, though variously, emphasize the central importance of such figures as Galileo, Kepler and Newton in astronomy and physics, Descartes, Locke and Kant in philosophy, Luther (even earlier) in religious protestation, and the popular revolutions in France and America (Habermas 1987, Lemert 1995, Toulmin 1990, Touraine 1995). The industrial revolution in northern Europe which initiated the large-scale rationalization of production and its social consequences is also regarded, although again with varying degrees of emphasis, as being central to the enactment and consolidation of the emergent modern project. Within these accounts lies a general agreement that the 17th century had produced a 'new philosophy' and science based on shared 'assumptions about rationality' (Toulmin 1990). Toulmin argues convincingly that a 'counter-Renaissance' took place in 17th century England. It was a revolution in which the new philosophers 'set aside the long-standing preoccupations of Renaissance humanism' and its interest in 'practical knowledge of the oral, the particular, the local and the timely' (Toulmin 1990: 30). By the 18th century abstract, logical rigour, exactitude and intellectual certainty achieved ascendancy in intellectual and cultural life. The earlier Renaissance traditions of idealism, humanism and heterodoxy, although retained to some extent in the emerging social sciences, were eventually permeated with, or subjugated by, the effects of the rationalization emphasis in the philosophy of Descartes and the science of Newton.

The percolation of the 'new philosophy' and science throughout humanistic forms of knowledge endeavouring to understand and shape the natural and social world led eventually to the privileging of the rational, disembodied abstractions with which we associate Cartesian science. The principles of a general, universal and certain philosophy established the dominant theoretical and methodological discourses of modern cultural practice. The privileging of rationalization as the dominant form of cultural practice gave rise to the political, economic and technological constructions of modern Europe and Western societies. The vast accomplishments of rationalizing modernity, though generally hailed for their advancement on earlier epochs, have been shadowed by the travesties and human and ecological disasters which have occurred in their wake. In more recent years criticism of the modern trajectory and its failures has become more widespread and heightened. Much of this criticism has been associated with mid and late 20th century disenchantments and dissension, especially after Nazism and the Soviet gulag, and atomic weaponry. Marxist thought and Frankfurt School critical theorists have been followed more recently by a postmodern criticism which extends these critical theories to the extreme. Postmodern criticism asserts a break with the modernist project altogether and expresses incredulity toward its grand narratives of rationalization and humanism.

But critics of modernity have a much longer history. As monolithic and apparently global as modernity – in its rationalization forms – now appears, competing and critical discourses have existed throughout the modern epoch. Many, recalling the Renaissance critics Erasmus and Montaigne, have challenged the very conceptions of modernity we have widely come to accept (Toulmin 1990, Touraine 1995). Most of these criticisms once found expression in Romantic and antinomian movements, and nonconformist religious movements (Calhoun 1995, Thompson 1993, Toulmin 1990) from the 17th century onward including various manifestations today. More well-known critics include William Blake and the English Romantic poets Byron, Wordsworth, Coleridge and Shelley. They include also the writers John Ruskin, William Morris and Elizabeth Gaskell, and Friedrich Schiller in 19th century Germany, who portrayed dissenting and critical perspectives of the abstract rational imperatives of social order and the new industrial production. Older Protestant religious communities such as the Frisian-founded Mennonites, mystical sects, and anti-technology worker groups found dissenting commonalities, often ironically, with later feminists and 'postindustrial', 'small-is-beautiful' ecologists and hippies of the 1960s and 1970s. These movements illustrate some of the better-known counter-modern expressions, which again find commonalities with many contemporary 'New Age' alternative explorations in spirituality, meaning-making and lifestyles.

However, serious academic interest in counter-modern activities of this nature as resources for understanding contemporary social conditions and practices is a relatively recent development (see, for example, Heelas 1996, Melucci 1996, Thompson 1993, Toulmin 1990, Wexler 1996b). While many theorists are currently attracted to postmodern discursive deconstruction and some counter-modern explorations – which include, for Beck (1992, 1997), the 'modernization of barbarism', the opposite of civilization – most economists, scientists and technologists appear largely undisturbed from their task of ensuring further advancement of rationalizing modernity's rapidly globalizing project. But there are some efforts in the sciences to engage in debates more salient in the humanities and social sciences (e.g. Latour 1993, Lindley 1993, Zohar 1990), and to explore limits or alternatives to rationalizing modernity. For the moment, though, the possibilities for social knowledge and practice are constrained by old and new orthodoxies continuing to appeal for legitimacy through the constructs of a certain, dominant, form of modern knowledge and of modernity. Whether modernity is exhausted and archaic or vibrantly rehabitable, it is the Cartesian rationalized, secularized, technologized and universalized construct of modernity upon which we more or less agree.

The question of whether or not we have ever been modern (Latour 1993) or whether modernization has ever been more than partial (Offe 1996) according to our generally accepted view, increasingly draws our attention. The assumptions and assertions of modernity in social practices and in shaping human character are of such wide acceptance that serious doubt requires serious explication. My reflection begins with a discussion of a particular product of modernity, that of sociology. My consideration of the tradition of sociology and the principal ideas of some of its central figures, prefaces a discussion of the sociological treatment of the social practices of institutions and organizations. Institutions and organizations, central to sociology's subject matter since Saint-Simon and Comte, are often regarded in much current literature, still influenced by functionalism, as somewhat ahistorical and naturally extant objects or, more recently, as narrative constructions devoid of extra-linguistic structure. In many schools, particularly business schools, the history of organizational thought and practice is regarded as of little practical importance. Indeed ahistoricism has been endemic in organizational analysis for decades, as others have pointed out (Mouzelis 1967, Reed 1985). Its current form seriously exacerbates the prevailing condition of myopic, ideological managerialism dominating organizational analysis.

But central to my telling in this chapter of a history of sociological and organizational thought is the excavation of the modern story of rationalization, evolutionary progress and universality. This reflection represents a story of modernity which we are now leaving. At the same time, these reflections draw us to recompose resources of sociological and social theories from which our analyses and understandings of contemporary organization practices may be critically constructed. Moreover, a reflexive social analysis of organizations contributes to the task of imagining and constructing new social arrangements – especially of practices of work and production – serving sociocultural and planetary ends.

Preparing Modern Sociology

The climate of the 'new philosophy' of the 17th century and the relative triumph of Cartesian rationality over idealist, metaphysical and speculative knowledge led, by the early 19th century, to a project of a social science. The foundation of a social science is associated with the social philosophers Saint-Simon (1760–1825) and August Comte (1798–1857), who endeavoured to establish a 'science of social physics'. Between them, the term 'sociology' was coined. Other schools of thought of the 19th century, including the utilitarian social and political philosophies of John Stuart Mill, and Alfred Marshall's economics, assisted in the formation of sociology. The modern sociological institution arose out of the confidence of modern philosophy and science which sought to extend the systematic application of reasoned minds to all social phenomena and problems. Knowledge and understanding, social improvement and civilization would, its theorists believed, thereby be accomplished. Once they had succeeded, as John Locke expressed it, in 'clearing away the underbrush that stands in the way of knowledge' (cited in Toulmin 1990: 3), confusions arising from theological and ideological matters would be resolved, and a rational social order established.

The social contexts in which Saint-Simon, Comte and the utilitarian philosophers worked were marked by political and social revolution: the French Revolution in 1789, and the industrial revolution beginning around the turn of the 18th century. These societal events and their consequences presented the central questions to be explored by social philosophers at the time and by subsequent generations of social theorists. They constitute the foundational rationale for the quintessentially modern project of sociology.

August Comte, drawing on the rational philosophers of the 17th century, especially Montesquieu and Condorcet, as well as Saint-Simon, sought to develop a rational, 'positive', systematic science of society (Comte [1855] 1974). With Saint-Simon, Comte endeavoured to discover the 'laws of social physics'. Comte believed that the essential task and accomplishment of positive science was its subordination of rational propositions to empirical facts. Science, for Comte, must relinquish the search for ultimate causes and universal principles and search instead for general laws ascertained and verified by empirical investigative methods. This rigorous grounding of knowledge and understanding in observation and certainty, as opposed to speculation and questionable validity, constitutes Comte's positivism. Comte divided all natural phenomena into two categories: organic and inorganic bodies, both of which are ordered according to their measure of complexity. Their order is 'determined by the degree of simplicity, or...generality of their phenomena' (Comte [1855] 1974: 44). Various sciences might study these bodies but a 'positive philosophy' takes the task of coordinating the different laws arising from the empirical observations of the different orders of phenomena. A positive social science 'endeavors to discover...the general relations that connect all social phenomena' (ibid.: 473). The establishing of systematic relations between phenomena and 'the whole of the existing situation' enables explanations of the discrete phenomena and the whole to be established.

Comte's ordering system applied in similar fashion to the societal order, in which he postulated an evolutionary progression according to the development of human rationality. Human society progressed from theological, and metaphysical, illusions to its highest stage of scientific-positive polity. At this highest stage, a society, uniting the principles of order and progress, is achieved. Comte's absolute doctrine of positive science led him later to seek a 'science of morals' that would instil in human beings – who were becoming, he believed, 'devoid of religious attachments' – a system of guidance for human action. Morality, necessary to secure social order, has to be instilled by social institutions, and these institutions must be the repository and authority of higher morality. Comte's scientific theory and method influenced other major theorists of his and succeeding generations – notably John Stuart Mill and Herbert Spencer. But of more direct significance for the development of sociology was Comte's influence, principally his positivist science and social morality, on another French social philosopher and theorist, Emile Durkheim, half a century later. Discussion of Durkheim will resume after a brief comment on the contribution of utilitarian philosophy to the emergent social science and sociology.

The philosophers Hobbes, Locke, Mandeville and their associates, in the 17th and early 18th centuries shared an endeavour to create a secular, rational ethic based on principles derived from 'natural propensities' inherent in all human beings. Although these philosophers differed in their assumptions about human nature, they generally agreed that individual human beings possess naturally given rights and interests which they are naturally disposed to seek and satisfy. This generally composed the principle of 'the greatest happiness for the greatest number' for which utilitarian philosophies are well known. In the early 19th century these liberal ideas found fuller development in the work of Jeremy Bentham and John Stuart Mill. Mill was influenced not only by the Scottish and English liberal utilitarianism of his forebears but by continental European thought, especially the idealism of Hegel and Kant, and the progressive scientific method of Comte.

For Mill, early liberalism had neglected the institutional nature of society and the historical growth of institutions. This neglect undermined the utilitarian insistence on freedom of individuals to seek happiness and self-interest. A good society must do more than permit individual freedom: it must provide the opportunity for a free and satisfying life to be lived. The role of institutions in assisting or hindering the realization of the liberal society of the utilitarian vision must be more fully understood and their social arrangements changed. For Mill, in *Utilitarianism* ([1861] 1976), the theory and means of utilitarian social philosophy were inadequate to pursue a comprehensive study of social institutions. Mill found some redress for this deficiency in Comte's general science of society which contained both a general law of progressive growth and a scientific method for its analysis. Mills differed from Comte on several matters, especially over Comte's compelling interest in morality and social unity, as against Mill's insistence on individual psychology as the basic unit of social scientific analyses. But Mill's liberal individualism and his adoption of Comte's positivist scientific method affected the social philosophy and emergent social science of the 19th century. Importantly, Mill, in *The Logic of the Moral Sciences* ([1843] 1988), proposed a social scientific method based on the deductive method of physics, that added to Comte's theory of induction. General propositions may be inductively established from the observation of facts. Subsequent propositions may be deductively established by reference to the laws governing the conditions of those facts. Inductive and deductive methods supplement each other and are the proper procedure for social science. For Mill, the task of sociology is to ascertain from the study of history the empirical laws of society from which deductively the laws of human nature may in turn be ascertained.

Another major figure of this period, Herbert Spencer, made a further significant contribution to the development of sociology. Sharing the principles of utility and liberty with the liberal social philosophers, Spencer, however, parted from Mill in placing at the centre of his philosophy the concept of organic evolution. Publishing *The Social Statics* ([1850] 1972) nine years before Darwin's *Origin of Species* (1859), Spencer endeavoured to link 'psychological processes with biological survival' (Sabine 1961: 721). He pointed to similarities in the development of organic and social systems, 'from an indefinite incoherent homogeneity to a definite coherent heterogeneity' (Spencer cited in Sabine 1961: 722). Spencer's social evolutionism, developed further in later publications (*Progress: its Law and Cause*, 1857; *On Social Evolution*, 1972), argued that the growth of society toward higher order differentiation would lead to the 'good' society. For Spencer, moral improvement was akin to the biological adaptation and greater differentiation which ensure the survival of the fittest.

For Spencer, human society is like an organic body comprised of biological-type structures, functions and needs. These constituent parts, operating in interdependent relation, comprise a self-regulating system. Drawing heavily on biology and evolutionary theory, Spencer at the same time sought to retain from liberal philosophy the emphasis on the primacy of the individual in social relations. His social biologism led him to the view that the study of society is premised on the assumption that 'the properties of the units determine the properties of the whole they make up' (Spencer cited in Levine 1995: 145). It is these central ideas – the biological organism and evolutionary model of human society, and the central emphasis on the human individual as the primary unit of analysis – that were foundational in the development of sociology. Although Durkheim was later to reposition the role of the individual in society (society as prior to individual), the matter of the individual–social relationship remains of central importance. Spencer's development of biological analogies and the relationships of organic parts to the whole anticipates sociological structural-functionalism developed some 70 years later. For Spencer, societies are 'essentially parallel' to biological organisms, but they also differ from organisms. In society there is no 'social sensorium' (cited in Levine 1995: 145), no equivalent of an animal brain in society's central regulative organs. It is society's primary constituent units, human individuals, not their corporate sum, which maintain consciousness and take actions. This important caveat to the biological organismic model was overlooked in much 20th century sociological theory, especially the highly evolutionist theories of structural-functionalism.

Notwithstanding the generative bases in the liberal utilitarian and empiricist traditions, a counterposing, or some would argue, complementary, idealist tradition, especially that of the German philosophers, contributed to the construction of sociology. Theorists in the tradition of Hegel, most obviously Karl Marx and Georg Simmel, encouraged the development of grand theory and analytically interpretive theories of social phenomena. The work of these theorists, and that of Le Play, Weber, Pareto, Tönnies and others, contributed a humanist, idealist, dimension to the establishment of the discipline of sociology. But discussion turns now to Comte's disciple, Emile Durkheim, social scientist and social philosopher.

Emile Durkheim (1858–1917)

Durkheim is generally known for his foundation and advocacy of a scientific sociology. But he was also a moral philosopher and, some argue, the development of a sociology of morality was his central preoccupation (e.g. Bellah 1973). From his first book, *The Division of Labour in Society* ([1893] 1964), to his last, *The Elementary Forms of Religious Life* ([1915] 1965), Durkheim, in the tradition of Descartes, sought to investigate the original elemental state of all things social. His efforts throughout were directed by the hope that elemental understanding would indicate the sources of possibilities for the improvement of society. Sociology, for Durkheim, was meaningless without the aim of social improvement. Durkheim's social philosophy was concerned with the relation between science and religion, and the individual and society. Although these concerns had long occupied philosophers in various ways, Durkheim's *oeuvre*, in the view of many later commentators, offered a distinctive and controversial contribution (see, for example, Aron 1967b, Bellah 1973, Giddens 1972, Levine 1995, Nisbet 1974, Zeitlin 1990 for elaborations on this theme). In addition to the influence of Comte and the French heritage, Durkheim was influenced by the utilitarian and liberal philosophies of his proximate generations. Following Comte, Durkheim's science was concerned with establishing a verifiable method for the investigation of social practices. Moreover, in disagreement with the utilitarian views that humans behave in accordance with the principle of maximization of self-interest, Durkheim proffered a social theory of modern moral social cohesion. His moral social order proposed the exertion of a higher order, secular, authority over individuals which simultaneously constrained and enabled a higher order of human freedom.

Durkheim's earlier books *The Division of Labour in Society* ([1893] 1964) and *The Rules of the Sociological Method* [1895] translated into English 1938) have exerted much influence on the development of a scientific sociology. *The Division of Labour* addressed the changes brought about by modern industrial society and its characteristic expansion of rational economic production and urbanization. In this book Durkheim further developed Comte's scientific method, as well as incorporating the notion of societal stages of development. Drawing on the biological organismic metaphor, derived also from Spencer (and found throughout Aristotle, Aquinas and social Darwinists), Durkheim postulated the conditions for social integration, and social pathology, in a social system characterized by high specialization and complex interdependence. For Durkheim, traditional society is characterized by a simple, 'mechanical' solidarity or cohesion. Mechanical solidarity is characterized by low social differentiation and high resemblance among individuals. A generalized conformity among all members of the society is a fundamental requirement of social cohesion. Religion and law provide the central systems of constraints, and kinship groups the primary social bonds. Society, comprised of undifferentiated individuals and clans, is held together by an enveloping and intense *conscience collective*.

In contrast to the mechanical solidarity of traditional societies, Durkheim theorized, modern society is evolving a qualitatively different form of social cohesion. Durkheim conceived of social organization in modern industrial society as functioning according to a system of interdependencies in organic, rather than mechanical or causal, interrelation. A complex 'organic' solidarity emerges in which societal functioning resembles the functioning of an advanced organism. Organs, parts and physiological processes relate reciprocally and interdependently to ensure the functioning of the organism. '[T]he structure of societies where organic solidarity is preponderant is entirely different. These are constituted, not by the replication of similar homogeneous elements, but by a system of different organs, each one of which has a special role and which themselves are formed from differentiated parts' (Durkheim [1893] 1964: 132). Advanced societies are characterized by a functional interdependence between specialized parts (individuals) and regulation by higher moral constraints.

The emergence of highly differentiated societies with an elaborate division of labour and specialization of function promotes a greater role for the individual – as the utilitarians were aware. Free from external and imposed arrangements individuals are increasingly exposed to diversity and difference in their relations with each other through a differentiated and specialized division of labour. Traditional *conscience collective* is weakened, but it does not disappear: 'Only it more and more comes to consist of very general and very indeterminate ways of thinking and feeling, which leave an open space for a growing multitude of individual differences' (Durkheim [1893] 1964: 172).

Differing with the utilitarians, Durkheim argues that a transmutation of the *conscience collective* takes place, rather than its dissolution in egoic individualism. This transmutation manifests as a social cohesion of moral individualism rather than giving way to a disaggregation of individuated actors. For the individual, voluntary, moral duty replaces mechanical, dedifferentiated, coercion. For Durkheim the rise of a moral individualism accompanies the specialized division of labour, and the organic solidarity so generated is 'spontaneous'. An economy of differentiation requires a morality of cooperation, hence for Durkheim, organic solidarity is a 'more rational', 'more humane', moral social order. Organic solidarity is of an emergent nature, it is not yet fully realized. The social problems presenting at its incomplete stage – especially anomic pathologies affecting individuals dislocated from traditional social arrangements – will diminish or disappear. These problems result from maladjustments of the evolving social organism and the incomplete development of the division of labour. Anomie and external inequalities would gradually diminish, Durkheim believed, as the division of labour developed and social institutions changed accordingly.

Although Durkheim endeavoured to address the persistence of injustices and inequalities – including the forced division of labour – through his later works, his theorization of a progressive, social organic functionalism described in *The Division of Labour* and the method of scientific social inquiry developed in *The Rules of the Sociological Method* received most attention from subsequent generations of sociologists. In *The Rules of the Sociological Method* Durkheim insists that social philosophers must engage in detailed empirical study of social phenomena which he postulated, must be treated as 'facts'. Society, for Durkheim, can and must be treated as a phenomenon given in nature. Social phenomena share the properties of physical objects in that they exist independently of the observer. 'Social facts are capable of objective representation…which excludes subjective impressions' (Durkheim [1895] 1972: 65–66.) Furthermore, human ideas, values and purposes that exist in the human psyche can be conceived as 'natural facts' which can be studied scientifically (Durkheim [1895] 1972: 58–60).

The sociologist must begin a study of any given area of social reality with a conceptualization and definition of those objects under gaze. The object must be observable in the manner of the other sciences, but what is crucially characteristic of a social fact is not just its externality but that it exercises a constraint on individuals. 'A social fact is to be recognized by the power of external coercion which it exercises or is capable of exercising over individuals' (Durkheim [1895] 1972: 64). These facts exist independently of individuals and they come about by the association of individuals in social groups. They can be categorized and classified in genera and species and as such comprise the subject of a general social science. Durkheim's scientific sociology holds the assumption that society is different from the reality of individuals – every social fact is the result of another social fact and not a fact of individual psychology. 'A whole is not identical with the sum of its parts. It is something new…' (ibid.).

While Durkheim always retained interest in broader philosophical questions much of his work has been seen as contributing to the branching of sociology into two strands: the social philosophical and the social scientific. He has been used and criticized by each of those strands of thought. But, significantly, it was his interpretation by Talcott Parsons in the mid-20th century and the development of structural-functionalism that more or less positioned Durkheim for several generations as the founding father of structural-functionalism. Durkheim's concern with ethical and moral institutional constraints upon the individual and the central importance he gave to the role of religion and the sacred in understanding society have frequently been ignored. A revived interest in Durkheim in recent years is now evident (see, for example, Gane 1992, Hamilton 1990,

Pickering and Martins 1994). In particular, attention to Durkheim's theorizations of religion, 'social energy', social cohesion and action may offer much more to contemporary social analysis than his strict empiricism.

While the Durkheimian heritage has been largely confined to the socio-logical tradition, the tradition of theory and political practice invoking the name of the famous 19th century thinker, Karl Marx, is considerably broader. His work and that of numerous Marxist theorists over the gener-ations is vast and complex.

Karl Marx (1818–1883)

An asserted orthodoxy in the sociology of organizations established from the mid-20th century has typically regarded the influence of Marx and Marxian theory as of considerably less significance and as functionally disruptive to the programmatic agendas of a problem-solving, Durkheimian-inspired, Parsonian-elaborated, organizational science. But the sociological tradition and social theory more broadly, although displaying a similar ambivalence toward Marxist traditions of theory and critique, have been irrevocably influenced by Marx's work. The influence of the Marxist heritage evidently endures even amid the present popularity of diverse critical contributions in social theory, including the postmodern. Most obviously, Marxist-influenced thought remains current in sociologies of work, production, tech-nology and industrial practices in contemporary conditions (e.g. Aronowitz and DiFazio 1994, Castells 1996, Gorz 1999, Rifkin 2000).

Marx's work is typically regarded as presenting an early or 'youthful' phase and a later, mature, phase. While some (e.g. Fromm 1964) have criticized this splitting as exaggerated and as effecting a relegation of Marx's humanism and idealism to his youth, and his interest in economics and politics to his mature years, it is a distinction that many Marxist scholars retain as useful in understanding the development of Marxism and its influence in social and political affairs (e.g. Anderson 1976, Aron 1967a, Aron 1967b, Bottomore 1964, Tucker 1978). The early period between 1841 and 1848 produced a number of important works including *The Poverty of Philosophy*, *The Economic and Philosophic Manuscripts of 1844* and *The German Ideology*, and the long pamphlet *The Communist Manifesto* (1848). In his second period Marx's two most important works are *A Contribution to the Critique of Political Economy* (1859), including its famous preface, and *Capital* (1867).

The young Marx, formally educated in European philosophy, was notably influenced by Kantian liberalism and the religious tensions of his era.[1] But the most enduring philosophical influence upon Marx's work was that of Hegel. Marx inherited the Enlightenment creed of 'innate goodness of man, human perfectibility, the power of human reason' (Bottomore 1964: viii). But he developed from that humanism a theory of society which held that in all social classes under capitalist social conditions man's latent and creative powers are stifled and repressed. What is characteristic of modern capitalist societies for Marx is the presence of structural contradictions or antagonisms that render vast groups or classes of people in conflict with each other. Capitalism, for Marx, keeps the vast majority of men as 'labouring beasts', and prevents the fulfilment of greater human potential.

In *The Economic and Philosophic Manuscripts of 1844* Marx, in response to Hegel, develops a theory of political economy. For Marx, man in capitalist industrial society has lost control of the products of his own activity which instead appear as inhuman ruling powers over him. This condition, for Marx, following Hegel, is one of 'alienation'. But Marx importantly departs from Hegel in proposing, not a spiritual or ideal energy of true being from which man is alienated, but a material, productive human being. For Hegel, history is the process of 'the self-realization of spirit (Geist) or God.... Spirit is self-creative energy imbued with a drive to become fully conscious of itself as spirit' (Tucker 1978: xxi). Spirit may become its nature as self-conscious being by the processes of knowledge and recognition, especially of illusory conditions and falsities. Alienation, in the Hegelian schema, refers therefore to the processes which prevent man from reaching self-creation and self-realization as spirit.

Marx's proposition was an inversion of Hegel's metaphysical idealism ('placed upon its feet'), and postulated a materialist conception of history that put human experience at the centre. The primary sphere of man's being is not his spiritual or ideal life but rather his economic life – the foundation on which all else rests. The economic sphere is the primary site of man's self-alienation. Man is essentially a producer and material production is the primary form of his producing activity. History is a 'history of production' in which labouring man creates a world in material productive activities. This 'materialist conception of history' is a dialectical process of development through opposition and conflict.

Man, for Marx, is potentially a 'free conscious producer' but has been constrained from expressing himself freely in productive activity by the institutions of work and production under capitalism. Man has been driven to produce by need and by the requirements of ruling classes to accumulate capital. In this sense then, working man's productive activity has always been involuntary – it is degraded from creative activity to mere labour in production. The worker is forced to sell his labour power to owners of capital and plant. Both parties enter into an instrumental relationship, estranged from each other by their inherent conflicts of interests. The worker must expend his energies in the production of objects over which he has no ownership or control. Producing involuntarily and estranged from the products of his labour, the worker is thus estranged from his human nature and his labour is 'alienated labour' (Marx 1844a). In these conditions 'the worker sinks to the level of a commodity and becomes indeed the most wretched of commodities' (Marx [1844a] 1978: 70). '[T]he worker becomes a slave of his object...the more the worker produces, the less he has to consume; the more value he creates, the more valueless, the more unworthy he becomes' (Marx [1844a] 1978: 73). Alienation becomes the normative state of the worker:

> In his work, therefore, he does not affirm himself but denies himself, does not feel content but unhappy, does not develop freely his physical and mental energy but mortifies his body and ruins his mind. The worker therefore only feels himself outside his work, and in his work feels outside himself....His labour is therefore not voluntary, but coerced; it is *forced* labour. (Marx [1844] 1978: 74)

But this state, for Marx, is neither necessary for human productivity nor an intractable totality. Alienation may be overcome by a revolutionary change in the social conditions that produce and maintain it. Bourgeois society, Marx theorized, had reached the stage through its technological development and modern industrial organization in which the socialization of the means and ownership of production was possible. A revolution of the proletariat would accomplish the repossession of man's alienated social powers and the 'transcendence of human self-alienation'. Such a proletarian revolution would accomplish the end of all classes and overcome the antagonistic character of capitalist society. It would therefore be of benefit to all people and would lead to social arrangements in which the 'free development of each' person is made possible.

Some years after the publication of these critical philosophical theories Marx's mature work in both *Capital* (1867) and *A Contribution to the Critique of Political Economy* (1859) more fully developed a critical theory of political economy. A considerably greater emphasis is placed on economy over idealist philosophy. In these works, seeking to realize the philosophy of his youth (or as some would have it, reject it), Marx elaborated a detailed empirical social science. Drawing on empirical accounts of the practices of industrial labour and factory systems by contemporary economists, and those of his collaborator Friedrich Engels, Marx formulated a critique of the division of labour in its industrial capitalist form, of wage labour, and of human exploitation. The industrial conditions of the day clearly illustrated for Marx the severity of alienation and dehumanization inherent in capitalist production and economy. These conditions and the social relations that produced them may be, and inevitably will be, socially transformed. Revolutionary activity, Marx postulated, may hasten the historical necessity and inevitability of societal transformation to socialism.

In the Preface to *Critique* (well known for its succinct summary of Marx's essential ideas and his reflections upon them), Marx summarized his sociological theories, and his economic interpretation of history:

> The general result at which I have arrived…can be briefly formulated as follows: In the social production of their life, men enter into definite relations that are indispensable and independent of their will, relations of production which correspond to a definite stage of development of their material productive forces. The sum total of these relations of production constitutes the economic structure of society, the real foundation, on which rises a legal and political superstructure and to which correspond definite forms of social consciousness.… It is not the consciousness of men that determines their being, but, on the contrary their social being that determines their consciousness. At a certain stage of their development, the material productive forces of society come into conflict with the existing relations of production.… Then begins an epoch of social revolution. (Marx [1859] 1978: 4)

The famous preface outlines Marx's distinction between the economic base and the superstructure, the latter containing the legal and political institutions and social institutions of ideologies, philosophies and values. It also indicates Marx's view that social reality determines human consciousness, that ideas and values must be explained in terms of the social relations they constitute. Marx's views opposed evolutionist notions of society organized around a central regulative principle of rationality. Society was organized around institutionalized class interests presenting as rational, universal interests. These institutions of power, mystified by rationalization, obscured the necessary consciousness among actors capable of contesting those institutionalized relations.

Finally, however, it is in *Capital* that Marx the economist is given fullest expression.[2] This expression differs, in some ways markedly, from the youthful Hegelian humanism that lies at the heart of considerable Marxist debates through the decades. The differences have inspired the adoption of various scholarly and political positions and a proliferation of Marxist-inspired movements and schools throughout the 20th century. For some commentators, Marx's thought presents an economic and technological determinism; for others, Marx is revealing the historical and cultural specificity of economic and social conditions, and their means of change.

Capital focuses on economic practices of value, exchange, exploitation, profit and accumulation. It is also an effort to offer a historical sociology of capitalism. For Marx, the division of capitalist society into two opposing classes – one which owns the means of production and the other which owns only its labour power which is sold to the capitalist owners and employers of that labour – is a necessary condition of capitalism. The laws of capitalist economy require extraction of surplus value from commodified labour power to procure capitalist profit and accumulation. The working class, which procures only enough payment necessary for subsistence and reproduction, is necessarily exploited in the generation of surplus value and profit. Marx theorized, like the classical economists, that over time there is a tendency for profit to be accumulated at falling rates. But he proposed that the falling rate of profit was both a law of capitalism and the mechanism of its inevitable destruction. His prediction, which he contended was scientifically formulated and theoretically demonstrated in *Capital*, inverted the liberal economists' view that humans acting in their own interests act in the interests of the group. For Marx, each person acting rationally in her or his own economic interests contributes to the destruction of the group or societal interest.

Essentially, Marx believed that capitalist society is characterized by contradiction, antagonism and class struggle. A revolution of the proletariat against private ownership of the means of production and bourgeois ideology would bring about a post-capitalist society in which the conditions for human self-fulfilment would be created. Many critics have pointed out that the uncertainties entailed in such an unspecified event as the destruction of capitalism and the rise of a progressive societal successor compromise, at least, Marx's scientific sociology and economics. Yet notwithstanding its spurious scientific purport and its considerably variable emphases in political party and intellectual theorizations, Marxism contines to inspire critical theorists and political practitioners of varying agendas. The spectre of Marx illuminates even the theories of its strongest opponents or deconstructive rejectors of the political as conceived by modern social thought (see Derrida 1994). Of similar intellectual, if not practically political, significance is the work of Marx's compatriot German social theorist and sociologist, Max Weber.

Max Weber (1864–1920)

Max Weber was, of course, influenced by Marx and his work necessarily required an extensive engagement with Marx's historical materialism and economic sociology. Yet also of influence was another German theorist of Weber's generation, Hegel's student Georg Simmel, with whom Weber shared philosophical and ethical interests. Both thinkers opposed the rising naturalistic social science of the liberal British and positivist French thinkers, and both maintained a compelling commitment to understanding possibilities for individual life in the face of overwhelming forces of social organization and technology.[3] In the hermeneutic tradition of German philosophy Weber sought to understand and interpret human actions and experiences in terms of their intrinsic human meaningfulness.

Weber's accomplishment is immense and encyclopaedic. His work includes philosophical and epistemological studies in the social sciences, history, politics, economics, and science; sociology of religion, and a general sociology of economy and society. The following discussion focuses selectively on a few encompassing themes in Weber's work which exerted a more direct influence on the later development of organizational sociologies. Weber shared with Marx an interest in the origins and development of capitalist economics and society but he rejected 'the doctrine of the more naive historical materialism' ([1904–05] 1958: 55) and notions of immutable, universal laws of history. To the material factors shaping human history Weber poses the question of the influence of religious conceptions in determining economic behaviour and economic change. In probably his most widely known work, *The Protestant Ethic and the Spirit of Capitalism* ([1904–05] 1958), Weber not only elaborated his theory of modern Western (or occidental) capitalism and the influence of religious sensibilities upon economic rationalities, he presented a succinct statement of his sociological method, and the rudiments of his general theory of modern society.

> The capitalist economy of the present day is an immense cosmos into which the individual is born, and which presents itself to him, at least as an individual, as an unalterable order of things in which he must live. It forces the individual, in so far as he is involved in the system of market relations, to conform to capitalist rules of action....Thus the capitalism of today, which has come to dominate economic life, educates and selects economic subjects which it needs through a process of economic survival of the fittest....In order that a manner of life so well adapted should be selected at all, i.e. should come to dominate others, it had to originate somewhere, and not in isolated individuals alone, but as a way of life common to whole groups of men. This origin is what really needs explanation. ([1904–05] 1958: 54–55)

The Protestant Ethic and the Spirit of Capitalism elaborates such an explanation. For Weber, groups of individuals sharing a social nature and daily life orientate themselves to an ethic, 'a manner of life', which supports the social structures in which they survive. There is a simultaneous recursive relationship between individual subjects and social structures. In modern capitalism a certain type of subject with certain moral and social values is selected. It is a subject dedicated to rational economic activities by, in the first instance, irrational, religiously inspired, motivations.

Weber defined capitalism in the plural – every capitalist society presents differences from another. Capitalism involving the pursuit of profit and wealth has been present in various forms of society: in antiquity, in the East, and in medieval Europe. But its form in the modern West, that requires the maximization of profit, the rational organization of work and production, and the reproduction of capital through continual reinvestment, is unique and relatively recent. The desire for profit and wealth, common in all societies, is satisfied in modern capitalist society, for Weber, by discipline and science. These imperatives are most eminently epitomized in the bureaucratic organization. For Weber, the continual accumulation of wealth for its own sake and not for its means to achieve material luxury, and not tempered by the norms of tradition, is peculiar to modern Western capitalism:

> the earning of more and more money, combined with the strict avoidance of all spontaneous enjoyment of life, is above all completely devoid of any... hedonistic admixture. It is thought so purely an end in itself....Man is dominated by the making of money, by acquisition as the ultimate purpose of his life. Economic acquisition is no longer subordinated to man as the means for the satisfaction of his material needs. ([1904–05] 1958: 53)

This drive toward maximum accumulation of profit and asceticism captures the spirit of modern capitalism. It may be traced directly to the influence of forms of Protestantism popular in northern Europe and the newly developing United States of America, following the success of the Reformation. In particular, the Puritan Protestant sects following the teachings of Calvin, emphasized a notion of calling, of salvation of the elect, and of a disciplined, frugal lifestyle. In Weber's interpretation of Calvinism,[4] the idea of calling refers to the moral obligation upon an individual to fulfil his or her duty in worldly affairs. The doctrine of the predestined salvation of the elect (predestination) exerted, in Weber's view, a tyrannical influence upon believers. A mysterious, unknowable God decreed by his own, unknowable, means who were among the damned and who among the elect. Man's only recourse was to obey his Church leaders, to perform his duties diligently and unceasingly, and to believe he was among the chosen. An individual's success in worldly affairs, undertaken with sober, ascetic industriousness, was taken as a 'sign' of God's favour. The accumulation of wealth was thereby morally sanctioned.

The virtues favoured by capitalism and Calvinism encouraged the selection of the faithful, hardworking, self-disciplined worker necessary for capitalist efficiency and accumulation. Methodical, constant work came to be understood as obedience to calling and duty. Weber's theory of Calvinist, productive subjects provided an economic motivation for the accumulation and reinvestment behaviour of capitalism earlier identified by Marx. Yet, Weber observes, the capitalism so founded eventually eradicates the religious ethic aiding its development. *The Protestant Ethic* ends with Weber's observation that turn-of-the-20th-century capitalism, as exemplified in the United States of America, was increasingly 'stripped of its religious and ethical meaning... [and that] victorious capitalism, since it rests on mechanical foundations, needs its support no longer...the idea of duty in one's calling prowls about in our lives like the ghost of dead religious beliefs' ([1904–05] 1958: 182).

Notwithstanding the intensification of materialist rationalities – and the 'iron cage' that is our modern fate – Weber insisted on the importance of religion and irrationality in shaping subjective and collective identities and actions. The role of material and economic resources and activities is not definitive in understanding culture and history. Weber saw social life as a 'polytheism' of values in contest with one another. While there was no universally valid hierarchy of values, choices could and must be made among them. Weber saw different domains and roles in social life as types of conflicting 'life orders' (*Lebensordnungen*) possessing different values and orders of behaviour. But his construction of this schema was to serve the purpose of an 'ideal typical' means of orientation. 'They are not intended to show that there is no standpoint from which the conflicts could not be held to be resolved in a higher synthesis' (Weber [1915] 1946: 323).[5]

Two further features of Weber's general sociology, his theories of social action and of bureaucracy, exerted a considerable influence in organizational sociology. In *Economy and Society* (1922) Weber described sociology as the 'science of social action', and such action, according to his scientific method, may be explained, comprehended and interpreted. 'Sociology...means the science whose object is to interpret the meaning of social action...and the effects which it produces' (Weber [1922] 1989: 7). Social action, as Weber defined it, is human conduct that is assigned meaning by the agent and 'involves a relation to *another* person's behaviour' in such a way that 'the relation determines the way in which the action proceeds' (ibid.). He postulated that there are four types of social action: 'i) rational in the sense of employing appropriate means to a given end ('*zweckrational*')... ii) rational in the sense that it is an attempt to realize some absolute value ('*wertrational*')... iii) affectively (and in particular *emotionally*) determined... iv) *traditional* behaviour' (Weber [1922] 1989: 28).

This list, which includes 'the two types of rationality to be found in human actions', is not, Weber made clear, intended 'as an exhaustive classification of the different forms action may take'. Rather, these are 'ideal types' which are defined as: 'pure abstractions conceived for sociological purposes, to which real action may approximate to a greater or lesser degree' (Weber [1922] 1989: 30).[6]

The importance of Weber's classification, and the emphasis on rationality as the measure of human actions and their institutions so constituted, is much debated (see opposing views in Runciman 1989 and Aron 1967b, for instance). But the typology enabled subsequent conceptual systems to be explicated in his comprehensive social science. For Weber, the chief characteristic of modern society was rationalization, specifically expressed by an expansion of the sphere of *zweckrational* actions, actions rational in relation to goals, into all spheres of life. Economy, production, social life and individual life tend toward *zweckrational* organization. Affective and traditional rationalities are eroded and suppressed. Instrumental rationalization, which Weber saw as both an accomplishment of modern capitalism and a denudation of human being, manifests in multifarious forms. In everyday political and bureaucratic organization it is most readily observable. The modern bureaucratic organization, which accomplishes the rational organization of work and production, embodies the capitalist aim of the maximization of profit and accumulation. It accomplishes, too, the instrumental rationalization of human beings that diminishes their individuality, their creativity and their autonomy. Bureaucracy accomplishes the domination of persons by the rational-legal systems embedded in its organizations. Persons are thus trapped in an 'iron cage' from which escape seems impossible. These observations led Weber to conclude that the 'disenchantment of the world' by pervasive rationalization is the fate of modern society and its citizens.

Although criticized in various quarters (especially for his controversial thesis on Protestantism), and misunderstood in others, Weber's analysis of modern industrial society and the human fate within it continues to influence subsequent generations of social theorists and sociologists. While Weber's reception among a generation or more of English-speaking scholars and students, especially in North America, was markedly shaped by his translator and interpreter, Talcott Parsons, in the 1930s, Weber was also seriously read by other social theorists – those of the Frankfurt School of critical theory – who more latterly gained transatlantic attention. This tradition, discussed below, draws much on Weber's theorizations of domination, of the unpredictability of social action, and the increasing rationalization and instrumentalization of all spheres of life.

The Last Great Edifice of Classical Sociology

The turn of the 21st century presents a discipline of sociology that appears to be characterized by a multiplicity of interests, philosophical attachments and methodologies of inquiry and analysis. There is now scarcely agreement as to the main currents in contemporary sociology, and the classical ideas are undergoing a thorough reconsideration. Fewer than 30 years ago Anthony Giddens could confidently claim that '*the* problem in sociology [was] the question of classes and class conflict' (Giddens 1973: 19; original emphasis). Such assertions, whatever their probable validity, are now rarely made. On the contrary, the points of agreement among sociologists centre around the notion that the discipline is now in a prolonged state of crisis and the lack of widely shared views as to the discipline's central problems. The question of crisis is discussed in the next chapter, but for the moment I wish to emphasize an important continuing general agreement among diverse sociologists in the recognition that all of the main traditions have been significantly influenced, although to varying degrees, by the foundational theories of the great triumvirate, Durkheim, Marx and Weber. Other theorists such as Simmel, Tönnies, Pareto, Sorokin and Freud, and their descendants have also significantly influenced the discipline of sociology, and their traces are discernible today. In addition, schools of sociology have developed differences as a result of the influence of national conditions and ideological preferences among their leading protagonists.

Since sociology's beginnings in 19th century social science, sociological theorists have attempted to define and uphold a disciplinary boundary and to establish a more or less operational consensus as to the nature and aims of the discipline. Their attempts have been erratically successful and their demarcations persistently permeable. For many commentators, the divisions within sociology are wide and even unbridgeable. But for others, the divisions within schools of interest and method may be seen as positions in a dualism evident in sociology. On the one hand is a general orientation toward a philosophical, humanist, interpretive sociology, and on the other, a pragmatic, instrumentally rational, administrative, practical sociology. Arguments of this sort are elaborated, for instance, by Berger [1963] (1972) Gouldner (1970), Nisbet (1967) and Ritzer (1992).

The early appeal of grand general theory was quietened, but not dissipated, by the widely influential mid-20th century generation of sociological theorists (some would say first generation of sociological theorists proper e.g. Mouzelis 1995). Yet their predominant efforts to consolidate sociology as a social science and to normalize a body of general theories and delineations of the discipline shaped the normative practices and products of sociology and sociologists. An emphasis on generating general theories and conceptual tools for empirical studies and analyses of social life, notwithstanding the tenacity of the interpretive imperative, prevailed for several decades. Numerous efforts by historians and sociologists of sociology have produced taxonomies along various axes of philosophical orientation (e.g. order, control, conflict, class), specific subject matter (e.g. demography, ethnicity, religion, organization, family, health) and methodological approaches to investigation and analysis (see e.g. Bottomore 1975, Levine 1995, Nisbet 1967, Ritzer 1992). For many commentators the multitude and diversity of perspectives represent a now familiar concern that the discipline is in crisis. In this view, both confidence in, and the efficacy of, the sociological project are waning. On the other hand, for others, the diversity, fragmentation and mutability of the sociological tradition attest to its survival and validity in contemporary societies and bode well for the future of sociology (e.g. Lemert 1995, Levine 1995).

The expanse of sociological endeavours includes a number of more or less distinctive sub-traditions, although their range, distinction and importance is a matter of disagreement (see, for example, Levine 1995, Nisbet 1967, Ritzer 1992). Moreover, the appeal of various sub-strands in sociological thinking, such as phenomenology, symbolic interactionism, social exchange theory, and conflict theory (including Marxism), varied considerably between the United States, Europe and other parts of the world. However, despite the influential contributions of these different perspectives to social knowledge, a dominant paradigm shaped the overall discipline of sociology, and certainly that of organizational sociology. Since the mid-20th century the dominant paradigm in sociology has been that of systems theory and structural-functionalism. Even after the end of the century, when many sociologists claim that functionalism is officially defunct, the appeal of at least certain elements of that tradition endures in a revised and rehabilitated form (e.g. Bourdieu 1988, Mouzelis 1995). Its manifestation also in a crypto-functionalist appropriation of postmodern ideas is a matter I discuss in subsequent chapters.

Structural-functionalism is associated most of all with Talcott Parsons, whose theory erected the 'last great edifice of classical sociology' (Touraine 1988). Parsons' work reveals a deep evolutionary assumption which enabled him to imagine that society had reached a state in which it is organized in a stable and coherent fashion around the principles of instrumental rationality. Order now prevails.

Talcott Parsons (1902–1979) produced two major books: *The Structure of Social Action* (1937) and *The Social System* (1951) which remain significant, and somewhat controversial, in sociological theory. The influence of these works, as well as Parsons' interpretations of Weber, appears synchronically throughout sociological and organizational writings. Moreover, Parsonian frameworks are widely evident in other social sciences including political science, psychology, education, economics and business studies. Parsons was explicitly concerned with the 'problem of order'. His first book, *The Structure of Social Action* (1937), pursued this problematic by setting his discussion in the context of deficiencies of classical social theorists' accounts of order. Subsequent theorists and analysts of sociological traditions have argued against the accuracy and validity of many of Parsons' imputations (e.g. Gouldner 1970, Levine 1995, Zeitlin 1973)[7] and still more have argued against his ahistorical, politically unconscious, 'bourgeois' frameworks and positivism (e.g. Gouldner 1970). But the importance of Parsons' work is rarely questioned. As Anthony Giddens reminds us: 'Even the severest critic of Talcott Parsons must recognize the extraordinary nature of his contributions to social theory over a period of half a century' (Giddens 1982: 76).

In *The Structure of Social Action* (1937) Parsons developed a narrative that postulates the convergence of the economist Marshall, and the sociologists Pareto, Durkheim and Weber. The convergence, for Parsons, occurs around a mediation of extreme positivist and idealist positions long evident in German philosophy and social theory. Parsons' exhaustive effort to prove their convergence is summarized in five theses (Parsons [1937] 1968: 719–726). The four theorists converge around agreement on 'the outline of what in *all essentials* is the *same* system of generalized social theory' (pp. 719–720, original emphasis) and their '[t]heoretically important differences…[can be] reduced to three circumstances' (p. 720). These differences Parsons briefly described as being those (only) of terminology, extent of analytical development, and mode of statement.

With this grand sweep of convergence, major controversies and divergent theorizations had been synthesized and dissolved. The convergence provides the postulates and solutions to his problem of order – in theory and in society. Parsons posited a theory of social action and social order based on society's 'common value system'. Seeking to counter what he perceived as an overly naturalist science that denied the role of human values, consciousness and action in human affairs, *and* the idealist, anti-materialist positions of other theorists, Parsons also sought to define and secure a coherent discipline of sociology in the social sciences according to his grand unifying schema. This accomplishment was destined to exert considerable influence over the field of sociology for generations, and despite valiant opposition in some quarters, it remains influential in the normative interpretation of the classical theorists in many universities to the present day. Parsons' selective reading of Marx, even more apparent than his reading of his chief protagonists, scornfully and sporadically addressed the complexities of materialism and idealism in Marx's thought. Ultimately Parsons relegated Marx's thought to the idealism of its Hegelian heritage (Parsons [1937] 1968: 488–495). Marxist materialism, and clearly the disruption to Parsons' unitive sociological project it poses, were glossed over. Parsons' devotion to the appropriation of Weber prevailed throughout his work. But it was his appropriation of Durkheim's thought that inspired Parsons' theories of social systems and functions.

Durkheim's imputed move from materialist positivism to a sort of idealist empiricism in his persistent questioning of the nature of social 'facts', and his ultimate privileging of moral values and constraints, assured his primary place in the Parsonian schema. Durkheim's *conscience collective* for Parsons, imposed normative, external constraints on the individual that were internalized by cultural and moral education and socialization. This collective transcendence, evident in sacred religious ritual performances, over individual profane interests, sustained and ensured social order. Therefore, for Parsons, the Durkheimian resolution of the problem of order, and of action, is demonstrated. Durkheim's persistent concern with the problems of conflicts of interests, coercion, and social inequalities and pathologies in modern industrial society is largely ignored. However, having more or less adopted from Durkheim an overarching theory of normative functional integration, Parsons proceeded on a path from a theory of social action drawn from Weber to a functionalist conception of social systems.

Parsons utilized Durkheim's descriptive functionalism of an organic social order as the basis for his theory of systemic functionalism developed in *The Social System* (1951). Moreover, he sought to emulate Durkheim's effort to establish sociology as a social science with a systematically researched and generalizable body of knowledge. Durkheim's organismic analogy – which viewed social systems as like living, holistic organic systems, maintaining a complex interdependence of parts for the survival of the whole – was readily transferred and elaborated by Parsons. Others too, importantly the anthropologists Malinowski and Radcliffe-Brown, were variously influenced by Durkheim and biological and natural science, and their scientific positivism.[8] A current of functionalist thought was popular in many disciplines in the academy, but the definitive elaboration of a general systems theory of society is the legacy of Talcott Parsons.

Structural-functionalism

From his synthetic theory of social action Parsons developed an analysis of society as a system of functionally interdependent variables. Indebted to Pareto's systems theory and Durkheim's functionalism, Parsons described in his introduction to *The Social System* (1951) his effort to develop a 'conceptual scheme for the analysis of the structure and processes of social systems' (Parsons 1951: vii). He began with the matter of interactions between individual actors which, he proposed, may be seen as a system. The simplest of interaction systems is the 'dyadic' one, between Ego and Alter which, although they are organisms, interact at a social and not a biological level. These interactions are simultaneously social and cultural in that they involve values, norms, goals and motivations that arise in cultural and personality systems. Therefore, for Parsons, a sociocultural system arises in which a complex interdependence of analytically, but not empirically, discrete systems occurs. Between the social, cultural and personality systems is a 'common sector' (the 'central value system') that 'consists in the value-patterns which define role expectations' (Parsons 1951: 540). Parsons posited a 'fundamental relationship between need-dispositions of the personality, role-expectations of the social system and internalized-institutionalized value-patterns of the culture [as] the fundamental nodal point of the organization of systems of action' (ibid.). Each of these systems has needs, boundaries and motivations.

The satisfaction of each of these subsystem needs is necessary for the whole system equilibrium to be maintained. The system – social or organization – whole is a complex arrangement of interdependencies among subsystems. Each of these subsystems is subject to four 'functional prerequisites' that must be met if the system (social organization) is to 'survive'. The system must be able to adapt to and allocate its resources, to define and achieve its goals, to integrate its constituent parts and maintain solidarity, and to transmit and maintain its patterns of interaction. (These functional prerequisites are popularly known as AGIL: Adaptation, Goal-achievement, Integration, and Latency.) Parsons described the means by which social systems are organized to meet these needs according to system and environmental inputs and outputs, stability through adaptation to those environmental resources and coordination of individual actions to contribute to higher system needs. Higher system needs require all subsystems, e.g. organizations in society and individuals in organizations, to contribute through boundary exchange to higher system needs of stability and equilibrium. In turn every social system must meet the needs of its constituent subsystems, including individuals, in order to survive. Systemic degeneration or failure of the 'central value system' will undermine the internalization of system norms and values among individuals and subsystems. Therefore a high degree of institutionalization of patterns and values is required to avert degenerative impulses. Conflicts are disequilibrating impulses that are, and must be, managed and resolved by higher order regulative mechanisms.

Parsons' structural-functionalist systems theory generated both a proliferation of sociological studies in this vein, and eventually a chorus of criticism as well. The first criticisms raised against the Parsonian schema focused on problems within his functionalism itself. These criticisms point to embedded assumptions in the Parsonian schema that suggest teleological arguments and explanations. In particular, Parsons' notion of 'functional prerequisites'; his concept of equilibrium, that assumes a tendency toward organic homeostasis and 'social' harmony in the whole; and his assumptions concerning problems of conflict and change drew much critical attention.[9]

Functionalists themselves, including Parsons,[10] recognized many of the first order problems. Robert Merton's contributions to structural-functionalism posed modifications and additions to the Parsonian variety. Merton offered a less grand theorizing than Parsons' schema and attempts to provide a more limited and applicable range of conceptual tools to the analysis of social practices. Merton's 'middle range' theories add to a systems theory functionalism concepts that endeavour to account for unintended consequences of actions and to explain relations between subsystems. Merton postulated the concepts of 'latent' or unintended functions; 'dysfunctions' as well as 'manifest' functions; and 'functional alternatives' (Merton [1949] 1968). Functional alternatives refer to alternative social or organizational arrangements that may be just as functional as those currently operating.

Refinements to Parsons' schema by Merton (ibid.), Selznick (1949) and Gouldner (1954a), among others, contributed to the establishment of a combined systems theory and structural-functionalist approach to the study of organizations, and other social practices, that ascended to paradigmatic orthodoxy by the 1950s and 1960s. Among the many variations between systems theories and structural-functionalist approaches, especially with respect to relative emphasis placed on system boundaries, roles of individual actors, formalized rationality, and questions of causality and change, a general body of social systems approaches is readily discerned. Many sociologists and other social scientists regarded structural-functionalism of various types as holding sufficient merit for widespread application to social analysis and social problem-solving, and for integrative usefulness in post-World War II decades of societal restabilization and reconsolidation.

A general criticism of structural-functionalism that eventually gained much momentum and, some would argue, quietened the overt use of structural functionalism and identification with that tradition, began to emerge in the 1950s. For critics, Parsons' slighting of the problems of power, conflict, inequality, excessive constraints and coercion delimit functionalism to analyses and applications that serve not a generalized common goal but those of particular classes and elites. The functional accommodation of social stratification, the assertion of normative unity around a common value system, and the illegitimacy of conflict, is a conservative defence of the status quo and an ideology obscuring domination. These criticisms, shared by many, were prominently elaborated in Alvin Gouldner's influential book, *The Coming Crisis of Western Sociology* published in 1970.

Eventually, definitive assaults on the paradigmatic hold of structural-functionalism in sociology came about with the events which many call the 'crisis' in sociology (Giddens 1973, Gouldner 1970, Lemert 1995). The crisis, which was precipitated by a number of complex and intersecting factors, changed the shape and directions of sociology. The crisis in sociology, and its relevance to the development of the sociology of organizations and organization studies, are discussed in Chapter 4. In the meantime classical theories of organization which had developed in the early 20th century were definitively affected by post-war functionalist, integrationalist, sociology. Parsonian structural-functionalism and its derivatives found a well-prepared audience among organization analysts seeking to establish an organization science. Chapter 3 discusses the classical theories of bureaucracy and organization and the pursuit of a scientific sociology of organization. But my narrative for the remainder of this chapter attends to two further matters: the presence of other currents in sociological thought, especially symbolic interactionism and phenomenology; and the critical theory of the Frankfurt School.

Phenomenology and Symbolic Interactionism

Notwithstanding the dominant influence of systems theory and structural-functionalism, the schools of thought of phenomemology and symbolic interactionism exerted important influence. Attempting, with Parsons, to understand the subject-actor and social structure, the phenomenologists and symbolic interactionists nevertheless departed dramatically from Parsons. In de-emphasizing the social structure in favour of subjective experience, they theorized the subjective and intersubjective construction of social realities. The philosophical perspective of phenomenology, with its focus on consciousness, has been influential in several arenas in the social sciences and humanities. It is most associated with the foundational work of Husserl and Scheler, and later with Merleau-Ponty, Schutz and Goffman. In many respects it has been more significant in anthropological traditions, but its influence in sociology has provided an important bridge between the two social sciences and encouraged a field of micro-sociology. The relationship of phenomenology to sociology emerged through its sympathetic, though psychological, association with the theories of Weber and Marx, especially those concerning nature and *Verstehen* (understanding).

For phenomenologists, each society has unique objective conditions in which its participants have unique experiences distinct from those of another society. These experiences and the viewpoints they engender create different, yet equally valid, perspectives on life and reality. They may be understood as phenomena possessing particularity and (to a degree) independent validity. For Schutz, whose express effort was to develop a synthesis of sociology and phenomenology, the social world of everyday life is always an intersubjective one (Schutz [1932] 1967). More precisely, Schutz' work may be considered a synthesis of Husserl and Weber (as Zeitlin 1973 argues) both of whom believed in the social construction of values and meaning and – Weber especially – insisted on understanding life as it is actually lived. In order to develop an interpretive sociology, Schutz elaborated Weber's condensed theory of subjective meaning and of intersubjectivity by adding insights from Husserl's phenomenological psychology. For Schutz, each individual shares a life-world (*Lebenswelt*) with others who co-construct that world. The world of objects is constituted according to the meaning it has for us. These meanings are constructed from a mixture of biographically determined appraisals and socially pre-structured interpretations given subjective definition. Interpretive sense is made of the biographical and cultural material by means of a common language of communication.

Meanings, language, motivations, conscious and unconscious perceptions, and interpretations of self and intersubjective relations comprise primary subject material for phenomenologists. These phenomena are subject to flux and momentary subtleties in meaning-making and interpretation. The sociologist must first endeavour to understand the meaning of human actions ascribed by the actors themselves. For Schutz, any social and cultural group establishes its own 'domains of relevance' by which phenomena are sorted and made cognitively manageable. Socially grouped relevances and typifications provide pre-established frameworks of meaning-making. These ideas and approaches to micro-social phenomena shared much with the school of symbolic interactionism.

Associated with George H. Mead and Erving Goffman and American pragmatic philosophy, notably with John Dewey, symbolic interactionism became popular in the Chicago School of sociology (Charles Cooley, Robert Park, E.W. Burgess, Herbert Blumer). Mead, for example, in his book *Mind, Self, and Society* (1934) endeavoured to overcome the traditional dualism between mind and physical nature. His method was a dialectical conception of the relation of humans to each other, and of humans to nature. Individuals are co-constituent of their environment, and the environment conditions the individual's sensitivity and action. For Mead, 'selves must be accounted for in terms of the social process, and in terms of communication' (1934: 49). For Mead, the self was a socially, and personally, interactive construction. It was not a unidirectional product of socialization into a predetermined social system.

Erving Goffman's influential book *The Presentation of Self in Everyday Life* (1959) spans the interests of both phenomenological and sociological traditions. In this work Goffman studies situations of inter-actions between people using 'dramaturgical principles' that focus on the non-verbal, unintentional, contextual expressions from which we infer meanings and impressions. For Goffman, people put on performances in their everyday actions and interactions with others. These performances are guided by what the actors regard as the official values of the society in which they live, but there is no socially institutionalized requirement that actors believe in the roles they play out. These acting roles inevitably present tensions and conflicts between the individual and social roles, and they stimulate further interactive manoeuvres and rituals (Goffmann 1967) among the players.

In Goffman and the ethnomethodologists, the classical sociological idea of society as a central system of institutional and behavioural regula-tion is set aside. In emphasizing attention to subjective social experience they encouraged micro-sociological inquiries into the practices of every-day life. But their explanation of behaviour by the play of interactions departs from the classical sociological notion of a social space organized by institutionalized norms. Social actors become actors playing roles strategizing their positions *vis-à-vis* others in an unstructured movement of currents. These ideas diverged significantly from the heritage of clas-sical sociology; but their uptake in micro-sociologies and social psycho-logies rarely recognized this important disruption. Phenomenological and symbolic interactionist theories influenced organizational analysis, parti-cularly management and organization behaviour studies, largely through the Human Relations school (discussed in Chapter 3), sympathetic to sub-jective worker experience in organizations. Moreover, a revised and revital-ized version of these traditions exerts a contemporary influence through late 20th century postmodern approaches to organizations.

Alongside these pragmatic sociologies, more popular in the United States, was a tradition that a number of commentators broadly designate as Western Marxism, which includes the comparable, although often independently developed, work of theorists from Lukács to Gramsci, and importantly that of the school of critical theory known as the Frankfurt School. Though scarcely well known in organization studies today, the Frankfurt School has exerted a significant influence in critical social analyses of diverse social practices.

Frankfurt School Critical Theory

The influence of the Frankfurt School, and that of Western Marxist criticism more broadly, in studies of organization, work, technology and industrial studies has been especially evident in recent years (see, for example, Alvesson and Deetz 1996, Burrell and Morgan 1979, Casey 1995, Fischer and Siriani 1994, Reed 1985). The writings of the Frankfurt School gained most popularity in the 1960s and 1970s during an effervescent period of student and intellectual protest in many Western countries. The Institute of Social Research was established in Frankfurt, Germany, in the 1920s and continued to operate in exile in the United States following World War II. The Institute sought to establish a context for interdisciplinary study by bringing together philosophers, sociologists, economists, historians and psychologists to pursue great philosophical questions. It hoped to counter the division of labour in the humanities and social sciences which was producing fragmented results and avoidance of great questions. The Frankfurt School now refers to a broad tradition of critical theory which finds unity in shared criticism of capitalism and commitment to alternative, non-authoritarian and non-bureaucratic, paths for social development (see, e.g. Arato and Gebhardt 1982, Held 1980, Horkheimer and Adorno 1972, Kellner 1989b for substantive discussions).

The Institute's key figures include Max Horkheimer, Theodor Adorno, Erich Fromm, Herbert Marcuse, Leo Lowenthal and more recently, Jürgen Habermas. All of these theorists, and their descendants in contemporary critical theory, engage in dialogical discussion with the works of classical Western philosophers, Kant, Hegel, Marx, Weber, Lukács and Freud. The aim of their interdisciplinary research was the pursuit of 'questions concerning the conditions which make possible the reproduction and transformation of society, the meaning of culture, and the relation between the individual, society and nature' (Held 1980: 16), which may be pursued across the humanities and social sciences, and in any domain of human inquiry. Central to their project, following Lukács' effort to retrieve Hegelian Marxism from its determinist and positivist interpretations, was a renewed attention to Marx's early work. Drawing again on German idealism led to a restored inquiry into human subjectivity, for which Freud's work was of paramount importance.

Similarly, Weber's writings, especially those on rationalization and bureaucratization, were recognized as significant contributions to contemporary sociology and social theory. The critical theorists endeavoured to further develop these critiques and to develop an epistemology of a critical understanding of society that was largely absent in the classical Marxist tradition.

Although the various figures associated with the Frankfurt School wrote on diverse matters, the school is most often recognized for its social philosophy and social psychology rather than for its association with programmatic critiques of political economy. In particular the critique of 'instrumental reason', of technological domination of nature and humans, of the capitalist mode of production, the commodification of cultural production, and the structural obstructions to humans 'coming to consciousness of themselves as subjects' represent the school's best-known themes and the core problematics towards which their critical *oeuvre* is oriented. Their complex arguments are developed in many works, including Horkheimer and Adorno's *Dialectic of Enlightenment* ([1947] 1972), Horkheimer's *Eclipse of Reason* ([1947] 1974), Marcuse's *One-Dimensional Man* (1965), Fromm's *Escape from Freedom* ([1941] 1965), and Adorno's *The Authoritarian Personality* (1950). These works are among the most well-known to English-speaking readers, although in several cases their translation into English was delayed.

For the Frankfurt School, modern capitalist society enmeshes the individual in a concentration of economic and political activities that are increasingly interlocked – 'it is a *verwaltete Welt*, a world caught up in administration' (Held 1980: 77). The concentration of economic activity in giant enterprises, state capitalism, and the incorporation of monopolistic trade unions have, in Marcuse's representative argument, established a system which 'tends towards both total administration and total dependence on administration by ruling public and private managements, strengthening the pre-established harmony between the interests of the big public and private corporations and that of their customers and servants' (Marcuse 1965: 35).

In order to understand (and transform) the role of individual enmeshment in this near totality of instrumentality the Frankfurt theorists formulated, beyond an economic and political ideology critique, a sociology of mass or popular culture. Differing from both classical Marxists and conventional cultural criticism, and closer to Freud's view, the critical theorists conceived of culture as emerging out of the organizational basis of society. For Marcuse, culture 'signifies the totality of social life in a given situation, in so far as both the ideational reproduction... and of material reproduction ("civilization") form a historically distinguishable and comprehensible unity' (Marcuse 1965: 94). Marcuse endeavoured, along with his Institute colleagues (although eventually in isolation from them in the United States), to analyse the ways in which cultural phenomena interact with other social dimensions. The critical theorists sought in artistic culture possibilities for protestation and liberation from the existing conditions of domination and repression. The turn to aesthetics heralded by some of the Frankfurt School theorists was a consequence of an increasingly despairing analysis of the prevailing political and economic conditions and the intractable march of instrumental reason and capitalism. As popular revolutionary practice also waned, the resort to aestheticism represented a compensation for the impasse of Marxism in societal practice and its imbrication in the modern Enlightenment project. This tendency recurs in a succeeding generation of cultural theorists who share the Frankfurt School's pessimism regarding social systemic domination.

In an effort to understand the failure of the European proletariat to protest against Fascism, and the apparent increasing integration of the working class into capitalism, the Frankfurt theorists sought to understand the socio-psychological formation of the individual. Reflecting Weber's interest in the relation between the individual and society, the Frankfurt School theorists pursued these questions through the theorizations of Freudian psychoanalysis. Each of the major theorists developed distinct contributions – Fromm, for instance finally pursuing a more social psychoanalytic theory incorporating both Marxism and metaphysics. Marcuse, on the other hand, through his efforts to refine the Freudian position, posited the possibility of a non-repressive social condition in a transformed, post-scarcity, Western civilization. Importantly, Marcuse introduces the notions of 'surplus repression' and the 'performance principle'. He accepted most of the Freudian thesis: the centrality of the unconscious, the role of instincts, infantile sexuality, and the conflict between individual and civilization. But he differed with the Freudian view of the conflict between the 'pleasure principle'[11] and the 'reality principle' in the psyche's dynamic, that must be resolved through the ultimate prevailing of the reality principle. The repressive transformation of instincts, which leads for Freud to civilization, leads, for Marcuse, to excessive or surplus constraints on the individual, and on nature itself (Marcuse 1962). The 'performance principle', that is, the particular form of Freud's reality principle under capitalist conditions, leads to surplus repression: the political and economic domination of sexuality. Marcuse proposed that under transformed social arrangements the capitalist necessity for surplus repression would become obsolete and a reconciliation of social conflicts would be made possible.

But he despaired of the possibilities for political practices generating such transformation in the post-war United States where he lived, and where sustained intellectual, politically emancipatory, practice never achieved the power of a social force.

Marcuse's propositions were not uniformly shared by his Institute colleagues. For many commentators, it is Horkheimer and Adorno's concern with the rise and domination of instrumental rationality – an instrumentality that prevails over all oppositions – that most characterizes the 'negation' of critical theory. Yet the Institute's theorists shared the view that critical theory's principal tasks are to show the historical specificity of apparently inexorable laws, and to reveal the potentialities for the expansion of realms of human freedom and justice. In Horkheimer's essay 'Traditional and Critical Theory' (1972), published in the 1930s, the Institute's project is elaborated. For Horkheimer, traditional theory since Descartes favours foundations and ahistorical 'basic facts'. It is a projection of the 'bourgeois ideal' of the unified values and laws of the capitalist market. Traditional social theories are forms of social practice which reproduce dominant forms of capitalist activity. Traditional theory, and its scientific practitioners, are unaware of their conformist, uncritical submission to dominant instrumental values. Critical theory is grounded in oppositional critical activity which necessitates a contextual understanding of all social phenemona, and aims to achieve the transformation of society.

With the publication in 1947 of Horkheimer and Adorno's *Dialectic of Enlightenment* emphasis shifted somewhat from political economy to philosophical critiques of science, technology and instrumental reason. In this book the authors trace the trajectory of the Enlightenment and conclude that its modern products of science and Marxism are potential instruments of domination and subjugation. The project of reasoned emancipation has ended in Fascism and intense instrumental capitalism and produced the 'administered society'. In a view that is later shared by the French theorist Michel Foucault, Horkheimer and Adorno conclude that 'power and knowledge are synonomous' ([1947] 1972: 4). For Horkheimer the dominant forms of reason in the administered society, epitomized in bureaucratization, require 'the fullest possible adaptation of the subject to the reified authority of the economy' (Horkheimer 1972: 56). The struggle for the individual 'in a world of apparatuses, machinery and manipulation [is] not to be annihilated at any moment' (ibid.).

Notwithstanding the concluding pessimism of most of the Frankfurt School theorists, their themes continue to be developed in the work of more recent theorists.[12] Importantly, their turn to the cultural sphere was followed by many others.

Feminist Critical Theory

As critical theory turned increasingly to the cultural arena, it tacitly diminished the centrality of the economic and political concerns of classical Marxism. In their place was an elevated theorization of the aesthetic, and of cultural and identity politics. An apparent impasse of the political and economic deepened. A culture of capitalism, many critical theorists concluded, foreclosed practical political alternatives. While Western Marxism in social theory moved toward the cultural sphere, an emerging feminist criticism in the 1960s and 1970s restored an insistence on the materiality – this time of a bodily and sexual nature – of political practice, as well as recognizing the significance of cultural practices.

Although possessing a long history (see Eisenstein 1983, Fuss 1989, Jaggar 1983, Rossi 1974, Spender 1982) and increasingly systematically developed in the mid-20th century, notably by writers such as Simone de Beauvoir and Virginia Woolf, feminist criticism as a social movement was more visibly and effectively launched in the 1960s and 1970s. This new wave of critical theory developed substantive feminist analyses of sexual oppression and gendered power relations which instituted inequalities, prejudice and discrimation. Feminist social criticism and cultural theory, and the popular women's movement similarly challenging masculinist social and cultural institutions, gave rise to a now vast literature on all aspects of women's lives hitherto unconsidered by dominant traditions of knowledge.

Feminist critics sought to develop new paradigms of social criticism that called into question and variously rejected the traditional philosophical underpinnings of Western social thought. Exposing the partial and gendered nature of purportedly universal, gender-neutral thought and the historical and cultural contingency of knowledge remains a primary platform of feminist critical theory. As well as providing grand-scale critical theory, feminist theory also significantly attends to the historically specific, the local, the particular, and the different. A vast body of feminist thought addressing and advancing contemporary questions in science, culture and social practices continues to develop. From analyses of everyday life to science and philosophy, feminist critical theory effectively challenges a once exclusive mainstream (e.g. Benhabib et al. 1994, Fraser 1989, 1997, Harding 1986, Keller 1984, Kristeva 1980, Smith 1990, Spivak 1990) and contributes new philosophical notions and theoretical schemata in understanding diverse social practices.

The rise of feminist criticism and the new demands resulting from its expositions contributed to the growing assault on classical sociological theory and on the institutional practices of sociologists in the academy.

These developments are discussed in the following chapters, but I wish to point out here that the development of feminist criticism into a social movement contesting the cultural stakes of society – that is, contesting the knowledge, values and norms by which social rules are set at any historical time – practically revealed the weakening hold of classical modern conceptions of universal, rationalizing modern society. The entering, throughout the 1980s and 1990s, of feminists into the postmodern debate has further implications for feminist thought and practice (e.g. Benhabib and Cornell 1987, Diamond and Quinby 1988, Fraser 1997, Nicholson 1990), and for social and cultural analysis more broadly. Not surprisingly, feminists have developed different views on the usefulness of postmodernism to the feminist project. An extensive and, for some (e.g. Fraser 1997), an unnecessarily divisive debate currently ensues. By the 2000s there are signs, perhaps, of a movement away from intra-theoretical opposition to the more bivalent sociocultural theory advocated by Fraser (1997).

A Modern Orthodoxy

Across and within the competing paradigms of modern sociology a prevailing recognition of modernity in its form of progressive instrumental rationalization provides a grand unifying imperative which structures sociological activity – and its criticism. The project of modernity and the privileging of rationalization is the lens through which all visions of society and organizations have been viewed. Yet within this grandeur, there are degrees of intensity with which modern imperatives and agenda have been enacted and valued. Clusters of theorists have formed around apparent enthusiasm for, or criticism of, modern societal rationalization. From theorists of general systems theory and structural-functionalism to Marxists, Frankfurt School critics and early feminist critics, the modern project is assumed to be monolithic and intractable. At best, critics imagined, are humanistic efforts to refine and delimit technocratic rationalities and excesses to stave off annihilation by modern totalities.

Against the vast backdrop of modernity, succeeding generations of sociologists – organizational sociologists in particular, as thoroughly modern social scientists – tended to elide disjunctures in modern enactments and to assume that their task was to produce empirically based or 'pure' theoretical analyses of social problematics for ultimate policy development and administrative application. Within sociology various theoretical and instrumental paths to such analyses and results were developed. Their association with particular ideological attachments has been variously criticized over the decades, from C. Wright Mills' criticism of the sociologist as 'organization man' to Gouldner's criticism in the 1970s, and Lemert's (1995) insightful traverse more recently. The traditions of organizational analysis to which we now turn eminently attest to the institutionalized assumptions and values of their antecedents. But they too eventually encounter a reflexive interrogation, and crisis.

Notes

1. Marx descended from a heritage of rabbinical families yet his father, pressured by the harsh constraints imposed upon Jews by the Prussian regime, converted the family to Protestant Christianity in the 1820s.

2. *Capital* consists of three volumes of which only the first was published by Marx, in 1867; the latter two were published posthumously by his friend Friedrich Engels. Together the volumes of *Capital* present Marx's great work on political economy, society, government, and human being.

3. See Simmel's great essay 'The Metropolis and Mental Life' ([1903] 1971) in which his critical explorations of modern life and the struggle for individual freedom and autonomous activity in the midst of increasing cultural domination are readily understood a century later.

4. There has been much debate over Weber's interpretation of Protestantism, especially his interpretation of Calvin which was done substantially through secondary sources – 18th century followers of Calvin – many years after Calvin's death. See, or instance, Giddens' preface to a 1976 edition of *The Protestant Ethic*, and Lemert (1995).

5. Note this important qualification to Weber's polytheism which does not support, as du Gay (2000) claims, a notion of the irreducible plurality justifying domain-specific 'commandments' and refusing choice and 'sacrifice' of some domain values for others.

6. The 'ideal type', one of Weber's major concepts in his social science, is a construct designed, as (Aron 1967b: 207) succinctly expresses it, to 'render subject matter intelligible by revealing (or constructing) its internal rationality'. 'Ideal types' are constructions to contrive a standard of measurement and to give interpretive meaning to otherwise diverse, unintelligible flux. The concept offers, in the Weberian hermeneutic, a partial comprehension of an always incompletely known whole.

7. Levine (1995: 46) commenting on Parsons' *The Structure of Social Action*, takes the view that: 'For all its grandeur and sweep [it] must be judged a deeply flawed work of scholarship.' For others, such as Mouzelis (1995), although he accepts Parsons' flaws, the usefulness of a revised Parsonian functional scheme remains demonstrable in sociological theory.

8. Zeitlin (1973) points out that that there was a number of less well-known sociologists contemporaneous with Parsons who employed a 'traditional functionalism' to social analysis. Their variations shared an interest in systemic functionalist and determinate relationships among variables and patterns.

9. Many of these criticisms have been variously rejected, refined or retained and serious defences of functionalism are offered by, for example, Cohen 1968, Mouzelis 1995, Bourdieu 1977, 1992.

10. Zeitlin (1973: 24), although concluding that 'Parsons' analytical scheme, together with the doctrine of functional prerequisites and system equilibrium... resolves itself into a futile quest for some indeterminate requirements of a vaguely conceived "equilibrium" of an ill-defined social system', wonders subsequently if there was a 'second Talcott Parsons' who 'turns his back on his general analytical scheme' (1973: 35–50).

11. The Freudian notion of the 'pleasure principle' refers to an innate tendency to want to avoid or minimize pain and maximize pleasure. For Freud, 'the resistance of the conscious and unconscious ego operates under the sway of the pleasure principle: it seeks to avoid the unpleasure which would be produced by the liberation of the repressed' (Freud [1922] 1955: 20). The 'reality principle', refering to consciousness of real world information, opposes the pleasure principle.

12. Jürgen Habermas is a major contemporary theorist associated with the now disbanded Frankfurt School. For Habermas the pressing concerns lie now in negotiating processes in which 'communicative action' in a condition of deep pluralism may devise a generative politics toward achievements of social agreements that may, against the totally administered society, meet human interests (Habermas 1984, 1987).

3 Classical Traditions of Organizational Analysis

The Sociology of Organizations

The proliferation of complex organizations defines a characteristic pattern of 20th century modernity. Etzioni's oft-quoted statement that 'we are born in organizations, educated by organizations, and most of us spend much of our lives working for organizations' (Etzioni 1975: 1) has a certain normative appeal, in that we regard organizations as bounded entities operating in the real world. We accept, more or less, the predominance of complex organizational forms as a characteristic feature of rationalizing modernity. Organization, the Parsonian-influenced sociological tradition agreed by the mid-20th century, refers to rational social action in the form of systems of 'complex bureaucratic organization' devoted primarily to the attainment of specific goals or values (Blau and Scott 1962, Etzioni 1970, 1975, Merton [1949] 1968, Parsons 1960, Selznick [1948] 1969). A number of sociologists continued an emphasis on organization as social relationships, and differentiated between sets of general principles and sites of action, in for instance bureaucracy, the company or the factory, throughout the structural-functionalist period of dominance (notably, for example, in Bendix [1956] 1974).

Notwithstanding the different levels at which analyses of production and administration were pitched, classical approaches to the bureaucratic organization encouraged attention to general, abstract principles of organization. These inquiries are often most associated with Weber's theorizations of bureaucracy. Marxist sociological approaches addressed principles of organization as they appeared in concrete social practices of the state, the large political party apparatus, as well as in the social relations of production in the industrial workplace. Concerns with the exploitative deployment of institutional power and legitimized domination, as well as with sources of contest and recomposition of organizations, remain primary foci for some analysts of bureaucratic organization today, even as a managerial tradition of organizational analysis favouring instrumental productivist agendas dominates.

There are many explorations of the sociology of organizations, and of bureaucracy that adopt various vantage points from which their narrations are constructed. Among the more exemplary are Eldridge and Crombie (1974), Mouzelis (1967), Burrell and Morgan (1979), Clegg and Dunkerley (1980), Hassard (1993), Reed (1985), Silverman (1970). There are preferences for emphasizing chronological, systematic developments, or thematic and methodological breaks and continuities, or ideological and professional delimitation throughout the 20th century. The perspective developed in my account, one shared largely with Reed and Hassard especially, stresses the historical social context of the development of studies on organizations. But in discussing the selective interests of defining elites in establishing arenas of investigation and discourses of legitimation, and in the next chapter discussing their counter-movements, my account also emphasizes the *historicity*, as Touraine (1988, 1995) describes it, of organizational practices – of the dynamics of historical contest among multiple actors over the terrain of knowledge, action and outcomes.

My account follows initially the differentiation long demarcated by Bendix ([1956] 1974) and Mouzelis (1967) – before the relative simplicity of the contest was superseded by the complex plurality of the decades of crisis – of two traditions in organizational analysis: the sociology of bureaucracy, and management and organization science. The following sections reflect on each of their histories, their levels of focus, and their eventual confluence.

Classical Theories of Bureaucracy

The classical theories of bureaucratic organization begin properly with Marx. Others, including John Stuart Mill, had expressed an awareness of organizational and insititutional activities affecting wider social and political conditions, but their theorization was never developed. Marx's theories of bureaucratic organization need to be understood in the context of his general social and political theory of historical materialism and class conflict, and initially in his critique of Hegel. Marx's primary interest in bureaucracy was in its relation to the power structures of capitalist societies in economic, political and state administrative arenas. The state administrative apparatus, practised through the edifices and ideologies of bureaucracy, does not represent general public interests which (as Hegel proposed) are above sectional interests, but class-specific, particular, interests.

For Marx, bureaucracy is the 'spiritualism of the state' which is the 'actual spiritlessness' and 'crass materialism' pertaining in 'passive obedience, of faith in authority, of the mechanism of fixedly formal activity, fixed principles, views, and traditions' (Marx [1844a] 1978: 24). This comprises the 'state formalism' of bureaucracy which 'constitutes itself as an actual power and becomes its own material content'. 'Bureaucracy' is [therefore] a web of practical illusions or the 'illusion of the state' (ibid.: 23). Bureaucracy is a rational instrument of domination that the ruling class exercises over other social classes. Because of its role in maintaining capitalist class domination the expansion of bureaucratization is inevitable. At the same time the bureaucracy must mask its 'true nature' from itself, and from the general populace who must believe it is an instrument of public service. Therefore, rather than being an abstract, politically neutral means of accomplishing practical economic and administrative tasks, bureaucracy is a state and corporate apparatus of particular control. The order of things the bureaucracy imposes on society perpetuates class division and domination and obscures its specific class interests in so doing.

As the rationally organized instrument of mystified class interest, bureaucracy is parasitic and oppressive of society. It is not only a powerful apparatus of ruling class domination which instigates the institutionalization of bureaucracy, but exerts a power of its own, through impersonal control, and unaccountable silence toward members of the public. Bureaucrats in turn are dominated by the legitimized authority hierarchically structured and obsessively adhered to in bureaucratic organizations. They are thus, like the social classes dominated by bureaucratic organizations, alienated from themselves and from other humans. For Marx, a radical transformation of administrative arrangements was socially necessary, and the working class would, after the proletarian revolution, accomplish such a transformation. Breaking down old class divisions and the 'withering away' of the state would render bureaucracy redundant. Those functions of bureaucracy still required under communism, Marx proposed, would be those of the management of things and not people. Persons freed from the imposed division of labour would cooperatively perform the necessary tasks of their society.

Successive Marxist theorists put forward further developments of Marx's theoretical propositions as actual revolutions failed to deliver the radical transformation envisaged. Attention turned to efforts to analyse the persistence of the bureaucratic form and practice. The role of the bureaucratic organization in the state and in society and its relationship to revolutionary, progressive change was subsequently much debated among Marxist theorists. Well-known among them were Lenin, Lukács, Trotsky and Rosa Luxemburg, each of whom addressed the practical problem of how the proletariat was to proceed in organizing revolutionary activity in order to take over the state bureaucratic apparatus. Lenin explicitly encouraged the overthrow of bureaucracry as a first task of the proletarian revolution and proposed 'instant revocability of every civil servant' (cited in Mouzelis 1967: 12). After the Russian Revolution of 1917, and the manifest absence of the withering of the bureaucracy, Lenin revised his theory. He accounted for the continuity of bureaucracy as a feature of economic under-development that would be remedied by increasing industrialization.

Lenin's theoretician colleagues proposed further refinements.[1] Trotsky, in opposition to Lenin, proposed that the restoration of bureaucracy in post-revolutionary Russia indicated serious contradictions in the social system and the Party. For Trotsky the party bureaucracy had assumed the oppressive tasks of the former state bureaucracy. The workers had lost any power they ostensibly won during the Revolution and that power once again resided in elites. The party apparatus and state bureaucracy became indistinguishable. Its rule is one of purely political power. For Trotsky (1937) the bureaucracy had betrayed the Revolution. Bureaucracy itself possesses a vested interest in maintaining privileges, hierarchies and obedience. Rosa Luxemburg ([1904] 1972) similarly denounced the elitist and counter-democratic tendencies in the party bureaucracy imposing a revolutionary consciousness upon the masses. Against the formalized order of activity advocated by Lenin, Luxemburg advocated the spontaneous struggle and organization of the workers. This spontaneity was regarded as a safeguard against the imposition of another form of domination in place of the old. She stressed, in order to prevent chaotic spontaneity, the importance of self-discipline in coordinating action. Luxemburg insisted on a limited role for leadership and organizational formalization as these undermine democratic freedom and organic organizational activity. The bureaucracy required vigilant restraint by the people.

The highly influential Marxist scholar Georg Lukács, contributed to this debate with an essay on the 'problem of organization' (Lukács [1923] 1971). Lukács argued that the role of class and revolutionary consciousness among the proletariat and the Party was crucial to the success of social transformation. While his theory of consciousness has been criticized as an apologetic for the Party (see Eldridge and Crombie 1974) the importance of his notion of heightened class consciousness in disciplined collaborative organization reverberated in the works of later thinkers, including the Frankfurt School and, in counter-position, Althusser.[2]

The concerns of the revolutionary sociologists – although developing into only rudimentary theories – preface the questions later so thoroughly and systematically investigated by formal sociologists, most especially Max Weber. Indeed Weber's sociology displayed throughout his constant concern with the practices and effects of domination. In his essay 'Politics as a Vocation' Weber captures the essence of his concern. In the context of a discussion of the state and the 'legitimate violence' used to ensure that the dominated obey the powers that be in order for the state, and other organizations to exist, Weber poses his question: 'When and why do men obey? Upon what inner justifications and upon what external means does this domination rest?' (Weber [1919] 1946: 78).

In response, Weber points to the paradox in modern industrial society in which subordination to the industrial way of life had contradicted the humane aspirations of the Enlightenment from the beginning. The bureaucratic condition in modern society, that is rationally structured and productively efficient, contained within it the modern paradox of the delimitation of modern self-autonomy and creative satisfaction, and the necessary condition of subjugation to domination. Domination, for Weber, is a type of power relationship in which the ruler imposes his rule upon others believing in his right to do so, and over persons who consider it their duty to obey. The existence of these believed rights and duties renders the power exercised legitimate in the eyes of both parties. The presence of legitimacy is very important. It enables the domination to be exercised as authority: legitimized domination. Systems of domination, when exercised over large numbers of people in society or in production, require a complex administration. An administrative apparatus enables the formalized and routinized execution of commands. The administrative staff carry out, and bridge, the interests and relationships of the ruler and the ruled. Weber distinguished different types of organization and explicitly described the ideal type of the 'purely bureaucratic type of organization'. Yet he stated clearly the importance of a discrete concept of organization that emphasizes the social relationships, as well as the rational instrumentality, of organizations:

A social relationship which is either closed or limits the admission of outsiders will be called an organization (*Verband*) when its regulations are enforced by specific individuals. The incumbency of a policy-making position or participation in the functions of the staff constitute 'executive powers'. Whether or not an organization exists is entirely a matter of the presence of a person in authority....More precisely it exists so far as there is a probability that certain persons will act in such a way as to carry out the order governing the organization....Thus, for our purposes, the organization does not exist apart from the probability that a course of action...will take place. So long as there is a probability of such action, the organization as a sociological entity continues to exist in spite of the fact that the specific individuals whose action is orientated to the order in question, may have completely changed. (Weber [1922] 1978: 48–49).

The significance of this statement – notwithstanding Weber's emphasis on rational instrumentality, and the value-rational orientation of modern men and women – is that organizations for Weber are a type of social relationship. They do not exist without authority and actor-meaningful courses of social action. These courses of social action contain tendencies in human behaviour which both favour and discourage total domination by social institutions. Bureaucracy is the reified form of that relationship and exerts its control over both the rational purposive goals of the organization, and the relationships between persons that ensure these practices are maintained and reproduced. Large-scale bureaucratic organizations in which personnel are disciplined by sets of rules and rationalized principles of production (Weber [1922] 1978) have therefore proliferated in all modern arenas, not only in economic and public administration but in religious and educational institutions as well.

The large-scale economic organization, for Weber, was second only to the army as the 'great agency which trains men for discipline'.

> [O]rganizational discipline in the factory is founded upon a completely rational basis. With the help of appropriate methods of measurement, the optimum profitability of the individual worker is calculated like that of any material means of production. On the basis of this calculation, the American system of 'scientific management' enjoys the greatest triumphs in the rational conditioning and training of work performances. (Weber [1922] 1946: 261)

Bureaucracy is an accomplishment of the development of capitalism, and continued capitalist social arrangements require bureaucracy. The expansion of capitalism required the routinization of production, rational-legal calculability of all inputs and outputs, and the impersonal, formalized control of specialized labour.[3] For Weber, capitalism is the mode of economic and social organization that most favours the expansion of technical rationality. He summarizes: 'The decisive reason for the advance of bureaucratic organization has always been its purely technical superiority over any other form of organization. The fully developed bureaucratic mechanism compares with other organizations exactly as does the machine with the non-mechanical modes of production' (Weber [1922] 1946: 214).

Weber's comprehensive theory of bureaucratic organizations clearly reveals his concern that bureaucratic rationality encroaches into all spheres of life and renders human subjects of bureaucracy dispirited functionaries. But Weber also believed that bureaucracy's 'purely technical superiority' did not render it politically superior or socially immutable. It is possible that the bureaucratic tool may be utilized according to different social arrangements from those of the capitalism that perfected it.

However, another classical theorist of bureaucracy, influenced by an Italian tradition of social thought, disagreed. Robert Michels,[4] most remembered for his famous 'iron law of oligarchy', proposed that elite forces control organizations irrespective of their commitment to values or democratic participation. For Michels ([1915] 1958), the very structure of large-scale organizations renders them oligarchic. The organizational hierarchy and exigencies of decision-making require specialist leaders who exercise *de facto* oligarchic rule over the rest. Increased complexity and formalization of rules and tasks alienates the ordinary rank and file of the organization from the distant tasks of the impenetrable power centres of the organization. Once a leader or elite group gains a position of dominance their primary interests become that of maintaining it. The pursuit of elite leader or elite group interest is undertaken even when those interests may be wholly oppositional to those of the organization.

Michels' theorization emphasizes the importance of both structural determinants and psychological factors in producing this tendency. The acquisition of power generates defensive behaviour in the self-interest of the holders and is rarely relinquished lightly. The political domination of the bureaucracy, both internally and externally, was inevitable. Michels' controversial political criticism of bureaucracy was ignored in many circles of organization theory, but his description of goal displacement and the constant dyamics of power have been retained in later theories.

These classical theorists, and others of the early 20th century, differed in some key respects from each other, but a view that society was evolving from traditional social arrangements to modern rational society was held in common. For the classical modern theorists, modern society was conceived as organized around a central principle of rationality in which the dynamics of order and change acted in tension. Society rationally negotiated these dynamics in various ways, and with varying effects of power. But challenges to these notions powerfully arose in the mid-20th century in work inspired by a functionalist turn in sociological theory. Favouring an evolutionist conception of society organized around a systemic order, Talcott Parsons' sociology generated an emphasis on system, function, integration and stability. At the same time the classical sociological theories of organization encountered growing criticism for their lack of precision or prescription, and for their theoretical distance from the concrete organization and its compelling day to day problems.

A competing tradition in organizational analysis arising among practitioners in the affairs of commerce and production and industrial engineering drew increasing attention from sociologists of organization. While the practical tradition tended to ignore the philosophical and societal contexts thematically central to the classical tradition, its emphasis on empirical knowledge encouraged some sociologists of organization to address omissions in classical theory or to empirically test their claims. Most of them took as their starting point Weber's ideal-type bureaucracy and Michels' iron law of oligarchy. This development in sociology of organization produced further challenges to both classical theories of society and new conceptions of dynamic social ensembles. Before I discuss these challenges I wish to consider the other tradition in organizational analysis: the managerial tradition in the sociology of organizations.

The Managerial Tradition in Organization Analysis

The managerial academic interest in organizations developed concurrently with classical sociology, and the sociology of bureaucracy. Although a convergence at the expense of sociology was widely asserted by the 1950s, there remained a plurality in the levels of analysis of the organizational problems addressed. But the practical appeal of managerial science and business organization theory has prevailed in most schools of organization theory and management studies and continues to assert a dominant influence in setting the agenda of contemporary debate on organizations. Some even contend that the sociology of organizations is now relegated to an apparently redundant humanist social criticism or to remnant forms of meso-level organizational analysis. This is, of course, disputed as the following chapter demonstrates.

Management Science

Managerial science clearly diverged from the broader sociology of organizations in its early development through its focused task of control and administration, as well as in the design and establishment of large-scale production organizations as the solitary prerogative of management. The early management theorists such as Henri Fayol and Frederick W. Taylor were industrial engineers. They were single-mindedly concerned with the practical tasks of efficiently managing and engineering organizational activity in order to achieve economically productive and profitable outcomes. The early organizational analysis, developed in the first decades of the 20th century and institutionalized in business schools, unhesitatingly assumed the vantage point of those in positions of authority. Senior management of large industrial or administrative organizations typically commissioned studies by teams of university researchers and defined the problems to be solved. Not surprisingly, therefore, the problem-solving imperatives of managerial interests produced a congruent organization theory developed for those ends, and a shift in sociologies of organization toward such grant-generating studies.

The expansion of capitalist production enterprises in the late 19th and early 20th century, the elaborate division of labour, the deployment of new machine technology and the growth in size and complexity of production organizations presented acute problems of coordination and management. A cadre of management personnel (notably with engineering backgrounds) arose as the management scientists of large-scale production organizations. Taylor, a member of the American Society of Mechanical Engineers,[5] devoted his attention to the problem of efficiency. He endeavoured to systematically codify the scientific principles of managing industrial works that mechanical engineers were practising. His famous book *Principles of Scientific Management*, published in 1911, premised that industrial organization is subject to the same scientific laws that govern other natural realities. These laws are discoverable by observation and experimentation and their application to working situations would enable the regulation of all production activities toward maximum efficiency and productivity.

Taylor's scientific management applied empirical and experimental approaches to the everyday problems of work, workers, machines and their organization. Taylor described a 'one best way' of scientific management which required the elimination of all non-rational means for organizing production and solving problems. The principles and techniques of Taylorism encouraged systematic job design according to the separation of the 'tasks of conception' from 'the tasks of execution'. Time and motion studies methodically determined the breaking down of work tasks into their simplest operations. But scientific management's extension of rationalization to all aspects of the production process, with clearly defined responsibilities for managers and workers, also required, for Taylor, a principle of cooperation. The class conflict evident in industrial workplaces was 'unscientific' and wasteful of time and energy. A scientific system of production and organization would, Taylor and his followers believed, demonstrate to workers the indisputable rationality of their management by officials and would eliminate bargaining and negotiations between workers and managers. Taylor's optimism for a scientific solution to labour problems and the elimination of trade unions was not empirically validated. Nor was the apparently irrefutable rationality of scientific management successfully persuasive among the workers. But the drive toward rationalization and movement of scientific management expanded all over the world, often generating fanatical devotees and ruthless experimentation. Modernity's assertions of unifying science and its promise of social cooperation and rational harmony were epitomized, even as they were contradicted, in the scientific management movement in industrial practice. Industrial worker opposition to the expansion of instrumental rationality eventually reflected that expansion, and the industrial workers' movement increasingly sought economic goals more than sociocultural ends in the organization of production.

Even as scientific management was criticized for its view of the worker as a mere component of the machine technology of production, the notion prevailed in its contemporary expression as 'human resources'. But the first industrial psychologists criticized Taylorist management theories for disregarding the worker's humanity, for considering irrelevant the worker's feelings, thoughts and needs in the pursuit of production goals. Workers, they argued, ought not to be reduced simply to tools of production, manipulable according to the same measures applied to materials, machines and plant. Yet for all its glaring deficiencies and machine-rational fixations, Taylorism and its variants continue to underpin a considerable body of management theories assuming scientific authority. The principles were applied to the administration of the entire organization, not just the shop floor, and attention to the design and management of formal organization structure and functions as subject to scientific system laws and imperatives ensued. At the same time, the consolidating classical management theory tradition readily employed Weber's ideal-type model of bureaucracy as a basis for formal, non-empirical theorizing.

Social Psychology of Industry and Organizations

The first industrial psychologists entered the managerial school in organizational analysis soon after scientific management ran into problems with workers and unions. Industrial psychology emerged as a branch of a social psychology field which in turn had developed from experimental and group psychology in the early 20th century (e.g. Brown 1954, Friedmann 1955, Kommarovsky 1957). It sought to address some of the human consequences of the inadequacies and omissions of classical management theory's organizing of production and its treatment of human workers. The classical management tradition concentrated on the formal aspects of organization and endeavoured to make as much as possible of organizational activity formally calculable, predictable and controllable. The organizational structure, viewed in terms of patterns of responsibilities and formal prescribed relations, rules, regulations, procedural design and disciplined workers assumed a primary focus. Informal aspects of the organization such as employee motivation, behaviour and desires were recognized only to the extent that they posed problems for the efficiency and rational control of the organization (Brech 1948, Burawoy 1985, Massie 1965).

The industrial psychologists sought to redress this bias against human workers and their machine-like status in production. But notwithstanding their humanist concern with the worker, their guiding orientation to the problem of human beings in production was directed by the industrial and management engineers primarily concerned with systems and techniques and human adaptations to system needs. While expressing concern with the worker's non-machine nature, the industrial psychologists focused on improving workers' productivity and efficiency. They focused on problems of motivation, the effects of boredom and repetition, interpersonal relations, and physical conditions such as noise, heat, lighting and rest breaks. Economic and power relations between workers, managers and owners of industrial organizations were assumed, more or less, as structurally unproblematic, and were not included in their constitution of social psychology. However, the practices of surveying workers' feelings and attitudes, and the improvement of some of their workplace conditions were sufficiently radical at the time to gain the support of the trade union movement. The movement to recognize and value the 'human element' in business organizations gained popularity, and became generally known as the Human Relations school in management and organization theory.

Although the term 'human relations' had many different meanings in the social sciences, the Human Relations school established, more or less, an orthodoxy around the work of Elton Mayo (1933, 1945) and his Harvard University team of investigators. Their influence began with the now famous, though always controversial,[6] studies conducted at the Hawthorne plant of Western Electric Company in the years 1927–1932. These studies, most extensively reported in Roethlisberger and Dickson (1939), began with a Taylorist approach that identified and manipulated physical variables affecting worker performance. The inconclusive results of these investigations led the researchers to employ new methods of research in social settings. The use of the interview as a method of inquiry among workers produced findings that indicated the influence not only of the individual psychological characteristics that a worker brings to the workplace that shape his (at the time only 'his') attitudes and behaviour, but also the importance of the worker's social relations within the workplace.

The research results shifted attention toward the characteristics of the organization, and the structure and culture of groups as determinants of workplace behaviour. This move from a Taylorist focus on physiological and individual psychological variables toward a social and organizational psychology focus became widely influential in industrial organizational research in subsequent decades. The recognition of the informal organization, the importance of friendship groups and shared values in the workplace and the part played by non-economically rational values in determining workers' behaviour comprised a significant contribution to classical, mechanistic management theory. The social psychological approach, however, did not depart from the overall orientation of management science and the singularly instrumentally rational goals of efficient production. Although many of the criticisms of scientific management were scathing, among them the influential work of Herbert Simon (1945) and Dwight Waldo (1948), there was little questioning of the institutionalized relations of production and organization. The Mayo-influenced school of organizational behaviour continued the classical school's interests in maintaining a separate elite cadre of managers more skilled in human relations and the management of emotion. Moreover, its continued exclusive concentration on intra-organizational elements and their harmony neglected extra-organizational environments in determining the conditions and the behaviour of and within the organization. Significantly, the role of trade unions in the plant and in the workers' lives was ignored.

Another strand in the Human Relations school, that of W.L. Warner and J.O. Low (1947) and the Human Relations group at the University of Chicago, made some effort to redress this omission. The anthropological and phenomenological orientation of the Chicago group's approach contributed analyses of cultural elements such as status, role, culturally patterned behaviours, religion and so forth, in their relation to industrial organizations. Their studies, including those of W.F. Whyte (1946, 1951) and Everett Hughes (1958), attempted to show how broader environmental elements impact on the organization and shape its behaviour. One of the significant contributions of this group was a view of trade unions that differed from the hostility evident in Taylorism and Mayo. This view, although largely reflecting the functionalism already popular in that discipline, encouraged a more favourable regard for the role of unions as constituent of the social system of the plant. Nonetheless the management perspective encouraged an approach toward unions that sought the diminishment of conflict and the promotion of participative collaboration (Gardner 1945).

Criticisms of the Human Relations school[7] typically focused on the school's lack of attention to broader organizational and institutional contexts. When these matters were discussed, they were done so in a superficial manner with their application to micro-level problems restricting a more comprehensive exploration. The eventual extensive research on leadership, supervision and techniques for adjusting the worker to his or her social groups characterized the interests of the school. Critics regarded the findings of the Human Relations researchers trivial and repetitive. The school was criticized for its lack of attention to organization structure and to the reality of industrial and economic conditions that positioned the organization as an economic organization (e.g. Drucker 1960). Moreover, its functionalism and the inherent conservative bias, illustrated in its view of conflict as an interpersonal pathology which could be cured by better communications or similar devices, naively precluded the consideration of conflict as a wider socially structured, or socially negotiated, practice. The school generally shared the classical management view (embedded in functionalism) that ultimately the interests of all organizational groups are the same. The neglect of power, structure and wider social relations, and their restricted methodologies clearly delimited the contributions of the school of organizational behaviour in relation to the field of organization science.

The Human Relations school also included a branch interested in the social relations of the workplace that include, as constituent of the relationships between workers, groups, supervisors and managers, the role of technology in the concrete context of jobs and workplaces. Combining a structural-functionalist formulation with the Human Relations attention to interpersonal relations, the Tavistock Institute became well known from the mid-1950s for its 'socio-technical systems' approach to the social psychology of work. This work focused on the relationships between the organization and its environment, and relationships within the organization between the technical systems and groups of workers (e.g. Emery and Trist 1960, Lawrence and Lorsch 1967, Miller and Rice 1967, Trist et al. 1963. See also Hassard 1993 for a review). Numerous developments from that influence include efforts at job redesign and job enrichment, quality circles, worker participation and teamwork that are still popular today.

In Europe there were efforts, especially after World War II, to encourage industrial democracy, typically in the form of joint consultative committees between workers, trade unions and managers in large industrial organizations. The goal was the reduction of conflict in the workplace and the reduction in the power of big trade unions in industry. But alongside the manifest managerial interests in human behaviour, in small group relations, and in the inter-relationships between micro-social systems and production technologies, a discrete sociological tradition in organizational analysis continued.

Organization Science – A Sociological Return

The sociological tradition increasingly took on the character of organization science. A scientific sociology of organizations sought to establish general foundations of the 'Theory of Organizations' (Selznick [1948] 1969), and to incorporate the Human Relations approaches within an overarching behaviourist organization science. Loosened from, but still useful to, a partisan management tradition of organization theory, this endeavour was to prove highly successful over the next decades. It was also to produce some remarkable findings that challenged classical sociological theories of society, even as much of its work was directed back into the development of organizational management theory and strategy.

Among the pivotal influences,[8] in addition to those discussed above, is the work of Barnard ([1938] 1964), Simon ([1945] 1976), Selznick ([1948] 1969, 1949), Crozier (1964) and Parsons. Barnard's *Functions of the Executive* ([1938] 1964) developed a functional framework of organizations that provided an analytical base adopted by later organization theorists for several decades. Barnard elaborated a theory that conceived of organization as 'a system of consciously co-ordinated activities' (Barnard [1938] 1964: 72), and argued that activity is coordinated in the pursuit of rational common goals. This approach entails the cooperation of all organization members and also requires the organization to maintain an 'executive stratum' to manage the tension between organizational goals and conflicting individual or informal group goals.

This functionalist explanation for the necessity of executive strata was retained by Barnard's followers. Simon's *Administrative Behavior* ([1945] 1976) postulated the organization system as able to provide an encompassing rationality that structures both internal operations of the organization and the psychology of individual workers. The rational acceptance of institutional goals reduces tendencies toward anomic pathologies among unrestrained individuals, and achieves for the social system a harmonious equilibrium between its constituent subsystems and the whole. Simon emphasized the role of decision-making and executive efforts to manoeuvre among the limitations of human decision-making mechanisms. He also noted the 'lack of realism' (p. xiv) in much administrative and organization theory and the avoidance of empirical work.

When empirical work was undertaken the findings generated some significant challenges for functionalist analysis. In his well-known study of the Tennessee Valley Authority, Selznick's (1949) application of structural-functionalist analytic tools to a bureaucratic organization produced conflicting results. His findings reported numerous unintended consequences, goal displacements, dysfunctions and conflicts that contradicted the overall official purposes of the organization. Furthermore, the organization was observed to be in a state of constant effort to satisfy organic system needs, to adjust to its external environment, and to achieve organic equilibrium with that environment. Selznick's study, like work reported by March and Simon ([1958] 1961), Blau (1955), Crozier (1964) and Gouldner (1954a, 1954b), showed that organizations, despite their formal adherence to bureaucratic rationalities and legitimation are really unstable, weakly coherent, fragile ensembles of compromises between constant sources of pressures, constraints and contestation. Similarly, Lipset, Trow and Coleman (1956) concluded from their study of a trade union that the degree of decentralization and member participation in the organization structure mitigated the tendency toward anti-democratic ruling elites. Moreover, Blauner's (1964) influential study proposed that the diminishment of rigid regimentation in factory production enabled by new automation technology reduces alienation among workers.

A theme emerging from these studies was one of *limited* rationality and of a diminished role for its central, unifying mastery of organizational processes and activities. Simon proposed a notion of 'bounded rationality' in which most human behaviour in organizations is '*intendedly* rational but only *limited* so' (Simon [1945] 1976: xxviii). Crozier (1964: 145) spoke of 'power as the new central problem of the theory of organization' and of managed uncertainty. March and Simon ([1958] 1961) proposed that the goal of organizations is to attain satisfactory rather than optimal or maximal performance and productivity. These findings emphasize the strategic movement between competing forces. The classical notion of a central, unified and total governing rationality is rescinded.

But the analysts do not conclude that instrumental rationality is in crisis or that organic, non-rational aspects of the organization will prevail. Rather, organizational rationality does function as long as it concedes notions of systemic whole and systemic stability and order. Instead, movement, change, flux and power are the dynamics with which managers and other actors within organizations ensure the efficient operation of the organization. Selznick appealed for an open systems-functionalist model as a solution to the problems of maintaining system stabilization, integration and harmonious cooperation. The growing recognition of bounded rationality and weak cohesion, and the contributions from organizational psychologies, eventually fuelled the development of a theory of strategic management as a neo-rationalist response to uncertainty and contingency. But in the meantime the search for a general theory of organizations prevailed.

For all the importance of theoretical and institutional developments within the knowledge traditions of social science and organization science, and the latter's concretely applicable body of organization theory, recognition of broader societal contexts shaping the direction of scientific orthodoxies and knowledge legitimation remained unexamined. The 'domain assumptions' (in Gouldner's 1970 term) within the field of organization science were themselves products of social and cultural contexts pertaining in specific historical conditions. But the historical and cultural specificity of organization activity and analysis escaped the grasp of most of the key figures in organization science at the time. The sociologist Robert Merton was among the few social scientists in the mid-20th century to express some concern over the social organization of sociological inquiry.

Robert Merton pointed out in 1959 that there are 'social determinants of sociological problems'. Historical events affect the value commitments of social scientists and 'lead them to work on a restricted range of problems'. The enormous changes in American society in the early 20th century following decades of waves of migration, social reform and industrial development led many American sociologists to a 'gross preoccupation with problems of social disorganization' (Merton 1959: xxxiv). This gross preoccupation assumed the status of a 'moral duty' under the guise of a value-free objectivity on the part of many social scientists. The scientific method, social scientists believed, would extend human control over the problems of the natural and social worlds. Organization scientists and their practitioner followers unreflectively assumed the practical tasks of bringing rational order to human activities, especially those of production and administration. The impingement of such historical events and societal imperatives contributed to a decisive convergence in organizational analysis by the 1960s.

Convergence

Useful Organizational Analysis

Historically and culturally specific social circumstances and conditions produce, and selectively illuminate, sociological questions and problems. The enormous social and economic importance of the large corporate organization from the 1940s and 1950s, and the constituting problem of order and control against counter-rational pressures, preoccupied sociologists and organization management theorists of those decades. The development of organizational analysis in the 20th century in both the sociological tradition and the managerial tradition indicates the importance of understanding organizations to a range of interested parties. And it indicates too, as Merton's student Alvin Gouldner later argued, the subjugation of critical, conflict-exposing theories within the dominant functionally and morally integrated organizational society (Gouldner 1970). The analysis of organizations converged around a practical problem-solving sociology and organization theory delimited by a shared framework of systems, order, function, control and scientific method.

A strong political agenda for social cohesion in the post-war decades based on economic expansion and consumption fuelled a drive toward applied, problem-solving social research. This drive was evident in many areas including education, urban planning, political science and organizational sociology. The rise of the large corporation in the early 20th century and the extensive technological developments most significantly effective since World War II instigated initiatives to address the complex management and organizational problems that consequently arose. Drucker, for whom 'the large corporation is a tool and organ of society', summed up the task in 1946: 'To make it possible for this new social institution [the corporation] to function efficiently and productively, to realize its economic and social potential and to resolve its economic and social problems, is our most urgent task and our most challenging opportunity' (Drucker [1946] 1960: 208). By the end of the 1950s the 'management boom' that emphasized the need for management knowledge and skill was widely operant.[9] Consequently, the education of managers was the fastest growing area of American education, with similar expansion evident in Europe.

Accordingly, the business schools sought to extend their rudimentary managerial organizational analysis and to broaden their traditional domains of economics, accounting, marketing, management and labour relations. The social and political interest in large organizations and their role in society, central to a sociological analysis, was unevenly accommodated or eliminated in the organization science subsequently developed in United States business schools. Weber's theorizations of bureaucracy and of social and economic organization were strategically selected for their prescriptive value and practical application. Yet at the same time there was wide concern among academicians about the lack of general theories and frameworks, and the lack of 'scientific stature' in administrative theory. It was this imperative that founded the eventually prestigious and widely influential journal *Administrative Science Quarterly* in 1956. Sociological theorists, as indeed theorists from political science and other social sciences, were drawn to the task. Sociologists of organization and industry retained elements of the critical concerns of their foundational theorists, as illustrated in the Weberian works of Bendix and Lipset, or the Marxist-influenced industrial sociologies of Mills and Gouldner. Likewise, an extensive British tradition in industrial sociology, including Dahrendorf (1959), Fox (1977), Goldthorpe (1968), Child (1973), Eldridge (1971) and Baldamus (1961), retained critical social perspectives. But the Parsonian synthesis of Weber and Durkheim set a dominant direction in forms of theory in an organic functionalist science of organizations and social institutions. The new journals in administrative and management science confidently bespoke and legitimized the new field.

In Search of a General Theory of Organizations

Both the sociology of organization and managerial organization theory converged in implicit agreement that the phenomenon of organization under discussion was the bureaucratic organization. But they differed in their philosophical orientations and lenses of analysis. Notwithstanding the conclusion of Blau, Selznick, Crozier and others of the limited, fragile rationality of the bureaucratic organization, both perspectives privileged the classical sociological construct of formal, purposeful, intentionally rational organization existing as a 'social fact'. Weber's theorization of bureaucracy became a standard for comparison, criticism and redesign. The concept of bureaucracy was used as a synonym for organization, although Weber himself had been careful to distinguish different organizational types. Ironically, Weber's theorization of bureaucracy and his emphasis on rational instrumentality assumed the status of a prescriptive orthodoxy. Although Weber had clearly distinguished between bureaucracy and organization – the latter conceived as a type of social relationship – it was his 'ideal type' bureaucracy that endured in the theoretical developments of subsequent decades. The amoral rational machine structure of organization coexisted with perspectives from organization behaviour which emphasized bounded rationality, the role of the informal organization and workers' personalities and needs. These problems of order and stability, and of change and action, focused the tasks of management and organization science.

The theoretical and methodological approaches of systems theory and functionalism, coupled with recognition of bounded rationality, came to assume an epistemological orthodoxy in the investigation of social and organizational problems. The contributions from social psychology on the dynamics of small groups and interpersonal relations, which developed to serve the administrative managerialism ascendant particularly in US and British organizational analysis, shared the general orientation of sociologists of organizations. An imperative toward adaptation, adjustment and conformity of fit among individual workers' 'personality systems' neatly accorded with the general organizational systems perspective. These approaches to organizations and the various levels of analysis were found by the 1950s to be lacking an overarching 'general theory of organizations'.

Although, as Reed (1985) and Perrow (1972) indicate, a foundation of a science of organizations was well argued for following the seminal work of Barnard ([1938] 1964), Roethlisberger and Dickson (1939), Simon ([1945] 1976) and Selznick ([1948] 1969), a general theory still eluded the organizational scientists. Selznick, in 1948, captured the general consensus at the time: 'formal organization is the structural expression of rational action....[T]he formal structure [is] subject to calculable manipulation, an instrument of rational action' (Selznick [1948] 1969: 358). 'To recognize the sociological relevance of formal structures is not, however, to have constructed a formal theory of organization.... The definition of formal organizations as cooperative systems only sets the stage, as an initial requirement, for the formulation of a theory of organization' (Selznick [1948] 1969: 361).

Selznick advocated the wide adoption of 'structural-functional analysis' as the basis of theory and method of analysis of organization. For Selznick, 'structural-functional analysis relates contemporary and variable behavior to a presumptively stable system of need and mechanisms' (Selznick [1948] 1969: 361). This approach is applicable, Selznick argues, to any level of systems, and their dynamic relations. A structural-functional analysis addresses the composite of mechanical structures and individual personalities that make up the cooperating, structured system of organization. The optimal means of understanding the complexities of formal and non-formal aspects of the organization was by way of an open, natural systems model. This model, Selznick argued, recognized organization systems as behaving as any living organism would in order to satisfy its system needs and adapt to its environment. Organizations defend and preserve the status quo as the consequence of a natural predisposition of organismic systems to conform to 'natural laws' of survival 'instincts' and self-preservation. Long-range change, in this model, occurs in an evolutionary manner largely independent of management plan and design. Selznick's Parsonian-based model set a framework for open systems analysis which subsequently flourished in organization theory. By the 1950s and 1960s the drive toward a general theory of organizations inspired considerable effort. Parsons, renowned for his synthesizing *oeuvre*, offered his suggestions.

Parsons' General Theory of Organizations

Both Selznick and Parsons sought to redress an over-emphasis on the rational structures and mechanistic processes of organizational activities which had prevailed, not only in the form of Taylor's scientific managers, but in organizational behavioural science. This prevalence had generated a managerial systems focus that under-attended to the non-rational, organic elements of social and formal organization. Although this over-emphasis on formal, mechanistic bureaucratic organization had been recognized by the Human Relations school in the 1930s and 1940s, the alternative emphasis in their studies (e.g. Brown 1954, Mayo 1933, Roethlisberger and Dickson 1939) on the informal, psychological and inter-personal aspects of organization either ignored the formal structural dimensions or referred the psychological adaptations of humans to that mechanistic structure.

Others, including Gouldner (1959), argued contrarily that a similar over-emphasis on organic systems had replaced the rational mechanistic model. What was required was a synthetic approach. Parsons attempted to offer such a synthesis. Parsons' structural-functionalist general theory of organization appeared in the inaugural issue of the *Administrative Science Quarterly* (1956) and in his book, *Structure and Process in Modern Societies* (1960). *Administrative Science Quarterly* was founded with the explicit task of pursuing a general administrative science and the formulation of a general organization theory. Parsons' grand theory of the structure of social action was the framework for such a theory, which other organization theorists from Barnard to Simon to Selznick had not achieved.

The model proposed in Parsons' 'Some Ingredients of a General Theory of Formal Organization' ([1960] 1969) begins with the criticism that attention to the structure of social action employed in organizational analysis had become narrowly constrained. It focused largely on internal structure and process, as Parsons describes it: 'such problems as line authority, staff organization, and the process of decision-making' (Parsons [1960] 1969: 197). The theory of bureaucracy so privileged concentrated on the managerial level of formal organization, failing to recognize the importance of, in Parsons' schema, two other distinct levels of organization: the technical and the institutional. For Parsons, every formal organization has certain 'technical' functions, comprising a sub-organization, which is oriented to technical matters such as 'materials' – physical, cultural or human and their processing in products (Parsons [1960] 1969: 197). The technical system is in a broad sense controlled by the management system, but in the functional differentiation of the complex system this control is not a 'one-way relation'. Both systems present specifications, 'needs', to the other in their operations for procurement and production.

At a third level Parsons formulates a wider social system in which the managerial system of the organization is positioned. This wider social system provides the 'source of "meaning," legitimation, or higher-level support which makes the implementation of the organization's goals possible' (Parsons [1960] 1969: 199). Essentially, for Parsons, this means that the managerial organization is controlled by the 'institutional' structure and agencies of the society in which the organization operates. A significant element in Parsons' effort was to indicate that the theory of bureaucracy employed in managerial organizational analysis focused excessively on the managerial level, emphasizing and generalizing uniformities specific to that level. Such focus omits crucial attention to the broader societal level. For Parsons 'it is a cardinal thesis of this analysis that no organization is ever wholly "independent"' (ibid.). The emphasis on the management system of a mechanical bureaucracy had produced work, 'that has been rather severely limited' (Parsons [1960] 1969: 199).

Ironically though, Parsons' contribution in his general theory of formal organizations, and his criticism of an over-emphasis on managerial systems premised on a mechanistic theory of bureaucracy, led less to the broader, societally and morally situated theory of organizations that Parsons sought and more to a comprehensive development of a natural systems model of organizations. The natural systems model does indeed emphasize the 'whole' and interdependent nature of the system and its parts, but de-emphasizes the rational instrumentality of modern organization. The rational features of modern organization that Weber, and before him Saint-Simon, recognized are those which make it distinctively modern. This important move has had a lasting influence, although for some it excessively downplayed the rational features of organization and of management, and continues to lead to 'anti-management' sociological theories of organization (Donaldson 1995) and for others overplayed a Durkheimian emphasis on spontaneous, organic social forms (Gouldner 1959).

The shift of emphasis that occurred toward natural or open systems models in organizational analysis privileged a focus on intra organizational structures with respect to their system functions and environmental relations. Weber's oft-forgotten interest in the irrational dimensions of human action were restored somewhat in the Parsonian natural systems emphasis on organizational 'behaviour' in accordance with a natural systemic order. But the preference for systems needs and functions, and the reinvigorated attention to non-rational features, although increasingly eliding the human subject as 'exogenous to the system', enabled the micro-psychologism of the organizational behaviourists to be systematically accommodated.

From General Systems to Strategy

The task for organizational analysts, and managers, subsequently became directed toward knowing and managing the irrational aspects of organizational personnel, processes and environments. Organizational science moved from a mechanistic bureaucratic systems model to an 'open systems' approach. Structural-functionalism, while ostensibly a natural science of complex organizations in which human rational intervention was limited, was nonetheless applied to the task of rendering rationally knowable and manipulable human irrationalities and organismic attributes in collective social practices. Although apparently rejecting the Weberian tradition's over-emphasis on rationality, the natural systems, structural-functionalist models that subsequently prevailed firmly retained the modern rationalist imperative exemplified in positive social science. Bureaucracy was replaced by a self-legitimizing organizational system and neo-rational, strategic management.

The natural systems theories drew important attention to the spontaneous mechanisms common to all groups, the complexities of human relational behaviour, and the rise of informal social organization within the formal rational organization. They were useful, too, as an ideology of functional unity and employee integration into the imagined whole for the 'common good'. Efforts to refine the model to better address the variabilities of concrete organizations have ensured the model's popularity in organizational analysis even into the present time. From population ecology models and organizational life cycle metaphors to 'contingency theory', open systems models continue to be widely invoked. Contingency theory emphasizes managerial strategy as being contingent on the relationships between the organization structure and a number of crucial variables, typically environment, technology, goals and size (well represented in Lawrence and Lorsch 1967). It represents the culmination of the open systems functionalist approach of the preceding decades combined with an authorial agentic role for management. Most importantly, contingency theory promotes an emphatic role of strategic managerial decision-making – even as it recognizes bounded rationality – over organization system, structure, culture and processes.

For many contemporary theorists strategic management has displaced the theoretical orthodoxy of systems theory and structural-functionalism in organizational analysis. As sociological notions of society organized around a central principle of rationality have given way, so too have organization system theories. Entrepreneurial models favouring strategy and asystemic currents of movement emerge in their place. But the old models, often coupled with neo-rational strategic management theory, retain a vigorous influence in contemporary analysis and practice. This functionalist-neo-rationalist model is found in works by writers such as Donaldson (1985, 1995) and in scores of textbooks in organization theory, organization behaviour and management (e.g. Daft 1996, Jones 1997, Robbins and Barnwell 1998).

Convergence and Discord

The 1960s and 1970s saw numerous efforts to consolidate a field of organization theory or organizational analysis. A synthesis of general systems theory, modified structural-functionalism in the form of contingency theory and neo-rational management found considerable popularity. In addition to the proliferation of organization research produced for business practitioners, a body of work on organizations which sought to retain a broader sociological character to its inquiry (e.g. Eldridge and Crombie 1974, Etzioni 1970, Perrow 1972, Silverman 1970) typically shared this general systems framework. Moreover, the managerial tradition in organizational sociology welcomed the theoretical sophistication brought by sociology and other social sciences to its field of study. Parsons remarked in 1960 that the field of organization and administrative science had gained 'many insights which the social scientists had developed', but 'an immense amount of work will be required before we can have anything that deserves to be called a theory of formal organization' (Parsons [1960] 1969: 213). The unifying imperative of a normative science and general theory of organizations provided a shared direction and purpose, even if the levels of analysis of management and sociology were divergent. By 1964 Theodore Caplow, in a typical organizational analysis work, confidently asserted:

> [H]uman organizations are a class of natural phenomena the attributes of which are not time bound or culture bound, and the workings of which are orderly, so that the sociology of organization is more susceptible to development as a science than other branches of sociology. This thesis grows less contentious year by year…. [A]mong those involved in the empirical study of organization it is nearly taken for granted. (Caplow 1964: v)

In the 1970s the distance which later became for many an irreconcilable chasm between administrative organization theory and a remnant sociological organizational analysis was not yet perceived as so wide. A scientific sociology of organization sought primacy over a humanistic tradition that was quickly contributing a critical and contestational body of work on organizations. But despite these grand assertions, efforts to produce general theories and 'foundations' of organization studies, such as March's 1965 *Handbook of Organisations*, revealed an eclectic mix, 'a babel of voices' (Eldridge and Crombie 1974: 12), that did not comprise a general theory at all. Drawn from psychological studies of managerial leadership, decision-making, interpersonal relations, economic and sociological theories of organizational structure, and various applications to problems of organizational change and strategy, March's early handbook revealed different levels of interest and manifestly disparate theoretical perspectives. While this plurality was drawn together with the intention of defining a prescriptive programme of practical relevance, and in that respect succeeded, it reveals strikingly the uncertainty and weak cohesion prevailing more normatively than abstract notions of order and integrated system. But the campaigns for unifying, universal science of organization continued.

The goal of constructing an interdisciplinary body of organization science for applied social prescription is aptly described: 'Modern organization theory represents a frontier of research which has great significance for management…it offers the opportunity for uniting what is valuable in classical theory with the social and natural sciences into a systematic and integrated conception of human organization' (Scott 1963: 26). Organization theory endeavoured to become a discipline in its own right in order to address particular problems in a similar manner to the sub-disciplines of production engineering, cybernetics, ergonomics, group psychology and so forth. This agenda was developed further in Etzioni's 1970 *Complex Organizations: A Sociological Reader*, notwithstanding the titular privileging of a sociological framework. This edited collection shares the orientation of Etzioni's *Comparative Analysis of Complex Organizations* (1975) toward organizational problematics of a practical nature: cohesion, compliance, control. Yet this orientation toward social problem-solving is scarcely confined to organizational sociologies. Etzioni's orientation is widely evident in United States post-war sociology, and for most of that generation is properly in accordance with the function of sociology in society.

A convergence around a politically conservative restoration prevailing in United States sociology and a practical managerialist problem-solving agenda among organization theorists dominated the field of organization studies. The various levels of analysis among psychologists, sociologists, management scientists, engineers and others were, apparently, accommodated. This situation was confidently described by Pugh (1966) as an 'interdisciplinary science of man in organizations'. But this development was not quite as smoothly inclusive and scientifically reasonable as its advocates would have it appear. The shared practical agendas, systems orthodoxies and positivist scientific methodologies foundational to the schools of organization science becoming established in many universities were drawn from across originating disciplines, but they were not so insulated as to be undisturbed by the crisis in sociology widely felt in the 1970s and 1980s.

Notes

1. The debates between Lenin and Trotsky are discussed, for instance in Poulantzas (1973). See also Lenin ([1902] 1963). For further discussion of the early communist theorists' views on bureaucracy and the state see Mouzelis (1967), Eldridge and Crombie (1974), Burrell and Morgan (1979).

2. For further discussion of Althusser's structuralism see Althusser (1970), Aronowitz (1981), Burrell and Morgan (1979). Importantly, as Mouzelis (1975) notes, the Althusserian movement in sociology with its strong structuralist, anti-voluntarist, and anti-empiricist orientation exerted no apparent influence on an organization theory still dominated in the 1970s by practical, managerial empiricism and humanist psychologism.

3. Weber's famous characterization of the 'ideal type' bureaucracy elaborated in *Economy and Society* defines a set of traits that are found in all bureaucratic organizations: the bureaucratic organization is a continuous organization structured according to 'the principles of office hierarchy and of levels of graded authority' to ensure a system of super- and subordination. The bureaucratic office is based on 'written documents ("the files")'. The bureaucrat possesses 'expert training' and carries out his (her) duties impersonally and full-time and is paid a salary. The office is managed by a system of rules and technical knowledge that regulate relationships (Weber [1922] 1978: 956–957).

4. Michels, although German by birth, was trained in Italy under the influence of the Italian school expounding a form of social realism, against the Romantic or idealist notions of German theorists, especially Hegel and Marx. Michels, following Pareto and Mosca, attended to the role and actions of elites, which were considered to play a defining role throughout history. See Levine (1995) for further discussion.

5. See Mouzelis (1967) for discussion on the precedent influence of the American Society of Mechanical Engineers on the subsequent development of the management societies that succeeded the ASME. The contemporary Academy of Management in the US can trace its lineage to the ASME. The ASME published papers dealing with the application of engineering principles to the administration and organization of the workshop and the office of the large enterprise. These interests continued in the journal *Harvard Business Review* founded in 1922, and later in the American Academy of Management.

6. The literature on the Western Electric studies is extensive. Critical studies include Brown (1954), Kerr and Fisher (1957), Landsberger (1958), Carey (1965) and Burawoy (1985).

7. Mouzelis (1967) identifies a third strand in the Human Relations school: the 'interactionist approach'. This approach placed greater emphasis on what people do and how they interact with one another within the organization. Their methods, stressing observation and measurement of human interactions, favoured a quantitative analysis and de-emphasized the role of sentiments among workers and the formal-informal organization favoured by the classical Human Relations theorists. In my view the differences between this strand and the others is somewhat over-stretched. Although the work of Whyte (1951) and Homans for example was important it is not significantly distinguished from the social psychology orientation of the school in general.

8. Compare with Reed (1985) and Perrow (1972), who both place significant emphasis on the influence of Barnard's (1938) book.

9. Drucker argues in his 1960 preface to *The Concept of the Corporation*, that the supply of management knowledge and skill, rather than money, was the basic contribution of the post-war Marshall Plan, and the chief contribution of various United States technical aid programmes.

4   Counter-Movements

Criticism, Crisis, Dispersion

The Crisis in Sociology

Conceptions of society as a system progressively organized around central principles of rationality prevailed as a dominant paradigm in sociology until the mid-20th century, and these conceptions remain widely held now. But the systems paradigm, and the conjunction of questions concerning order and change, were never the only ones, nor of such solidity that the emerging crisis in sociology predicted by Gouldner (1970) did not dislodge their primacy. While the crisis is scarcely over (see Lemert 1995, for example, on this debate), and for some now institutionalized as postmodernism, its consequences are enduringly manifest and manifold. The crisis, which was always broader than sociology, affected all areas of the discipline including the field of organizational analysis. The epistemological and methodological conventions that had become thoroughly established in the field were challenged and disrupted. The resulting disarray, welcomed by some and reviled by others, eventually created opportunity for reflexivity, dispersion and renewal.

For some analysts, the crisis that swept the social sciences from the 1960s was of the significance of a Kuhnian revolution (Gouldner 1970, Lemert 1995, Toulmin 1972) that ushered in tumultuous, disruptive and diverse challenges and new perspectives to a relatively stable, normal social science. The social sciences in the academy although comprising many different perspectives and methods operated with more or less shared understandings of purpose, rational science and disciplinary demarcation. Even as new disciplines had branched off from older ones, their institutional legitimacy depended on reproduction of academic and social scientific normative 'laws' and characteristics – an academic 'habitus' in Bourdieu's theorization (Bourdieu 1988) that in turn reproduced a relative stability of practice and profession. But the effects of dramatic social, political and intellectual changes from the 1960s onward disrupted the established habitus of the academy as well as the practical hegemony of certain theoretical orthodoxies. Beset by challenges to established beliefs about knowledge, truth, meaning, purpose and legitimacy, the modern project of sociology lost its confidence, and direction.

A trend of intellectual discontent had been evident much earlier, but during the post-World War II years of relative political stability, economic prosperity and confident reconstruction, critical analysis received little mainstream attention. For that period a stabilizing, reintegrative sociology, especially in North America, was professionally and politically favoured. A social science of policy development and problem-solving was readily served by a general social theory of structural-functionalism which abstracted social problems and prescribed their solutions. An encompassing imperative to maintain social system integration and harmony, critics argued, effectively obscured the embedded ideological interests of dominant groups in society.

Although a sense of crisis was expressed by some throughout the history of sociology, even in periods in which prevailing assertions of stability and cohesion were popular (see, for example, Lazarsfeld and Theilens 1958, and Merton 1975), it was not until the 1970s that the momentum and significance of diverse contrariness was unmistakable. Intellectual orthodoxies and academic knowledge institutions were challenged with unprecedented efficaciousness by insurgent new voices and competing political demands. Eventually the new (to the academy) voices generated a proliferation of competing perspectives and interests, methods, problems and career aspirations. Many of the new intellectuals in the academy argued against the 'histories of exclusion' reposited in academic institutions that posed particular gendered, ethnic and social class views and values as universal scientific truth. Initially reflecting a long-standing though subjugated Marxist-influenced political criticism through the 'New Left' political movements, the new intellectuals demanded political and ideological changes to the dominant knowledge traditions in the academy. The relative stability and homogeneity of modern scientific sociology that its exponents confidently insisted had triumphed by the 1960s was in trouble. The sociologist as 'organization man' – incorporated into highly centralized governmental structures preserving social order, as Mills (1959) and Chomsky (1969) among others prominently criticized – was under siege.

By the 1970s, commentary on these developments expressed cautionary concern. Eisenstadt and Curelaru described in 1976 developments in sociology that were 'minimizing the possibility of scholarly discourse on problems of common interest', and the continuing spread of these developments produced 'a *widespread malaise* in sociology; and acceptance of its being in a state of crisis' (Eisenstadt and Curelaru 1976: 311–312; emphasis added). Others expressed similar concern, and not only in sociology with its grand traditions of plurality, but across the social sciences and humanities. Comparable statements to that of Eisenstadt and Curelaru can be found among economists, political scientists, anthropologists, psychologists and historians (see Levine 1995). Dissension permeated the social sciences and troubled its senior spokespeople. A restoration of integration and consensus was implicit in the seniors' admonishment. Disarray portended disintegration and dysfunction of social knowledge systems and of modern economic and political systems.

For some, the state of dissension amounted to academic anarchy in which an unregulated, undisciplined proliferation of social research flooded a once tightly regulated and professionally controlled market. By the 1990s, the diversity of activities conducted under the general rubric of sociology was widely lamented. Randall Collins, speaking on behalf of many, reflected: 'We have lost all coherence as a discipline, we are breaking up into a conglomerate of specialties, each going its own way and with none too high regard for each other' (Collins cited in Levine 1995: 285). For others, the diversity and volume of the research output enabled by a deregulated orthodoxy and plural legitimation measures indicated a healthy state of discourse production and exchange. In some circles, including feminist ones, an acceptance of diversity was more or less assumed as a pragmatic solution to the seemingly irresolvable crisis that fragmented once-shared understandings and professional codes more valued and achievable among earlier generations of (typically male) social scientists.

The factors contributing to the crisis were many.[1] My discussion draws attention to the aspects of the crisis most effective in sociology of organizations. An intellectual crisis in professional sociology had already begun to arise and preceded the sociological institutional crisis fuelled in the 1960s by broader social and political changes. The emergent intellectual crisis and an emerging critique of modernity followed recognition of early and mid-20th century social and institutional failures that produced Nazism and Facism at the extreme, and urban social problems on a wide scale. An element of doubt in the socially progressive and emancipatory capacity of modern social institutions disquieted some professional sociologists even among the mainstream of the discipline. The confidence in a scientifically trained political and administrative elite, although restored after World War II, was less certain than it had appeared in earlier decades of the 20th century.

Criticism of the social sciences in the 1950s and 1960s initially took the form of a revived humanism in sociology and psychology (e.g. Berger [1963] 1972, Fromm 1961, Mills 1959, Rogers 1961) that continued in the course of a soft radicalism of the so-called 'new sociology' movement of the 1960s and early 1970s (see Gouldner 1970, Horowitz 1965, Wexler 1987). Moreover, ideas from traditions of critical theory, previously little known among English-speaking sociologists, were discovered by a younger generation of intellectuals and activists. Critical social theory devoted attention to the serious failures and problems of modern social institutions, and elaborated critical theories of negation from which alternative social understanding and practices might be devised. The Frankfurt School theorists offered refinements and developments to an older Marxist humanism and much-discredited Stalinist-Marxism. Similarly a loosely termed 'Western Marxism' encompassed numerous dissenting intellectuals offering criticism from a variety of perspectives, including French philosophy, and phenomenology.[2] These critical movements, expressing sociology's idealist and hermeneutic traditions, emphasized human emancipation from domination by social institutions and offered through their theories of negation insights into alternative social possibilities.[3] They sought a restoration of the subjugated but not silenced traditions of critical social theory and critical humanistic sociologies to a weakening structural-functionalist sociology in transatlantic universitites.

Sociological systems theory and structural functionalism, and positivist social science, were already under attack (e.g. Black 1961, Cicourel 1964, Goffman 1959, Horowitz 1965, Mills 1959, Zeitlin [1968] 1990). In addition, outside the academy a radical social criticism gained momentum. The 'culture of experts' in the social sciences, which provided professional intellectuals for government agencies in Western societies, was under increasing criticism for either failing to fully deliver the imagined promises of a functionally integrated and welfare state, or for their uncritical collaboration with state apparatuses of control. Critics targeted in particular the United States for its collusion with a 'warfare state' through the 1960s and 1970s Cold War and Vietnam War. Moreover, the 1960s to 1980s saw considerable demographic and structural changes affecting existing academic traditions and schools in the United States and Europe. The expansion of university education to admit formerly excluded populations (women, ethnic minorities, and children of the working classes), the building of new universities, the rapid expansion of existing scholarly traditions across the spectrum of arts, sciences, social sciences, medicine, law and engineering into new fields and programmes of inquiry led to the rise of new disciplines and sub-disciplines. These new disciplines, institutionally established by cadres of new professors with frequently oppositional agendas to their predecessors (Bourdieu 1988)[4], necessarily engaged in struggles for legitimacy and even ascendancy in their generational, and (occasionally) class, differentiation from the old guard in the modern academy. Although some argue (e.g. Levine 1995) that the 1970s saw a decline in state funding for social science research in the United States and Europe which greatly restricted social science activity, and even led to the closing of some sociology departments, it is difficult to account for the division in sociology by this factor alone. The crises of confidence and dissent were more readily strengthened by broader international social, political and cultural contexts. As Touraine (1988: 21) put it, the crisis arose from the 'growing difficulty of maintaining the very idea of society at the centre of studies on social life' when observations of the real world showed evidence of a social field of competing forces and demands.

The social and political changes reshaping the modern world inevitably generated new intellectual questions and demands upon established cultural institutions. Of considerable significance among them were the movements of anti-colonialism, and decolonization, occurring across the European-colonized world. Movements against colonialism had gained momentum even before World War II but the immediate post-war years saw an unprecedented surge in anti-colonial political events. As an earlier modern and colonial world retracted and reconfigured following wars or legal-moral assaults against established world systems of political, economic and cultural power the disjunctures generated crises of their own and fuelled the intellectual crisis in Western academies. Importantly, the idea of society as a systemic aggregate of institutions and processes of socialization equilibrated by an idea, especially in modernity, of the nation-state, was manifestly in trouble.

The composition and growing momentum of formerly unspoken or unheard subaltern voices among newer generations and classes of intellectuals and writers demanded establishment attention. Eventually, by the 1980s and 1990s, postcolonial discourses raised competing critical agendas from, most notably, race, ethnic, gender and geopolitical perspectives. Their entry into the academy in more than token numbers and their newly articulated perspectives challenged dominant cultural conventions and forms of knowledge. Institutional responses to these political and intellectual demands took various forms. In some instances changes were visible and dramatic, in others they were more accommodatory, dispersive or integrative. In general though, an irrevocable effect was discernible in many European and North American universities. It was an effect interwoven with the growing crisis in philosophical and scientific thought that discredited objectivist 'illusions' and universal true knowledge (see Toulmin 1972). At the very least, the manifest inability of social system theories and functionalism to deal with the context of social contradiction and turbulent dynamics led to that paradigm's rapid decline.

In the social sciences a further differentiation and clustering into increasingly diverse and often opposing sub-disciplines and pan-disciplinary clusters of social inquiry occurred. Eventually, the rapid differentiation and newly gained institutional and professional establishment led to disparate and discordant departures. These new, loosely clustered arenas of inquiry in many cases retained little of the core beliefs unifying their parent disciplines. The former bases and claims for credibility were destabilized and retracted, and a localism, and subjectivist particularism, offered instead. In many fields these events eventually generated, and settled into, a condition of historically agnostic paradigm plurality in which current generations of academic social scientists conduct and publish research for a readership schooled only in particular orthodoxies and conformist to aspirant-elite preferences of localized domains. The simultaneous retreat into and defensive proclamation of paradigm incommensurability, exemplified early in Burrell and Morgan (1979), that is now commonplace in many fields in the social sciences, and especially so in organization studies, is a result of what critical theorists perceived as an insurmountable intellectual and professional disputation over dominance and unified legitimacy. This incommunicative factional dispersion has had unintended practical consequences for restored elites in the academy and society – especially evident in the successful managerialist dominance of organization analysis.

The crisis in sociology readily affected organizational sociology which, in the United States at least, was still searching for a general theory of organizations. The field of 'organization studies', as a composite of diverse interests and approaches to analysing or affecting organizations, became established in the wake of sociology's crisis. The field primarily and practically encompasses the preceding two general traditions in the study of organization: that of sociology and that of management science. Not unexpectedly, the field is characterized by competition, compromise and professional institutional dynamics, and occasionally tolerant pluralism, in a struggle over legitimacy and delimitation. In many respects the field of organization studies is an exemplary case of loose association, tense or foreclosed dialogue among clamorous traders in fragments of grand theories, ideas and programmes struggling for status, power and institutionalization.

The Sociology of Organizations and Crisis

Disciplinary differentiations had emerged early in the founding decades of the social sciences. Indeed sociology came into being through a confluence of contributing intellectual traditions and its boundaries have always been difficult to define (Giddens 1982, Levine 1995, Smart 1999). The early sociologists, especially Durkheim, were most keen to establish disciplinary boundaries, rules of methods and content of investigation. As difficult to establish as that disciplinary demarcation has been, there was sufficient agreement on many aspects of the sociological domain to provide practical cohesion and shared cumulative knowledge. Among those domain interests was a long-standing and central problematic of sociology, shared, although with markedly different perspectives, by the distinctive traditions of Marx, Durkheim and Weber: the matter of social structures and institutions, and their relations to individuals. In the latter decades of the 20th century this core problematic of sociology, the matter of social practices of organizations and institutions, had become an increasingly contested arena in a new division of academic labour.

Despite the influence of a classical stream of criticism in sociology, as well as the general theoretical interest in social structures and organizations typical of the sociological project, a significant alteration in the discipline and practice of sociology has repositioned the problematic of organization. Of course, none of the disciplines in the social sciences can lay exclusive claim to areas of interest or methods of inquiry, and that is notably so in organizational analysis. But the modern social science disciplinary traditions have secured legitimacy by asserting claim to academic bodies of knowledge and professional expertise in at least some core domains of inquiry. Each of the main foundational traditions within sociology, and most especially the Weberian and Durkheimian strands, has attended to the phenomenon of organization as a central characteristic of modern industrial capitalist society. The dislodging of the problem of organization from its broader social and theoretical contexts of inquiry, in which the remants of sociology of organizations are reduced to a naive sociologism, has proved significant.

At once composite and consequent of the crisis in sociology, the social questions of bureaucratic organizations and institutional practices were, by the 1960s, loosened and practically dislodged from their intellectual moorings in classical sociological inquiry. Sociological inquiry into organizations had become characterized by scientific positivist empiricism and functionalist-derived applications to organizational problems. The focus of classical approaches, which was on the societal contextualization of organizations and a perpetual reflexivity, was rejected or ignored. Although the disruption was significant for the current state of inquiry into organizations, in an important sense it did not register much significance at the time. The move of organizational analysis away from the broader, especially humanist, traditions of sociology and into schools of business and management historically uninterested in the metatheoretical concerns of social theorists, only confirmed what later critics (Aronowitz 1981, Gouldner 1979) called the complicity of mainstream sociology in the repressiveness of the established order. Much of what comprised the sociology of organizations had, by the 1960s, already significantly discarded a central interest in meta-social analysis of organizations and a critical reflection on organizations in preference for a technical conception of organizational problems for a clearly defined managerial agenda.

However, the broader discipline of sociology had by no means entirely occluded or silenced contestational and critical perspectives. The traditions of Marxist sociology and critical theory had maintained an influence, especially in European sociologies. Industrial and urban sociologies, and some social psychologies, retained the critical Marxist problematics of alienation, economic exploitation and coercion, and domination (e.g. Baran and Sweezy 1966, Braverman 1974, Burawoy 1985, Fromm 1955, 1961). Moreover, the phenomenological and interpretive schools were contributing new critical perspectives. A renewed attention to humanist traditions of sociology, particularly in the form of a rediscovery of the classics (e.g. Glass and Staude 1972, Nisbet 1967) found a growing audience in the 1960s and 1970s. These influences continued to exert some intellectual demands on the sociology of organizations, at least for its practitioners to acknowledge the theoretical and moral tensions they posed. Even as the classical concern with bureaucracy had become closely focused on intra-organizational elements and merged with functionalist theories of organization, echoes of Weber's concern with intensified rational instrumentality and domination in organizational practices remained. Nonetheless, the migration to and integration with the dominant managerial approach to organizations in schools of business and economics was a relatively bloodless merger.

The dominance of structural-functionalism in the sociology of organizations endured even though, ironically, it was sociologists of organizations such as Simon, Sleznick and Crozier who had not only shown the weakness of functionalism and of the central rationalities assumed by classical sociology, but advocated a neo-rational strategic management in its place. Structural-functionalist sociology of organizations had already eschewed interest in broader sociological imperatives, especially the humanistic and socially critical. Some sociologists were fully aware of this path in the 1960s. The sociology of organizations had become, as Mouzelis (1967) described it, narrow, ahistorical, and inclined toward 'the mere accumulation of rigorously tested myopic statements' (Mouzelis 1967: 179). The field had developed a 'psychologistic bias' (ibid.: 172) that was ignorant of broader knowledge in the social sciences, and diverted attention from the 'organizational features of society as a whole'. Mouzelis' view sought to maintain the broader sociological imperative and opposed the narrow functional imperatives, managerial orientation and production problem-solving intent in which the sub-discipline was clearly absorbed. For Mouzelis: 'The crucial problem today is not so much how to increase what Mannheim calls the functional rationality of modern bureaucracies but rather how to safeguard…a minimum of substantive rationality and individual initiative; not how to make people more contented and cooperative with management but rather how to prevent them from becoming happy automatons in a "brave new world"' (Mouzelis 1967: 173–174).

That criticism, in 1967, was scarcely heeded. The concerns which had preoccupied the classical sociologists, and which Mouzelis insisted continued to need exhaustive analysis among his generation of organizational analysts, were ignored. Instead the rapidly establishing field of organization studies, greatly aided by its institutional housing in schools of business, management and economics, departed further from reflective sociological theory and critique. The manifest agenda of business schools needed little explanation. In that setting there was little use for a critical inquiry into organizations in their social relations, or of their substantive ends.

From today's vantage point the relative ease with which a new sub-discipline such as organization science, initially, and organization studies eventually, became established is in large part accounted for by the condition of post-war sociology. Critics such as Gouldner (1970), C. Wright Mills (1959) and Lemert (1995) identified professional academic sociology as significantly an American sociology in which the sheer size and relative homogeneity of the American discipline and its distinctive application to applied social problems overshadowed a European tradition that retained the humanism and criticism of the Marxist and Weberian schools. The critical reflexivity dimension of sociology had been weakened or silenced in the dominant American tradition. In the United Kingdom the expansion of universities and the establishment of business schools in the 1950s and 1960s shared some of the conditions evident in post-World War II America. Social reconstruction, integration and economic expansion assumed greater internal importance, especially as the remaining vestiges of empire broke free. But the drive toward professional homogeneity may not have been quite as effective in Europe as it generally was in the United States. Social integration around consumption and the monochrome politics of welfare democracy did not entirely relegate an *oeuvre* of modern criticism to the same fate as a politically defeated Marxism. Modern critical sociologies continued to provide analyses of social, industrial and labour relations practices. But the outcomes of these critical efforts, and the experiences of critical activists, contributed to th conditions preparing for the advent of postmodernism.

Criticism

Although the sociology of organizations and its hybrid successor organization studies had become increasingly diverse yet myopic, historically agnostic and for a time supposedly value-neutral, the liberal ideological trajectory met currents of criticism, opposition and resistance. That criticism took many forms on a continuum from conservative humanism to radical humanism, and also that of a radical, anti-humanist structuralism. It displayed varying degrees of systematic argumentation and coherence, reflection, caution, and occasionally direction. By the late 1970s the renewed interest in Marxism and critical theory following the 1960s cultural and political movements, and the influence of Gouldner's widely read *The Coming Crisis of Western Sociology* (1970), found expression in radical humanist criticisms of organization studies and organizational practices in society.

Humanistic Contestations

At the time in the 1960s when Mouzelis was admonishing the narrow psychologism and precious scientism of sociology of organizations in Britain, across the Atlantic a revival of humanistic sociology demanding a broader gaze upon human social affairs was already underway. Peter Berger's 1963 'Invitation to Sociology: A Humanistic Perspective', for instance, demanded that the scientific sociology enterprise restore its humanism – bequeathed from the Renaissance imperative of intellectual liberation – and in so doing become more 'sophisticated and also…more civilized'. Echoing C. Wright Mills in calling for 'an openness to the immense richness of human life [which] makes the leaden consequence of sociologism impossible to sustain' (Berger [1963] 1972: 218), Berger advocated a humanistic sociology that would be vitally informed by history and philosophy and aware of the limitations of science. Sociology is, or must be, in this view principally concerned with the human condition – with what it means to be human in particular social conditions.

Berger was fully aware of the difficulty of restoring a humanistic character to sociology as the discipline, especially in the United States, had become by that decade firmly fixated not only on science, but on the usefulness of its professional applications. In a blithely trenchant assessment, for a self-described conservative humanist (Berger and Neuhaus 1970), of the orthodox mainstream enterprise of sociology Berger remarks:

It is not easy to introduce a humanistic dimension into research designed to determine the optimum crew composition of a bomber aircraft, or to discover the factors that will induce somnambulant housewives in a supermarket to reach for one brand of baking powder as against another, or to advise personnel managers about the best procedures to undermine union influence in a factory. (Berger [1963] 1972: 218)

To rationalize these applications of the sociological craft as humane endeavours with nothing ethically questionable about them, Berger added, would require a *tour de force* in ideologizing. Of course, such a *tour de force* had already taken place and in the view of radical humanist sociologists (e.g. Gouldner 1970, Mills 1959) had rendered the conventional practice of sociology an applied science serving the interests of dominant classes. The humanistic critique of technocratic instrumentalism as the dominant mode of science and society found expression in other humanistic theories that filtered, albeit unevenly, through sociology and into the sociology of organizations. By the late 1960s and early 1970s a revived humanism in sociology, of both a liberal and a Marxist orientation, effectively contested the eliding of human action of the social sytems paradigm. But this humanist contestation, and for some its dramatic defeat (after the events in Europe in 1968), which in many ways assisted the cultural turn to postmodernism, met also an anti-humanist structuralist (and poststructuralist) current in the 1970s and 1980s. Organizational analysis by the 1990s was much affected by both. The dominance of structural-functionalism underwent, as Giddens (1973) portrays, a relatively sudden demise.

The humanistic challenge to the totalizing structuration of functionalism, and to the technocratic instrumentalism of managerial organizational analysis, first found expression in efforts to restore agency and action to the domain of social systems. Many critics of structural-functionalism (notably Dahrendorf 1959, Coser 1956 and Lockwood 1956) rejected the consensus and integration proposed in Parsons' overarching formulation. They developed theories of conflict and coercion which grappled with the interests of oppositional groups that had been ignored in the equilibrating normative state of functionalism. But these efforts by and large enabled structural-functionalism to account for its omissions and accommodate conflict. Its overall position within the service of a technicist imperative in social theory was untroubled. As Giddens (1973) argued, much of the criticism of structural-functionalism simply represented the other side of the structural-functionalist coin and was therefore subject to the same limitations.

Even the humanist critiques and alternative approaches which found expression in sociological inquiries drawn from phenomenology and symbolic interactionism were practically added on to an adapted natural systems theory. A growing influence of symbolic interactionist and ethnomethodological approaches to social practices in sociology began to appear in some organizational studies in the 1960s (e.g. Bittner 1967, Sudnow 1965). These efforts ostensibly rejected the positivist science methodology of mainstream organization analysis. Their focus directed attention to the complexities and immediacies of human subjective experiences and interactions through which they sought to analyse the 'network of meanings' that produced the 'negotiated order' of 'everyday life'. In so doing these theorists offered a hermeneutic or interpretive organizational analysis that recognized the relationships between sub-jectively meaningful courses of action and the social structures of inter-action and activity in which they occurred. These activities, their theorist-observers proposed, demonstrated the socially constructed nature of social processes and social reality.

Another humanistic critical inquiry took the form of psychodynamic analyses of organizational and work life. They focused on the effects on the worker of organizational structures and institutionalized relationships. Importantly, Maccoby's (1976) psychoanalytic study identified the 'psy-chostructure' of the organization which fits workers to organizational norms, including dysfunctional ones. LaBier (1986) further developed these notions and pointed to organizational conditions which produce psy-chopathologies in workers and serious emotional costs to humans partici-pating in conventionally organized workplaces. But their criticisms, and those of other insightful psychodynamic and psychoanalytic studies (e.g. Baum 1987, Hirschhorn 1988, Jaques 1976, Schwartz 1990), typically remained within the dominant framework of functional systems in need of improvement to mitigate their unintended effects on workers.

Silverman's (1970) book promised a more organized, serious critique of structural-functionalist orthodoxy by proposing that system perspectives and action perspectives were irreconcilable. For Silverman, organizational analysis required a 'paradigm shift' that reflected the sterility of orthodox theories and their failure to explain the relationships between social struc-ture and human action. Silverman (1970) endeavoured to avoid the fixation on micro processes that characterized phenomenological and symbolic interactionist approaches. Drawing on Weberian theories, Silverman attempted to offer an action frame of reference that moved from 'an exami-nation of the micro problem of particular actors to the macro problem of the systems of expectations…which they and other actors import from the wider social structure' (Silverman 1970: 165). In this manner he proposed to offer an explanation for organizational patterns of interaction, and of change occurring through such interaction, and the meanings people ascribe to their actions. But Silverman's critics (e.g. Burrell and Morgan 1979,

Reed 1985), though recognizing his important contribution, insisted that he failed to reconcile the Weberian action frame of reference and the ethnomethodological one. Indeed, his concluding remarks – that his framework is offered as an analytical method rather than a theory, a frame of reference from which 'questions about the nature of social life in any organization' may be derived and which require 'empirical studies to provide the answers' (Silverman 1970: 223) – indicated for Burrell and Morgan that his view is 'firmly in line with the positivist attitude...and clearly emphasises its location within the context of the functionalist paradigm' (Burrell and Morgan 1979: 201).[5]

Such was the vigour of the criticism mounted against structural-functionalism by radical critics of the late 1970s that any method advocating empirical investigation could be sniffed out as positivism, and as exemplifying the 'abstracted empiricism' so reviled by the humanist critics. In this view the schools of action approach, including symbolic interactionism, along with systems theories 'end up' as, in C. Wright Mills' term, 'abstracted empiricism' ineluctably produced by research methodologies derived from the natural sciences, and unable to theorize the complexities and contradictions of human actions and social practices.

More formally, in Giddens' view the demise of structural-functionalism had 'stimulated the resurgence of a crude voluntarism, linked to...a retreat from institutional analysis' (Giddens 1973: 15). The privileging of the importance of the practices of everyday life, of negotiated relationships and social order, and the focus on practical reason (as against theoretical reason), in interpretive sociologies has rationalized a 'withdrawal from basic issues involved in the study of macro-structural social forms and social processes' (ibid.). The trivia of everyday life and the phenomenal experience of social reality have displaced the long-standing central problems in sociology which, Giddens reminds us, are questions of social structure, and of social class. The dominant trends within sociology, and also within the Marxist tradition of social theory, had reached a point in the 1960s when they had become inadequate to undertake analysis of social problems. This situation indicated a condition of crisis in sociology. Sociologists of organizations – those most proximate to the task of institutional analysis – were seriously ill-equipped for the task and were immersed in either a rehabilitated structural-functionalism, or in the minutiae of micro-analyses, calmly indifferent to structured social relations. Marxist sociological thought was for Giddens in 1973 (and Gouldner 1970, Habermas 1975, Offe 1985, Aronowitz 1981, and others) similarly in crisis, especially after the failures of state socialism to implement alternative emancipatory economic and social relations.

Yet notwithstanding the apparent crisis in Marxism, a critical analyst of organizations, Reed (1985), argues that it was within this 'weakened sociological condition' that a rejuvenated Marxist perspective was to find fertile ground for the development of alternative theoretical frameworks. The field of organization science and its body of problem-solving theory, despite the generational hold on orthodoxy, was readily broken up. An arena for sustained critical approaches to organization studies was formed.

A Critical Disruption

The crisis in sociology experienced at many levels in the academy provided the historical juncture for disruptive organizational criticism of the sort not seen since the embryonic criticisms of institutional structure in Luxemburg, Trotsky and Lukács. The liberal, and radical, humanist revivals in sociology and psychology were already offering alternatives to systems and structural-functionalist orthodoxies.[6] Importantly, the action approach had offered some redress of the neglect, or elision, of human agency in social system activity. But for another cluster of alternative theorists there remained a glaring lack of attention to political and economic interests in the structure of social and organizational institutions. A number of critical theorists of organization from both Marxist and Weberian perspectives mounted a programme of serious contestation to the established orthodoxies of framework and method, and dominant interests, in organizational analysis. Their efforts sought to disrupt the hegemonic managerialism that had commandeered the field through sociological structural-functionalism, neo-rationalism, and behaviourist social psychologies of the Human Relations school.

Of course, there had been no shortage of criticism of the endemic managerial bias in industrial and organizational psychologies. Shortly after publication of the famous Hawthorne studies of Elton Mayo and associates, for instance, critics pointed to serious omissions and manifest biases in the studies. These critics, who included Daniel Bell in 1947, argued that Mayo and his associates 'uncritically adopt industry's own conception of workers as *means* to be manipulated or adjusted to impersonal ends' (cited in Brown [1954] 1980: 93). However as Brown noted, 'industrial psychology has always thought of the worker as "means to be manipulated"…and it is difficult to see why the work of Mayo…should have been selected for special criticism' (ibid.). There ought to be no surprise that the work of industrial and organizational psychologists carries a management bias. The circumstances in which it was conducted were those of management-commissioned studies seeking solutions to management problems in industrial and administrative organizations. Among sociologists such an expectation was readily apparent. Reinhard Bendix' influential study in 1956 addressed the facticity of class and authority structures in industrial organizations, and the managerial ideologies that reflect the bureaucratization of industries. In Bendix' assessment Mayo's contribution to managerial ideology has been pervasive (Bendix [1956] 1974: 319) and undisguised.

The practice of managerial organization scientists, who variously took notice of the prescriptions of the 'human relations' organizational psychologists, was conducted under the same rubric of rationalization and production: problem-solving for managers of large complex production organizations and administrative bureaucracies. The scientific representation of organizations as natural systems structured through rational action for functional ends obscured, the critical theorists argued, the managerial ideology of organizational science. A functionalist orthodoxy not only defined and legitimized the forms of organizational analysis throughout the field, it determined the context of any contestational theory or approach. For the new generation of critics in the 1970s and 1980s the 'stultifying influence', as Reed (1985) puts it, which functionalism exerted narrowly constrained the field and truncated its development. These critics sought not just a departure from functionalism but an exposition of its obscured ideologies of capitalism. These ideologies sought the universalization and normalization of a particular, historically specific economic and political *modus operandi*. The equation of capitalist ideologies with scientific rationality and natural cooperative sytems had produced a widely operant acceptance of a structure of social relations in which organizations were naturally a part.

By the late 1970s the renewed interest in Marxism and critical theory in sociology found expression in organizational analysis through the influential work of Clegg and Dunkerley (1980), Burrell and Morgan (1979), Salaman (1979), Reed (1985), and others, and through the work of critical industrial sociologists including Mills (1959), Braverman (1974), Baran and Sweezy (1966), Mandel (1978), Miliband (1977), and Burawoy (1985). Critical organization theorists orientated their criticisms of managerial organizational analysis according to a general perspective of contextualizing the practices of organizations in the wider structure of social relations of production. Drawing on Marx's theory of the 'labour process' of capitalism, and its further elaboration influentially by Braverman (1974), and later in partial counter-position by Friedman (1977), Edwards (1979), Littler (1982) and others, the critical theorists drew also on Weber, variously on Simmel, and on critical social psychologists such as Fromm and Rogers.

A central concern among critical theorists was an analysis of organizations as structures of social relations serving the interests of ideologically dominant classes. Resisting the ahistorical and apolitical positivism of conventional organization science, the critical theorists posed a contrary analytic. In this view, the mask of rational integration and consensus hides an administrative apparatus engaged in the systemic economic and political exploitation of the majority for the appropriation of maximum profit for a dominant capitalist minority. Organizations are rational instruments of class domination, and managerial organization theory is an everyday instrument of that domination at the sites of production.

Much of this important Marxist-influenced criticism of mainstream organization theory focused on the ways in which managerial organization theory devises forms of control over the labour process of production for the traditional capitalist ends of surplus value and capital accumulation. Marxist industrial sociologists, economists and trade unionists had elaborated such analyses throughout the development of organization science but their views were inadmissible to managerial organizational analysis. Critical organizational analysts endeavoured to expose the distortions and mystifications embedded in such practices (Burrell and Morgan 1979, Clegg 1975, Zey-Ferrell and Aikin 1981), and the linkages between institutions of production and administration, and relations of social classes.

Although the Marxist critics presented varying degrees of adherence to humanist Marxism and scientific Marxism (the twin tendencies within classical Marxism and the source of ubiquitous debate), the formulations offered by Althusser's reading of Marx in his anti-humanist, anti-empiricist structuralism began to influence critical organizational analysis and industrial political analysis in the 1970s. The influence of Althusser's two most important books, *For Marx* and *Reading Capital* (published in Paris in 1965 and translated into English a few years later) spread quickly. Althusser's structural analysis of capitalist society presented a striking oppositional schema to the humanist voluntarism of Marxist theory of the Western Marxism of Lukács, Gramsci, and the Frankfurt School.

Central to Althusser's Marxism is his emphasis on an 'epistemological break' in Marx's work which places Marx's later scientific works in distinct contrast to his earlier humanism. For Althusser, the mode of production is the 'structural causality' of things social. Humanism is an ideological illusion that obscures the scientific knowledge that grasps humans or social classes, not as conscious subjects of history but as involuntary 'supports' of social relations. For Althusser, men's beliefs that they were in any way free to act of their own volition was a delusion. Humans are remorselessly governed by laws of which they are unconscious. For Althusser, even under communism (still the preferred end of Marxism), people would still live in ideology: 'All human societies secrete ideology as the very element and atmosphere indispensable to their historical respiration and life' (Althusser 1970: 232).

Althusser drew from his reading of Marx's *Capital* a notion of the dialectic as a process without a subject; of tensions between structural forces that are without historical trajectory and necessity. He conceived of the social totality governed by the 'principal practices' of the economic, the political, the ideological and the scientific. Each of these practices engages in historically variable interrelationships and each exerts a variable degree of independence or autonomy. In the final analysis the economic is the most important but its degree of dominance is conditioned by the role of superstructural practices at particular historical junctures. For Althusser, the state as the principal 'ideological apparatus' ensures that the social formation reproduces the conditions of its production simultaneously with its enactment of social structural reality. Therefore, the ideological apparatus of the state extends into all levels of the infrastructure and superstructure of every society. Individuals are 'interpellated' as subjects of the ruling ideology and behave accordingly (Althusser 1970). They are ineluctably constituted by ideology, and ideology only exists through its functioning in the interpellation of subjects.

The determining role of ideology through any of the principal practices of the social totality comprised Althusser's notion of 'over-determination' which means that social affairs, and the lives of interpellated subjects, are determined by total systemic structural domination. For Althusser, 'individuals are always-already subjects'. Such over-determination of the social reality explains 'uneven development' in social forms in different societies, and requires the theoretical rejection of the notion of historical necessity and a revolutionary dialectic. Althusser did conceive of a process of social change which occurs as a consequence of antagonistic and contradictory interrelationships between structural formations but he, necessarily, forecloses the classical Marxist role for political activity, consciousness-raising class struggles, and revolutionary agentic societal transformation. Moreover, Althusser's separation of an apparently real, structurally determined, world from individual consciousness – which is not possible because of the prevalence of ideological illusion – presents an unbridgeable gap between structural reality and the human knowers of that reality. As the total theory accounts for all social reality there is no requirement for, and no scientific validity in, the conduct of empirical research.

Althusser's work attracted considerable interest. His anti-empiricism was welcomed in many quarters, including those of the few organizational analysts who early recognized the importance of structuralism (see, for instance, Mouzelis 1975), even as it attracted the criticism of armchair theorizing. The Althusserian critique of the crude reductionist interpretations of historical materialism, of the micro focus of the sociological pheno-menologists, and the proliferation of routinized empirical research and atheoretical generalizations of mainstream sociologists gathered a diverse sympathetic audience. Among sociologists of organization the influence of Althusserian structuralism was evident in the anti-empiricist criticism of, for instance, Burrell and Morgan (1979) as well as the radical Weberians and Marxists, including especially the industrial sociologists of the labour process. Importantly, the Althusserian theorization of the ideological apparatuses of the state drew attention to the role of industrial organizations, as well as administrative bureaucracies, in the power structure of society as a whole. Similarly, the emphasis on structure and power heightened attention to the processes of bureaucratization in society that were central to Weber's work, and assisted the shift from micro and middle-range functionalist sociologies of organization. But Althusser's abstract theory and his foreclosure of political action further distanced academicized Western Marxism from party political practice and class struggles for societal transformation.

Burrell and Morgan's influential book (1979) endeavoured to show how industrial organizations are key structural apparatuses in a capitalist mode of production. In accomplishing the appropriation of surplus value and capital accumulation industrial organizations simultaneously reproduce the necessary patterns of uneven distribution of consumption, and organization of economic power. The bureaucratic structure of the organization mirrors and reproduces the administrative arrangements of the superstructure of the capitalist society as a whole. In this manner Burrell and Morgan's critical analysis of organizations demonstrates the 'base/superstructure' elements in classical Marxist theory, although with some later qualifications of the economic determinism associated with that rudimentary metaphor. They argued that the economic domains are co-constituted by social and cultural practices which at the same time retain relative autonomy from each other. This emphasis led to a focus on contradiction and disjuncture within social practices, and particularly within those of organizations.

Subsequent to a primary aim of critical theorists to expose the con-tradictions and mystifications of capitalist economic organizations are efforts to construct a political economy of organizations and their rela-tions to the state. Clegg and Dunkerley (1980), drawing on Althusser, theorize the relations between production organizations and the state as networks of ideological apparatuses of the state. The state, as a formal organization, intervenes in order to control or regulate the internal contradictions of capitalist social relations of production. Such interventions produce unintended consequences and ideological crises, and these disjunctures provide possibilities for politics of resistance and altered social relations. Moreover, it is these disjunctures and the recurrent incompleteness of the class ideologies of control and repression through state apparatuses that critical industrial sociologists theorized in response to Harry Braverman's (1974) despondent prognosis for the labour process in production organizations of capitalism. Braverman, following Marx, attempted to construct a theory of social structure from the analysis of the capitalist labour process in advanced capitalist conditions. For Braverman, the vastly expanded role of automation and computerization in production accelerated the trend toward the displacement of human labour power, both manual and mental. Accumulation of capital is increasingly accomplished by technological developments and forms of control, and not just by more efficient extraction of surplus value from labouring workers as it was under Taylorist scientific management. Braverman elaborated this process through its various devices of Fordist assembly lines and industrial psychology to its consequences in a progressive deskilling and degradation of labour and workers in production. These processes lead to irreversible transformations in the labour process and the recomposition of class. Automation, deskilling and displacement of labour fuelled the fragmentation and disorganization of unionized workers and the working class.

Braverman's thesis generated considerable interest and controversy among industrial and organizational sociologists and labour relations analysts. While most agreed with the analyses of the impacts of the developing techno-capitalism many disputed the prognosis of an apparent totality of domination and ineluctable deskilling.[7] Burawoy (1985) proposes an alternative approach to Braverman's prognosis that is not a simple rejection of the deskilling thesis but a reassertion of working-class craft skill and solidarity against the power of the bosses more evident in British critiques of Braverman's labour process theory (e.g. Littler 1982, Salaman 1981, Thompson 1983, Wood 1982). Burawoy criticizes Braverman for assuming the capacity of capitalism to survive class struggles. Braverman, for Burawoy, assumes that the 'expressive totality designates the subordination of society to capital, so that everything appears functional to capital. There are no dysfunctional elements, tensions, or crises' (Burawoy 1985: 61). Although others, such as Offe and Ronge (1975), O'Conner (1973), Poulantzas (1973), Habermas (1975) and Aglietta (1979), argue that a serious examination of the capitalist state reveals considerable problematics confronting capitalism, Braverman dismisses these as ineffectual moral objections; which in any case are readily incorporated by hegemonic remystification and restoration.

Burawoy develops a comprehensive critique of Braverman, arguing that Braverman fails to understand the ways in which the appearance of totality and inevitability hide the conditions of domination. Understanding the conditions of the 'expressive totality' enables alternatives to that structured totality to be imagined and socially constructed. For Burawoy, drawing on the Italian theorist Antonio Gramsci,[8] Braverman's concern with the degradation of work and the domination of capital reflect the specific character of capitalism in the United States. In other countries, especially in Europe, workers have experienced greater control over the labour process and more effective political struggles. This variation in both labour process and political regime within capitalist societies undermines Braverman's conception of capitalism as monolithic and intractable. Burawoy poses alternatively a distinction between the labour process and the political apparatuses of production. He offers an analysis of these politics of production and their relationship to state politics and state apparatuses. The distinction enables him to account for the under-politicization of production and to redress what he sees as the tendency among a number of others to collapse them into the labour process (Burawoy 1985: 125). He accounts for a periodization and unevenness of capitalist development and the variability of crisis and state intervention in the labour process of production.

Littler (1982) shares many of Burawoy's perspectives and similarly attempts to analyse the labour process from the view of its historical variability and relative distinction from the socio-economic conditions of particular contexts. But his primary attention is to the level of the industrial enterprise and the labour process, conceived as the coordinated sets of activities and relations in which human labour transforms raw materials into useful products, and the political apparatuses of Burawoy's schema are under-addressed. Nonetheless, Littler and other British labour process theorists (e.g. Knights and Willmott 1990) develop key contributions derived from a synthesis of Marxist and Weberian theories on work organization. Importantly, they restore attention to agency and voluntarist dimensions in the labour process, and in the political economy. Reed (1985) captures this concern in a call for a critical theory of organizations in which an integration of labour process and political economy perspectives resists a 'too easy acceptance of the structural detemininsm… of more orthodox interpretations of critical theory' (p. 89). He summarizes the revitalized labour process theory as highlighting the tensions between a structuralist and voluntarist perspective within the critical theory tradition, a tension also shared to some extent in the mainstream organization theory tradition. A renewed focus on dialectical struggles and non-determinant structural and cultural relations encouraged attention to resistance and change. Critical analyses of this sort are developed by Barker (1993), Jermier et al. (1994) and Kunda (1992).

For Reed (1985) however, the underlying tension between structuralism and voluntarism is 'likely to weaken the internal logical coherence and explanatory power of a critical theory of organizations' (1985: 92). Apparently 'highly abstract and generalized' accounts of macro-level forces and structures of capitalist political economies, are for Reed, too abstracted from concrete organizations. Moreover, the more limited empirical analysis of changes in work organization 'can only be accepted if many of the key presuppositions contained within the former are rejected' (1985: 92). Although these alleged contradictions are not elaborated, Reed concludes that critical organization theorists share a similar fate to that of the systems and action theorists in facing a number of unresolved tensions and conflicts that weaken their theories and encourage fragmentation.

It does seem to be the case that the 'weaknesses' in the critical theory perspectives, which have drawn with varying degrees of emphasis on structuralist imperatives and voluntarist ones, have greatly hindered the formation of a grand, general critical theory of organizations – if that is what Reed (1985) was implicitly measuring them against. But (as Reed himself indicates elsewhere) the fundamental Marxist emphasis on dialectical struggle between irrepressible tensions results not in a fixed synthesis, but in on-going tensions and struggles, perpetually undermining the construction of totalizing theory, and social practice. The task for critical theorists and practitioners is to work out in diverse concrete sites of economic and cultural production the dynamics between structural conditions and voluntarist agency. As Weber and Freud, and others before them, analysed human and worldly conditions, they recognized the paradoxes inherent in human activity in which the structures humans create simultaneously and unintendedly dominate their creators. This disconcerting paradox of institutions has been, in one form or another, a constant theme in the constitution of modern social and scientific thought.

At one end of a spectrum of efforts to deal with the intractable problem of human agency or systemic determination is a scientistic social thought that postulates a hypertrophic rationality and deterministic systems theories (including functionalist and Marxist structuralism). A more recent iteration of this view proposes, beyond opposition, a schema in which the problem of human agency is elided in a postmodern turn away from the allegedly modern sources, and modern dilemmas, of human agency. A subjectless system apparently displaces the anxiety of modern subject selves through acceptance of their subjectification. That discussion is taken up in the following chapter.

Alongside, and occasionally intersecting with, the critical analytical interests discussed above is an important tradition of feminist organizational criticism that emerged in practice in the late 1960s. Fuelled by the radicalizing politics of the women's movement in much of the West, initially it took two primary forms. The first, radical, effort was to imagine and construct alternative organizations to those which had always been designed by men and for men. As society was structured in an inherently gendered manner of inequality, discrimination and exclusion, so too were modern production and administrative organizations. Some of these early feminist efforts to construct alternative value bases for organizations such as non-hierarchical structures, rotational leadership and inclusion of women's values and relational emphases formed the basis of academic theorizations and criticism in the 1970s. These early works in turn gave rise to a now extensive and influential body of feminist work in organization studies. As well as the practical influence of the women's movement's politics and experimentation the growth of formal feminist theory in disciplines in the social sciences and humanities encouraged an expansion of interest in all branches of social thought and practice.

In organizational analysis and sociology of work a considerable body of work was produced from the 1970s onward on topics exposing and addressing women's fraught experiences in working and organizational life. Initially, most of the attention focused on inequalities, discrimination, structural exclusion and moral argument on the role of women in society and work. Amid the eventually prolific literature of this period are, for instance, the work of Epstein (1970), Kundsen (1974), Fox and Hesse-Biber (1984), Garson (1988), Hochschild (1983, 1989), Kessler-Harris (1981), Knights and Willmott (1986), MacKinnon (1979), Wright (1987) all of which address women's experience of inequality and gendered oppression in the workplace. Calas and Smircich (1992, 1996), Hearn et al. (1989), Mills and Tancred (1992), among others, addressed organizational and management practices producing and reproducing unequal gendered experiences of work, and argued for the inclusion of women in management functions. By the 1990s, as the journal *Gender, Work and Organization* attests, discussions of gender practices in work and organization had reached a wide, mainstream management and organization audience. Most other journals in organization studies now regularly publish feminist analyses of aspects of organizational and management practice. In this sense, at least, feminist criticism finds an attentive audience.

In addition to the body of empirical studies on women in organizations and work which demonstrate and criticize women's inequality, sexualized or contested place in organizational life, is a growing literature which critically interrogates the fields of organization and management studies as implicated in the gendered structures of exclusion and inequality in organizational practice. A number of feminist analyses of the field of organization and management studies turn their attention to the knowledge practices of the field and theorize the relative absence of women thinkers from the production of knowledge. Calas and Smircich's (1996) influential work in this area indicates a crucial step in encouraging the field to develop a reflexivity that has rarely been evident. At the same time their work, while leading to a discussion of the new wave of criticism launched by postmodernism in organization analysis, reminds us of the important efforts of feminists to criticize the embedded masculine biases of conventional modern organization theory, as exemplified by landmark works of Rosabeth Moss Kanter's *Men and Women of the Corporation* (1977). Yet, beyond the liberal reformism of most feminist studies Calas and Smircich seek a continued project of a critical social analysis of organizations in society. For Calas and Smircich, 'feminist approaches to organization studies [are] one of the few spaces left for reflecting upon and criticizing the excesses and violence of contemporary global capitalism, as it impacts many people all over the world' (Calas and Smircich 1996: 242).

Critical Outcomes

Critical analytical approaches to organizations continue, in the spirit of Marx, to effect 'a ruthless criticism of everything'. Their extensive range now includes a body of critical social psychologies (e.g. Carr 1998, Casey 1995, Fineman 1993, Fineman and Gabriel 1996, Gabriel 1991 and Gabriel 2000). In response to the many currents of criticism, the mainstream in organization theory intensifies its strategies to defend itself against and to incorporate critical theorizations and alternative representations. But notwithstanding the influence of critical analysis, the distance between levels of analysis which addressed on the one hand the social relations and psychological effects of an instrumental productivism and its administrative apparatuses; and on the other, the practical problem-solving concerns of management organization theory, delineated the chasm that emerged between the theoretical and political orientations of applied theorists and critical analysts. The chasm did not fully develop until after the broader crisis in sociology filtered into organization theory. The crisis in sociology and the plethora of theories and approaches subsequently on offer effectively disrupted many established orthodoxies in the social sciences, including organization science. But the outcomes of the disruptive incursion of new ideas, which included a renewed space for critical approaches to organization analysis, also included the construction of a neo-rationalist trajectory of managerialism in organization studies which, once again, claims a singular legitimacy. Despite wide-ranging radical criticism in organization studies, the effects of the broader crisis in sociology intensified efforts to produce *useful* organizational analysis in business schools.

By the 1980s, interest in production, work, organizations and economy, once central to the discipline of sociology, had lost ground in the thoroughly disrupted schools of sociology. The crisis had effected a shift toward cultural studies as confidence in the grand social theories, and in classical notions of society, as products of increasingly suspect metanarratives, foundered and dissipated. Marxism, which shared the evolutionism of classical theory, even as it exposed class interests embedded in existing rational institutions, was similarly in crisis. The intellectual effects on organization analysis only became readily apparent in the 1980s (as the work of Hassard 1993, Reed 1992 and Willmott 1993b, for instance, attest). An institutionalized avoidance of broader social theories and intellectual movements somewhat insulated organization science from the disruptions and reconfigurations ensuing in the broader sociological disciplines.

Indeed organization studies, for all its heterogeneity and currents of criticism, maintained coherence and operative unity through an overarching commitment to an applied managerialist agenda. When it did respond it was not so much to the academic crisis but rather, in a more pragmatic manner, to the changing conditions of a postindustrial social and cultural shift affecting business and organization practices. While academic theorists now follow a cultural turn in social theory, a heightened attention to economic and business practices in a rapidly globalizing market society is more evident in expanding business schools. As the cultural turn to language, identity and communalism excites many intellectuals, the postmodernization and globalization of capitalist social and economic relations grabs the attention of many others. Cohorts of new graduates (particularly in the United States and United Kingdom) are attracted and recruited into new research programmes boasting clear research agendas, corporate-funded research grants and consultancy opportunities. These activities gain rising popularity in the face of the institutional and intellectual crisis of confidence in classical disciplines. As well, they attest to a growing trend of individualized strategic positioning of oneself in a market society. In Europe, especially the United Kingdom, critical opposition to the reconstruction of neo-rationalist and neo-functionalist agendas has taken a number of forms. Commentators on the field of organization studies by the 1990s routinely described the cacophony of voices and divergent ideological objectives, and variously lament, tolerate or celebrate the disunity and disarray in the discipline. The theme of crisis in modern society, and in social science, supplants the scientifically based cohesion and rational change once envisaged by Durkheim and Parsons.

Organizational analysis, loosened from classical academic disciplines and historical perspectives, is now disciplined anew by the heightened instrumentally rationalizing imperatives of hyper-modern management. The intensified rationalization of productivism, separated from non-instrumental sociocultural ends, deflects or absorbs the range of criticism and opposition it confronts. Methodological and theoretical pluralities, feminist criticism, and psychological criticisms, are more often than not utilized in a refashioned and re-presented pursuit of a monological managerialism intent on maximized profit and control of production. The business form of organization is now widely privileged as the model for various other forms of purposive organization to follow. Purposive organizations at one time established to serve other primary goals, such as hospitals, schools, public libraries, sports clubs, etc. are drawn in and evaluated according to the dominant business models of operation. The conception of organizations as commodity producers prevails over a plurality of rationales and forms of organization – even as competing sociocultural rationales emphatically arise, and in increasingly diverse expressions in contemporary social and cultural conditions. A marketiza-tion of the social sphere intensifies as modern society fragments. But the marketized social arena simultaneously encounters demonstrably contra-dictory demands and forces.

For some critics this singularity of the business model under the guise of diverse eclecticism in organization studies necessitates an insistence on paradigm plurality in which socially critical organization analysis may again develop and provide a meta-criticism of the institu-tions of business organizations and management in contemporary social conditions. As mainstream managerial organization and manage-ment studies shows little serious effort to address, or even recognize, the moral institutional dilemmas of contemporary organizational life (a recent exception is Charles Handy's 1997 effort, and a turn of interest in business ethics), debate in organization studies focuses predominantly on either the in-house state of cacophony and dissent, or the business as usual mode of addressing problems prefigured by a perduring managerialist gaze.

By the turn of the 21st century a seemingly triumphant (but by no means complete) managerializing of the study of organization assertively defines the disciplinary boundary of organization studies. The diversity of approaches, methods and perspectives on organization – from the view of organizations as structured entities and empirical objects, to the view that they are 'conversations' discursively and transiently formed, or 'virtually structured' fluidities – the field presents an underlying unity through the privileging among these disparate perspectives of the managerial focus and intent. Lost in the institutionalized privileging of the managerial agentic gaze is the sociological tradition's broader theoretical *oeuvre*, its necessary reflexivity, and its critical character. Many would argue that the latter were overshadowed in the heyday of Parsonian liberal structural-functionalism and the rise of professional academic sociology. But others, such as Giddens (1982), Lemert (1995), Smart (1999) and Lash (1999), maintain that sociology's *raison d'être* is reflexivity, and the dilemma that so thoroughly vexed its founding theorists, of science and morality, has been resolutely maintained in sociological theory and practice. Even Parsons, definitively remembered for his contribution to a universal, liberal organization theory, originally sought an investigation into the nature of the relationship between the social structure and the individual relationship; between moral agents and their social structural arrangements. Yet the complex problems of moral action and irrationality within instrumental organization, which both managerial and critical organization analysts have tended to under-recognize, arise again. While a defensive moral proclamation of righteous paradigm difference is not uncommon, a more rigorous, reflexive, social ethic of analysis of organization is rare. The advent of postmodernism in organization analysis has both exacerbated this situation and opened up unexpected possibilities for critical organizational analysis, and practice.

Notes

1. A comprehensive discussion of the advent and effects of the crisis can be found in Lemert (1995), Levine (1995), and Touraine (1995), for example.

2. For a full discussion on Western Marxism see, for example, Perry Anderson (1976). See also Merleau-Ponty (1973) for a strong critique of Stalinism and party elitism against democratic and popular interests from a Western Marxist perspective.

3. Nisbet's (1967) historical analysis of sociology emphasized that the sociological tradition contained a persistent imperative that was not solely expressed in the concerns which tended to assume primacy in sociology: the problem of order, and later of control. Rather in Nisbet's characterization of the age of Enlightenment: 'The dominant objectives of the whole age…were those of release; release of the individual from ancient social ties and of the mind from fettering traditions' (Nisbet 1967: 8).

4. See Bourdieu's important empirical work *Homo Academicus* (1988) for an elaborate exposition of the French case. This study of French academic culture and higher education

reveals how the old elite structure was profoundly altered by the insurgent political-demographic shifts in elite institutions.

5. Burrell and Morgan (1979) go on to argue that Silverman's later work adopts a more firmly interpretive paradigm, and claim that his 'early and later works are paradigms apart' (p. 201). These latter works, published only a few years after his 1970 book, apparently 'are quite out of keeping with the postions articulated in the earlier work' (p. 269). Burrell and Morgan do not seem to consider that such paradigmatic flexibility displayed by one influential organizational analyst is disruptive of their own endeavour to describe paradigms of exclusion and incommunicability. Silverman's and others' apparent adherence to a particular paradigm at a particular time with apparent preferential choice among them suggests that paradigms – as frameworks more than world views – may be 'useful' for specific ends. This reduction of paradigm to knowledge tool leaves unaddressed the meta-social and institutional arrangements in which paradigms are developed and deployed.

6. At this time the work of social psychologists such as Eric Fromm (1955), (1961), Carl Rogers (1961), Goffman (1967), Maslow (1968), was influentially contributing to the humanistic dimension in sociology. This influence also had an effect in organizational analysis primarily through the human relations school of organizational behaviour.

7. See, for example, Aronowitz and DiFazio (1994), Block (1990), Casey (1995) and Thompson (1983) for full discussion of these matters.

8. In 'Americanism and Fordism' Gramsci ([1935] 1971) precedes and sets in broad context Braverman's work on the labour process in the United States.

5 Postmodernism and Organizational Analysis

The opening discussion in Chapter 2 described the rise and eventual institutionalization of a way of thinking and reasoning that subsequent generations of Western scholars accept, more or less, as modernity. The categories of an allegedly unified, rational, progressive and exclusively humanist philosophy and science were the victors in a Renaissance contest now largely forgotten, although vestiges of this contest appear again and again in diverse expressions of Romanticism, religious obscurantism and antinomianism as other, insubordinate, discourses. The science of Descartes and Newton and the economy of Smith and Marshall compose the modernity, with all its repressed paradoxes of social and technological accomplishments, destruction and annihilation, ambivalences and anxieties, that much of our contemporary social theorizations are pitted against.

As the 21st century begins, and as rationalizing modernity continues its trajectory of instrumentality, distorted growth and unmanageable risk, many intellectuals intensify their efforts to break free of myriad failures and collective horrors for which we now call modernity to account. As ambivalence, to say the least, has deepened post- and counter-modern criticism proliferates. Yet efforts to theorize, or recognize, credible successors or alternatives to the present social arrangements are scarcely emergent. There is wide agreement among critical intellectuals that something went – or was always inherently – terribly, systemically, wrong with modernity. Its project of objective, universal reason not only inspired the technological advances in material standards of living for the West but its technocratic rationality delivered the horrors of the Holocaust, and Hiroshima, and planetary degradation. Philosophers and social theorists in recent decades struggle to formulate response and propose directions. For some, modernity, or a new version of it, is defensible and rehabitable (e.g. Beck 1997, 2000, Beck et al. 1994, Habermas 1987, Lash 1999). For Habermas, modernity's emancipatory project is unfinished and the possibilities in rational communicative action in pursuit of politically negotiated civil society are far from exhausted. For others, a revised 'second' modernity is theorized (Beck 1992, 1997, Lash 1999) and a critique of modernity which restores something akin to Renaissance humanism and creative dualism to subject-actors is proposed (Touraine 1995). But for others, the task is one of extrication from, rather than a rehabilitation of, modernity's socially failed yet apparently irresistible totalizing rationality and technocratic instrumentalism.

A current turn in philosophy and cultural theory popularly known as postmodernism has formulated a critical philosophy in which the tools for extracting ourselves from modernity are not those most refined by modern philosophy and science, as these are composite of the modern episteme and ineluctably culpable in rationalizing domination. Rather, the tools are those of discursive deconstruction of Western metaphysical assumptions and the privileged categories of modern reason and science and the social practices they have legitimized. Philosophies revealing the indeterminacy of meaning and the arbitrariness of grand narratives and truth claims, including those of the sovereign subject, have attracted a significant intellectual following. Many of the philosophers and intellectuals associated with postmodernism personally witnessed the failure of leftist social movements in which they had had some degree of involvement. At a time when there appeared to be no oppositional social actors and when the old ones, especially the workers' movement, had been converted into apparatuses of power, the new critics rejected modern politics altogether and turned to either excoriative or ironically celebratory criticism. They looked to cultural arenas and identity practices for counter-politics.

The postmodern turn away from the social as political arena has been both welcome and double-edged. Confronting the dilemmas and degradation of modernity which, if the modern project is at all rehabitable, requires active recomposition by many more than elite groups. The urgency of the task to construct new social theories and practices of a more just and ecological nature is in little doubt. Postmodernism poses deep opposition and warnings of the spectre of totalitarianism in every social practice. At the same time it has encouraged a lighter, carnivalesque attitude among many adherents who find a *cause célèbre* in deconstruction as revolt, in ironic abstraction and intractable, amusing paradox. In exposing the fleetingness of meaning, the randomness of history and the arbitrariness of the order of things social, as well as proposing the immediate incorporation of all resistances, postmodernism inspires bewilderment, extreme relativism or reactionary conservatism. Against apparent social systemic intractability, and the decomposition of a sense-making life-world, postmodern thought offers as compensation a playful, though never satisfying, *jouissance*. Although some theorists try to reclaim postmodernism for leftist critical theory it is difficult to discern from a linguistic playfulness and discarded subject, imperatives to social action beyond bewilderment and quietism.

Nonetheless, the contributions of many of the theorists associated with postmodernism are significant, and postmodernism's relation to a wider condition of postmodernity is, I think, of considerable importance. Although the postmodern anti-humanist contribution to movement beyond, or alternative to, the crisis of modern thought is limited largely to opposition, serious concern with the limits and possibilities of modern reason and culture cannot be simply disparaged as symptomatic of a narcissistic individualism in a current generation of disillusioned, disaffected intellectuals. Several recent developments in social theories influenced by postmodernism now indicate a somewhat more sober and serious engagement with its questions and the moral and ethical dilemmas to which it has given rise (among them, for example, Bauman 1993, 1997, Calhoun 1994, 1995, Fraser 1997, Smart 1999). The air of dilettante playfulness and ironic exuberance, encouraged by much of the writings of the earlier French 'new philosophers' of the 1960s and 1970s most commonly associated with postmodernism, has evidently waned. But once again in organizational analysis the turns in social and cultural theories find erratic, derivative recognition.

Any analytic discussion of postmodernism is beset with the problems of variable uses of the terms postmodernism and postmodernity and their periodization in transatlantic social thought. A number of analysts have attempted to clarify these notions (among them Anderson 1998, Best and Kellner 1997, Foster 1985, Huyssen 1984, Smart 1993) and their uses continue to elicit disagreement and debate. Moreover the notion of postindustrialism is interwoven with the notion of postmodernity. My discussion begins with a more general contextualization of the rise of postmodern thought in philosophy and in the broader humanities and social sciences. It then considers the influence of postmodernism on organization studies in recent years and the uses to which it is put in organizational analysis.

Postmodernity and Postindustrialism

Notions of the postmodern have been in use for many decades, not only in art, architecture and literature where most commentators locate its origins, but also in social theory and sociology. C. Wright Mills in 1959, early recognizing the coming crisis in sociology in *The Sociological Imagination*, used the term 'postmodern' in reference to the loss of modern ideals of liberalism and socialism amidst the post-war generation in the West. For Mills, the coming of postmodernism portended a period of decline: 'We are at the ending of what is called The Modern Age. Just as

Antiquity was followed by several centuries of Oriental ascendancy, which Westerners provisionally call the Dark Ages, so now the Modern Age is being succeeded by a postmodern period' (Mills 1959: 165–167).

Although those remarks of Mills did not spark a significant response among sociologists, literary criticism, particularly in New York circles, of the same period more readily invoked the idea of the postmodern. Again, the reference to postmodernism in literary criticism was at first pejorative (see the *Partisan Review* in the early 1960s for examples of this view) of an epigonic literature that mixed genres and repudiated the intellectual standards of modernism. The view that there was a decline in intellectual and scholarly standards and a lack of historical and philosophical knowledge and depth of inquiry was not uncommon at that time (see Mills 1959 again on this point, also Horowitz 1965, and my remarks on the 'crisis' in sociology in earlier chapters). Despite the efforts of Parsons and others to formulate unified scientific general theories, there was among other intellectuals a growing disquiet that the instrumental rationality increasingly privileged in modern thought and practice was deeply flawed. For some, though, the forms arising in its opposition were further indications of modern degradation and social failure.

However, by the 1970s the notion of the postmodern had gained more currency and notwithstanding controversy and criticism another, more favourable, view of the postmodern had taken hold. Some commentators (e.g. Anderson 1998, Best and Kellner 1997, Huyssen 1984) emphasize the role of the literary criticism of the late 1960s and 1970s, importantly that associated with Ihab Hassan in New York, whose later work drew much from Michel Foucault, in promoting a more favourable popular connotation of the postmodern. These writers welcomed the break from modernist formalism and rejected the conservative politics of modern criticism emerging in the middlebrow and erotic literature of the new generation. Many regarded postmodernism in literary criticism as an attack on both conservative modernism and its restrictive structures and rules. It signalled an emancipatory movement led by writers from cultural, gender and social class backgrounds formerly excluded by established cultural elites.

In archictecture similar ideas disrupting modernist formalism are found among influential American architects of the 1970s and 1980s, including Robert Stern and Christopher Jencks. Their enthusiasm for an eclectic, anti-elitist, vernacular architecture also drew them, and like-minded cultural theorists, to a rejection of modernist politics in preference for a pluralist choice unfettered by outmoded notions of capitalism, class, left or right, or even the avant-garde. Postmodern cultural conditions, they believed, enabled the emancipation of individuals all over the world (or perhaps more accurately the West) to choose among an abundance of symbolic resources to construct their own values, lifestyles and identities. A number of feminist theorists found in these cultural theories strong accordance with their efforts to emancipate women from oppressive social relations and naturalized subjectification.

The capture of the postmodern by architecture and literary criticism was to prove immensely durable. After the early reference to the notion of the postmodern in Mills, and a later more favourable view expressed by Etzioni (1968) in his championing of the post-war student movements in pursuit of democracy in a 'post-modern' period in which the established elites were declining, there was little concerted attention to the notion of the postmodern in social theory and sociology until after the publication of Jean-François Lyotard's *La Condition Postmoderne* which appeared in French in 1979 and in English in 1984. By the 1980s the linguistic movement of poststructuralism, which abandoned structuralist notions of signification, meaning and truth, indicated a convergence of poststructuralist literary theory and notions of the postmodern among English-speaking audiences. While the French theorists associated with poststructuralism, importantly Jacques Derrida and Michel Foucault, differed often considerably with each other, and did not affix the label 'postmodernist' to themselves, they have typically been viewed in Anglo-American popular discourse as comprising a unitary movement in philosophical thought. The receptivity to poststructuralism and postmodernism in cultural theory widened into debates over notions of postmodernity promoted in Lyotard's work, and also by Fredric Jameson, Jean Baudrillard and David Harvey.

Lyotard's influential book primarily addressed the epistemologies of the natural sciences. While there had been little attention to the notion of the postmodern at the level of society there had been considerable interest in the notion of 'post-industrial' society theorized differently by Alain Touraine and Daniel Bell in the early 1970s. Lyotard, although borrowing directly from literary criticism's notion of the postmodern, linked the idea of postmodernity with postindustrialism. As he put it: 'the status of knowledge is altered as societies enter what is known as the postindustrial age and cultures enter what is known as the postmodern age' (Lyotard 1984: 3).

The notion of postindustrial society had been debated in social theory and sociology since at least the 1970s, although there is considerable earlier discussion of the effects of new technology on production and economy from the 1940s onward among analysts of work and industrial relations (see Casey 1995). Postindustrialism is a term often surrounded with similar ambiguity to that of postmodernism. In the first instance, postindustrialism refers to changes in economic and production practices in advanced Western economies in which there is a shift from production based on primary and manufacturing sectors to a wholly unprecedented production of symbolic products and services. Moreover, there are alterations in the modes of accumulation in these conditions which enable flexible accumulation and post-Fordist economies and markets of production (e.g. Harvey 1989, Lash and Urry 1987, Offe 1985, Piore and Sabel 1984, et al.). Harvey, who theorizes the 'condition of postmodernity' (1989), links postmodernity with postindustrialism. For Harvey, post-Fordism in industrial practice allows for a reversal of the acute standardization and routinization of modern industrial practices through newly flexible and mutable production forms enabled by advanced manufacturing and information technologies. Moreover, 'the mode of regulation' of industrial practice ensures that a body of interiorized rules and and social processes operate 'that allow a highly dynamic, and consequently unstable, capitalist system to acquire sufficient semblance of order to function coherently...for a certain period of time' (Harvey 1989: 122). From the post-war years to the 1970s, the particular configurations of labour control, technology, consumption habits and political and economic power 'can reasonably be called Fordist-Keynesian' (ibid.: 124). Since the 1970s a period of rapid change in labour processes and technology, and capacities of 'over-accumulation', precipitated a shift from Fordism to a 'flexible' mode of accumulation and a condition of postmodernity.

The transition from Fordism to flexible production and accumulation has involved a radical restructuring of labour markets, an intensification of labour control and rationalization, and restructuring of production organizations. The requirement for human labour in increasingly automated operations has greatly diminished, fuelling the rise of structural unemployment and dispersion of mass worker and trade union activities. At the same time there is an emergence of new sectors of production, markets, financial services, and greatly intensified rates of organizational innovation, and of consumption required by a flexible accumulation regime. Many large production organizations have become less centralized and simultaneously globally integrated into transnational corporate capital systems and networks. Uneven development between sectors and geographical regions is evident, even as global markets for some commodities, including labour, vastly expand. Central to these processes is the role of information technologies and the informated knowledge produced in their operations. These events allow for the more flexible movement and accumulation of capital, able to deal with the new, the ephemeral and the contingent in contemporary Western capitalist society. The rigidity of Fordist production and the more solid values implanted under Fordism (Harvey 1989: 167–172) have given way. Flexibility, flux, uncertainty, risk and contingency are the dominant features of post-Fordist postmodernity.

For another theorist of the postindustrial, Jean Baudrillard, these changes indicate a shift in production from the material commodity form to that of the sign form. Knowledge and symbolic consumption have become the main driving force in the economy. Baudrillard (1975, [1981] 1988, 1983) argues that the symbolic has replaced the real as the object of value and consumption, and the 'simulacra' is the normative cultural form: 'it is on the level of reproduction (fashion, media, publicity, information and communication networks)...that is to say in the sphere of simulacra and of the code, that the global process of capital is founded (Baudrillard 1983: 99). The hyperreal is the displacement of the real by repeated reproductions of the real so that there is no longer original reality. For Baudrillard, the Marxist analysis of political economy no longer holds validity as production relations and processes have dramatically changed. In the shift from the 'law of commodity' to the 'law of the code' the social, labour, form of production has given way. '[L]abour and production...only function as signs as interchangeable terms with non-labour, consumption, communication etc.' (Baudrillard 1983: 131). The modernist proclivity to differentiate is circumvented in the postindustrial, postmodern implosion of difference and opposition, flexiblity and flux. The new forms of postindustrial production enable diversity, plurality and choice, but the structures – linguistic codes – of commodity production delimit and determine the grounds of their exercise.

Baudrillard has been championed by many as the quintessential theorist, or cultural icon, of the postmodern. His work has generated much critical response (e.g. Gane 1991, 1993, Kellner 1989a, Poster 1988, Smart 1993) and occasional efforts at application. He remains one of the most controversial figures associated with postmodernism. For Calhoun, Baudrillard's declaration of the 'death of the social', the replacement of social relations by the simulacra of hyperreality and the programmed seductions of consumption, 'leaves him facing nihilism squarely and advocating an attitude simply of "ironic detachment"' (Calhoun 1995: 108). This attitude lacks capacity for positive, generative critical engagement with the contemporary world. Although a significant theorist and exemplar of the postmodern, Baudrillard has seldom been directly drawn into postmodern organizational analyses. But his work remains influential in theorizing the blurring of distinctions between production and consumption, and the flux and flexibility of economic relations. Other theorists propose notions of 'disorganized capitalism' (Lash and Urry 1987, Offe 1985) and of post-capitalism (Drucker 1993, Handy 1997) to describe conditions similarly recognized by Baudrillard, but without necessarily agreeing with Baudrillard's account of the abyss of abstract power. Beck's *Risk Society* (1992) and Castells' trilogy on *The Information Age*, for instance, elaborate the themes of postindustrial social conditions.

Lyotard's *Postmodern Condition* addressed some aspects of the debates on postindustrialism. But more particularly it endeavoured to interpret the knowledge practices of the sciences which were facing the challenges posed by philosophers such as Kuhn, Lakatos, Toulmin, Popper and Wittgenstein. Lyotard theorized the connection between advanced information technologies and postmodern eclecticism and pluralism, and argued that society can no longer be conceived as either organic systemic whole, as for Parsons, or as dualistic antagonist fields of conflict, as it was for Marx, but must be conceived as a web of linguistic communications. For Lyotard, these linguistic communications are comprised of a multiplicity of different language 'games' competing, or incommensurable, with each other. Among them, the 'narratives' of science and of reason, which had achieved legitimation by a web of mystifications and grand mythical assumptions of the Enlightenment, were each just one language game among many. This condition, and the incredulity toward the formerly totalizing grand narratives of dominant views of modernity as rationalization it generates, comprise a postmodern condition. The postmodern condition both reflects and encourages an epistemology of instabilities, paralogy, and indeterminacy. For Lyotard, the forms of knowledge thus produced assist our ability to tolerate the incommensurable and the proliferation of paradox.

Lyotard's theorization of postmodernity, though reaching a wide and popular academic audience and taken up as virtually the definitive statement on the matter, was much criticized (among the critics: Anderson 1998, Callinicos 1989, Habermas 1987, Harvey 1989, Jameson 1984a and b, Kellner 1989b). But the vantage point and authority of the philosopher, and the already growing interest in the French *nouveaux philosophes* especially after the failures and confusion of the events in Paris in 1968, assisted the dispersion of the book's thesis, typically in isolation from Lyotard's other works, across the world.[1]

The 'New Philosophers'

The *nouveaux philosophes*, although differing in many ways from each other, shared common ground in their criticisms of Marxism and socialism as it was practised in the then existing communist states of Europe. The new philosophers were championed by the mass media and some of them attained a celebrity status rare among intellectuals. This popular prominence and their rhetorical condemnations of Marxism led to the criticism that they were, as Smart (1983: 67) puts it: 'disc-jockeys' of ideas, 'intellectual playboys as beneficiaries of the rise to prominence and power of the information apparatus, the mass media'. For the new philosophers, the failure of radical politics demonstrated in the events of 1968 signified the disintegration of Marxism as social criticism and political practice. The events revealed not a dialetic movement but rather 'a fundamental shift in understanding and consciousness and [the] emergence of a "cultural fracture"' (Smart 1983: 68). The cultural turn had begun.

The new philosophers argued that modern reason is synonymous with domination and generates totalitarianism in various forms. Foucault linked the rationality of modernity, in both its liberal and Marxist forms, with the rise of Nazism and the gulag. This view was heralded by Weber's, and the Frankfurt School's, critique of instrumental rationality as the destiny of both capitalism and socialism. But for Weber the prognosis did not foreclose the possibility of reasoned, and moral, political and democratic practice, and the delimitation of technocratic rationality. Adorno and Horkheimer famously, despairingly, disagreed.

After *The Postmodern Condition*, which more properly addressed only the state of cognitive development in scientific knowledge, and not the postmodernity of art or politics, Lyotard's subsequent work turned to these broader questions.[2] Lyotard theorized the postmodern condition in culture as one in which modernist objectivist illusions were shattered. A jubilant freedom of invention ensued, free of the privileging of any meta-discourse of progress, reason, spirit, romantic unity or systemic equilibrium. Participation in constant language-games contests and constructs the cultural and political fields of human activity. Capitalism, not Marxism, provided the spaces for libidinal and hedonist desires to be pursued. By the end of the 1990s Lyotard regarded the triumph of capitalism over rival systems as an outcome of a 'natural selection' of the energies of capitalism and human desire. His thesis avoids the obvious criticism that it is another iteration of a grand modern narative, because, Lyotard argues, it is postmodern in that 'it has has no finality in any horizon of emancipation' (Lyotard cited in Anderson 1998: 34). By now, critics contend, the postmodern was no longer the exuberant emancipation of desire, difference and indeterminacy, it was perpetual disenchantment, melancholy and nihilist degradation (Anderson 1988, Calhoun 1995, Wexler 1996b).

However, Lyotard's influence through his recognition of postindustrialism played a part in the development of the notion of postmodernity as historical epoch which, for many analysts, encompasses postmodernism as cultural ethos. In many respects Lyotard's *Postmodern Condition* described a condition similarly identified as postmodernity by Harvey (1989), and others (Bauman 1992, Jameson 1984b, Lash and

Urry 1987). The interconnections and overlapping of postmodernity, as post-Fordist flexible accumulation and as hyper-capitalist marketplace of competing narratives and values, with the theorizations of postindustrialism developed through the 1970s and 1980s are evident. Post, or late, modernity's political and economic developments are reflected in philosophical movements of postmodernism in the academy and counter modern challenges in cultural practices in contemporary urban life, which include heightened individualist pursuits of identity, and neo-traditionalist ethnic, religious and communalist movements.

Theorists of postmodernity and postindustrialism, and generally of latter-20th century changes in economy and production, have considered the theorizations of postmodernism as epistemology and as politics, but a celebratory embrace of the postmodern more apparent in cultural theory has been largely absent. The Parisian philosophers, made popular by the media as well as their seminars after the 1968s events and defeat of the left, exerted a wide influence in English-speaking academies. Their influence found its way into many social sciences as well as arts disciplines by the 1980s through circuitous, initially transatlantic, routes. Now, in organization and management studies an eclectic *oeuvre* of writings self-described as postmodern approaches to organization and management, and a comparable body of criticism, ambivalent responses, as well as pragmatic application, have rapidly gained influential ground. Little, if any of Lyotard's work (other than secondary readings of *The Postmodern Condition*) has been directly influential in the field of organization studies.

The work of Lyotard's compatriots, Michel Foucault and Jacques Derrida, appears to have exerted more direct influence in postmodern organization studies. Foucault and Derrida did not write specifically on postmodernism nor on a condition of postmodernity. Indeed, Foucault claimed not to understand what was meant by the terms postmodern or poststructuralism. Nonetheless, his, like Derrida's, philosophy is most typically associated with poststructuralism in linguistic theory and postmodernism as social criticism. It is indeed an irony of contemporary social analysis that the sociality of production, organization and work has turned to the acclaimed authors in cultural studies even as many of those theorists explicitly eschew the social and economic in favour of textual analyses and recognition of identity over socio-economic struggle.

Foucault

Michel Foucault is an unwillingly invoked champion of the postmodern, or at least in the form in which it has become popularly deployed. Although he is typically associated with structuralism and poststructuralism, with methods of discourse analysis, and with analyses of power, disciplinary practices and sexuality, Foucault's philosophy and historical genealogy reveal a continuous theme concerning the problem of modernity in relation to the Enlightenment – with forms of rationality and forms of power. As a contemporary of Althusser, Foucault's work explicitly engaged with the legacy of Marx, and with the structuralist thought influential among post-war French intellectuals.[3] In many ways Foucault wished to avoid the excesses of theoretical abstraction and anti-empiricism characteristic of Althusserian structuralism and offered detailed historical analyses of the particular and the specific, but he retained a view that Marxism had inaugurated an epistemological mutation of history. The preoccupation with the sovereign subject, evident in Western thought since the ancient Greeks and Romans and strengthened under Christianity, had given way.

Foucault's complex *oeuvre* offers a vast social and political criticism through its many phases. His analyses of the power relations, structures and institutions of advanced industrial society, in particular the 'configuration of knowledge forms' that produce the power/knowledge systems and critical discourses of contemporary social life, included the 'normalizing' knowledge practices of the academy. His work developed an 'archaeological' focus and a genealogical method of the 'excavation of subjugated knowledges' by which he sought to uncover the 'myth' of continuity in history and to discredit the belief in holistic, universalistic theories of human social development (Foucault 1972, 1973, 1975).

Foucault's work, which clearly displays spectres of Nietzsche and Weber, is closely aligned with, though without reference to, that of Horkheimer and Adorno. While the latter theorists saw modernity as the 'eclipse of reason' Foucault rejected the notion that freedom is inextricably linked to reason, an idea that has been central to modern political consciousness. This Enlightenment notion identified truth with something whole, universal and transcendent. In *The Order of Things*, first published in French in 1966, Foucault argued that the universalism and holism of the Enlightenment was made possible by the 'situation of language with representation'. Language acquired the power to represent things that made up reality, and in so doing constructed that reality. For Foucault, 'the theoretical unity of [the] discourses' of the Enlightenment must in some sense be 'put in abeyance' (Foucault 1980b: 81). His project, for which he neither claimed nor sought scientific status, argued for the suspension and interrogation of unities. Foucault argued that history is random and discontinuous. There is no linear, developmental or causal relation between events in past times and those of the present.

Marxism, in Foucault's view, had failed as a system of thought and a social possibility after the revolutions in Eastern Europe which had ended not in socialist utopias, but in totalitarianism, precisely because of the totalistic, holistic vision within Marxist philosophy itself.[4] Marxism's pursuit of rationality and scientificity was a continuation of the Enlightenment heritage and complicit in the institutions and the effects of power that constructed and legitimized scientific discourses. The relationships between rationality and excesses of political power were evident everywhere in all modern political systems, both communist and capitalist. The social problems of societal modernization – complex bureaucracies, systems of discipline and vast forms of oppressive social control – were formative of and consequent on the cultural logic of modernity. As part of his exposition of the intractable flaws of modernity Foucault explored that which Enlightenment Reason had excluded: madness, chance, discontinuity, and phenomena which had not been accorded a history in established academic disciplines – sexuality, punishment, and marginalized groups such as the insane, the criminal and children. His effort was to reveal knowledge systems as regimes of power that operate techniques of exclusion and censorship. They comprise the 'dominant episteme' of particular and various epochs in Western history.

One of the great contributions of Foucault's thought was his rejection of the presupposition that social organizations contain one central power that is all-powerful. On the contrary, power is not always located in a 'definite number of elements' such as the state or state apparatuses, or other formal political or ruling class structures. In rejecting the notion of generalized repression or manipulation, Foucault sees power as operating everywhere, it is 'always already there', one is never outside it, 'there are no margins for those who break with the system to gambol in' (Foucault, 1980d: 141). The schema of power, right, truth is exercised through and functions as 'true discourse'. The theory of right and the pursuit of truth fixes the legitimacy of power, and effaces the domination intrinsic to it. People are subjected to the production of truth through power, and in turn, power cannot be exercised except through the production of knowledge presenting as 'true' discourse. Resistance, which power relations always generate and define, against the a priori existence of power (Foucault 1980d) is always already incorporated. All aspects of social life are governed by the exercise of power.

The subject is constituted by discourses of power – it is an extension of governmentality produced by the effects of normalization. The recognition of oneself as subject in order to exercise self-control and ethical ascetism is primarily a condition of subjectification. The constitution of the subject is a product of the 'whole technology of power over the body' (Foucault 1975: 30). Sexuality comprises a key source and effect of the operation of the power/knowledge schema. Sexuality is a product of power relations which 'materially penetrate the body in depth', without depending on it having to be mediated and interiorized in consciousness (Foucault 1980c: 186). The body is the irreducible materiality on which history continually operates. It is the primary site where power 'installs itself and produces its real effects' (Foucault 1980b: 97). In modern society domination and discipline are such a taken for granted part of everyday life that their unproblematic reproduction is ensured by the network of their operations as normalized governmentality. Today the instruments of domination operate in all forms of apparatuses, institutions, regulations. Without a 'uniform edifice of sovereignty' multiple forms of subjugation are effected. For Foucault, modernity's subject is a humanist delusion. Subjectification succeeds in the very moment of subject-selfhood. In his famous reflection that: 'man is an invention of recent date', and at the end of modernity, 'man [will] be erased, like a face drawn at the edge of the sea' (Foucault 1973: 387), Foucault poetically captures his rejection of humanism's subject. The subject, for Foucault, must be rejected because it mystifies and maintains the actual structural conditions of its absence.

Foucault's trenchant critical thought challenges the very idea of modernity – including the Renaissance humanism eclipsed by Enlightenment reason. It has exerted considerable influence among recent generations of social and cultural theorists. Yet, Foucault's schema of knowledge and power that pervades, and determines, human being and human doing in the world is readily criticized as presenting a totalistic, closed system. His insistence on the inevitability of power as domination and normalized governmentality precludes effective resistance beyond a micro-politics. His insistent rejection of the idea of the subject renders possibilities for social action that is not already determined, as well as for the construction of a self-project, untenable. If truth is necessarily an effect of power how is it possible to either see through the network of power/knowledge operations to some measure of the 'intolerable', which he advocated, or to conceive of some notion of 'other than what is'? Foucault himself refused to offer an alternative position for the possibility of collective human life. But he did in his later work propose an ethic of self-care and an ethical awareness of the intolerable. He claimed that his position 'leads not to apathy, but to a hyper and pessimistic activism' (Foucault 1984d: 343). By the 1980s he acknowledged an over-emphasis on power and determination throughout most of his work and latterly showed signs, after his search of Greek and Roman philosophical antiquities, of the spectre of the subject in his *Care of the Self* (1988a) and *Technologies of the Self* (1988b).

Foucault's social criticism finds company in that of Derrida, Lyotard, Deleuze and Guattari, Baudrillard, and many others. While Foucault would not necessarily agree with a Deleuzian celebration of postmodern culture, he would share the invitation to live without rules, the 'tyranny of reason', the quest for certainties, and the belief that we should rid ourselves of Facism in all its forms. He invites us to prefer pluralities over unities, difference over uniformity and to 'withdraw allegiance from the old categories of the Negative' (Foucault 1983: xiii).

Derrida

Jacques Derrida came to prominence in the late 1960s and early 1970s with the publication of his books on literary theory: *Of Grammatology*, *Writing and Difference*, and *Speech and Phenomena*. In these complex works Derrida, as philosopher and reader of texts, deconstructed the ideas and writings of philosophers to reveal the ways in which the text is constructed from non-synthesizable, always indeterminate, meanings. He demonstrated that the argument presented in the text involves a central paradox that cannot be resolved in the structure of language. It thus undoes itself. Derrida's readings interrupted the logical structure of established linguistic theory and elaborated a poststructuralist deconstruction of classical linguistic philosophy. For Derrida, Western philosophy holds a 'metaphysics of presence' that underlies all our thinking. Modern philosophy and conventional linguistic theory posit the notion that language communicates thoughts and ideas which arise from an original or essential locus of meaning. This, for Derrida, is logocentrism, a structure with a prefixed metaphysical origin which simultaneously obscures and denies the arbitrariness of its logos. We cannot hope to bring about the 'end of metaphysics' but we can critique it from within by revealing and subverting the hierarchies, rules and structures it establishes (Culler 1979: 154).

All texts give rise to at least a *double entendre* and potentially multiple readings and meanings. For Derrida this revealed the condition of *différance*, of always different meaning (Derrida 1978), which is 'a systematic play of differences'. It exposes the contradictions and undoes the argument or meaning implied by the author or speaker. *Différance* (the term itself a play on the words difference and defer) for Derrida, opposes or dissolves metaphysics and reveals the untenability of any claim to truth, transcendence or sovereignty. Derrida's philosophy, or method (although he disavowed the designation of his thought as a method which then becomes established) is that now widely known as deconstruction. In his work, *Positions* ([1972] 1982), Derrida discusses deconstruction as enabling the internal inconsistencies in a text to be revealed. In revealing the plurality of meaning, claims to a singular, unified meaning are destabilized and undone. Conventional linguistic analysis resides in metaphysical structures privileging reason, unity and determinacy of subject and object. These objectivist illusions, though normative structures of the social world, obscure the logical indeterminacy and undecidability of all social actions. Against the metaphysics of presence Derrida posits a continuously deferred or immanent meaning.

All essentialisms represent elements and forces of an imprisoning metaphysical tradition which need to be contested. The notion of the human individual as conscious, self-aware agent in the present is another objectivist illusion. Although structuralism had clearly argued for a 'de-centred subject' in its view that individuals are interpellated as subjects of ideology outside their awareness, Derrida claims poststructuralism enables a deconstruction of the immutable positionings of structuralism. An emancipation from such imprisonment is possible through a decentred subjectivity. The modern subject-self is replaced with a mutable, continuously repositioned subjectivity in a system of linguistic relations and strata. The fragmented subject is a continuous process rather than a fixed or even arrested node of relations. But its emancipation from that of the fixed positioning of structuralism is only partial. It is never free of the effects of discursive practices of subject positioning.

Derrida's linguistic philosophy and his reading of the text extended its reach to all discourses of the social, political and cultural arena. The now famous slogan '*il n'y a pas dehors-texte*' embraces a broad meaning of text. The view that there is nothing outside the text is now typically taken to mean there is nothing outside of culture. This breadth of textual rendition, however, does little to quieten critics who find the privileging of human discourse – devoid of extra-linguistic sensibilities and animal life – as the sole construction of the social world exceedingly problematic. Deconstructive analysis may be employed in all these arenas to expose inherent contradiction and intractable paradox which we cannot escape but can only repress. Yet for Derrida and his many followers this poststructuralist deconstruction offers a practice of resistance, a resistance to all narratives of authority and power and claims to truth. The unsynthesizability of plural meanings enables, it is asserted, critical opposition, a sliding out from under discourses of discipline and domination. While nothing is fixed, nothing is final, and anything is both possible and impossible at the same time.[5]

Derrida deliberately employs intentionally ambiguous and paradoxical practices in seeking both to deconstruct his own position and to ward off the possible resurgence of the tyranny of cultural institutions to fix, render certain or delimit ambiguity. Although Foucault, Derrida, Baudrillard, Lyotard and others associated with poststructuralism certainly emphasized the differences among them (including Baudrillard's call to 'forget Foucault'),[6] there are sufficient commonalities in their projects to position their works as indicative of the postmodern turn in cultural and social theory. Like the late Frankfurt School, the new philosophers apparently see little escape from society as domination. Resistance is an end in itself. Resistance, which for Foucault is always already incorporated, serves as a form of existential act as if it were a residue of subject expression possibly defying the disciplinary techniques of reason. Devoid of political possibility much of the resistance inspired by postmodern criticism eventually focused on aesthetics and identity as arenas for delimited acitivity. But postmodernism continues to be much debated by academics. Forms of literary criticism and deconstructionism are eclectically applied to diverse cultural, micro-social and organizational practices.

Critical Responses

Criticism of the philosophies of Lyotard, Baudrillard, Foucault and Derrida and the postmodernism associated with their thought, has been extensive and often excoriative. Initially much of the criticism came from Marxist and other modern critics of the left, as well as from analytic philosophies of the view that there must be perfectly good and reasonable solutions to paradox. A number of Marxist and feminist critical theorists explored the possibilities of recasting earlier radical concepts and critical theories in light of these French theorists', especially Foucault's, analyses. Others have rejected the new philosophies outright as reactionary and conservative. Still others revise and realign their views and endeavour to claim them for the tradition of left criticism. (See Best and Kellner 1997 as an example of the latter.)

For Jürgen Habermas, the new philosophers are 'neo-conservatives' – reactionaries against the process of societal modernization. In the postmodernist affirmation of non-identity, always deferred meaning, and the abandonment and implosion of normative rules, Habermas observes an 'anarchistic intention' and anti-politics (Habermas 1981: 5). Habermas claims that Foucault's work, for example, is conservative in essence; it is in the service of the hegemony it critiques by virtue of its pessimism. By making the current world system seem inevitable and claiming that all acts of opposition or struggle will be automatically assimilated into the system they oppose, Foucault offers no way out. He denies the possibility of envisioning future systems, and effective opposition and resistance are reduced to pessimistic, localized activism. A personal and private ethic is an insufficient political response to the failures of modernity, which for Habermas must be understood as aspects of the incompleteness of the modern project.

For Anthony Giddens, Foucault's notion of 'history without a subject' reduces human social affairs to events determined by forces in which those involved are wholly unaware (Giddens 1982: 222). The rejection of humans as actor-agents in a socially reflexively constructed world truncates, if not forecloses, the possibility for collective political life. Foucault's elevation of power to the primary position in action and discourse renders it a mysterious, ubiquitous phenomenon that pervades and precedes everything. The explication of meanings, norms and values as congealed or mystified power precludes the possibility of non-reified social life and the public contestation of social practices and values. But the disciplined society that produces 'docile bodies' has not entirely succeeded – there are many forces, groups and movements in society that are not so docile and continue to contest dominant powers of rationalizing modernity in institutions of production, administration and governmentality. (Foucault himself in his later work was to reconsider the question of the subject which he had posited as an effect of social practices of discipline and subjection.)

Other critics read in Foucault not so much a new, totalistic, reification of power as a theory of counter-practice, or at least of negation, to the official culture of modernity (e.g. Flax 1989, Foster 1985, Gane 1986). Foucault's concepts of 'surveillance' and discipline in the industrial and institutional spheres of the state offer ways of analysing new forms of production of information and knowledge and their relations of power in organizational practices. Moreover, Foucault's questioning of the discourses of power and their multiple sites and effects has been welcomed by many feminists and used to develop analyses of various social practices of gender and subjugation (e.g. Diamond and Quinby 1988, Flax 1989, Nicholson 1990). For Judith Butler (1990), Foucauldian notions and deconstruction methods are readily useful in the task of developing an anti-essentialist, plural, feminist identity project. They possess greater potential for liberatory practices of, for instance, sexuality and gender, and of established power relations in their myriad forms, than modernist theories and methods. But other feminists raise criticisms of the displacement of subjecthood (Hartsock 1990) just as feminism struggles to achieve for women equal subject status with men. Nancy Fraser (1989, 1997) takes umbrage at Foucault's equation of all forms of power as oppressive and for the lack in his schema of any normative dimension from which judgements can be made.

But many found a critical vantage point in Lyotard's incredulity toward grand narratives, the deprivileging of the narratives of reason and science, and the opening up of narrative sources of theorization and contestation. Derrida's poststructuralist deconstruction similarly attracted much following, and the association with postmodernism as cultural and aesthetic criticism assumed popular acceptance. Cultural theorists found Derrida's emphasis on *différence* illuminating in their explorations of identity, subjectivity, recognition and postcolonialism.

At the same time, another cultural critic, Fredric Jameson, interpreted postmodernism not only as cultural criticism but as a product of certain social and political configurations of the 1960s and 1970s. For Jameson, postmodernism comprises of objective alterations of the capitalist economic order. Postmodernism is not simply or only an aesthetic or epistemological shift, it is a sign of the dominant mode of production in the West. Jameson's 1984 essay 'Postmodernism, or the Cultural Logic of Late Capitalism' refers to the technological changes evident in production and financial exchange, and the predominance of transnational corporations and conglomerates across the world. Although similar observations by others refer to post-Fordist and postindustrial practices, for Jameson, these events indicate that modernization is virtually complete and the last vestiges of pre-capitalist social forms are obliterated. Culture has become coextensive with economy. Postmodernism signifies the closure of the distance between things – between object and subject – which modernism had differentiated. Everything is now absorbed into capitalism, and postmodernism demonstrates the implosion of modern differentiation and degradation. More importantly, the dedifferentiation of culture, which enabled some democratic dissolution of 'high' and 'low' genres in art and literature and the new freedoms of voice among previously excluded groups, such as women and ethnic minorities, signified a new relation to the market. Dedifferentiation, populism and the wide inclusion in production and consumption, ultimately indicated not a new individual, deinstitutionalized freedom, but a culture of accompaniment and complicity with the capitalist economic order. For Jameson, this condition of the postmodern is now hegemonic. In 'The Cultural Logic of Late Capitalism' Jameson strikes a note absent from the writers and critics of the postmodern at the time. Neither a celebratory nor condemnatory stance was taken. Rather, for Jameson, postmodernism is a new stage of captalism understood in classical Marxist terms – it is a historical event that cannot be rejected on ideological grounds. The task, in accordance with his classical Marxism, is a dialetical working through with the ultimate emergence of social transformation beyond it.

In many respects sharing Jameson's views, Huyssen, writing in 1984, argued that postmodernism in the United States presented a specific character and had adopted a 'peculiar' adaptation of French poststructuralism. For Huyssen postmodernism 'accrued its emphatic connotations in the United States, not in Europe' (Huyssen 1984: 363) where it indicated a break with modernism, and initially, an iconoclastic avant-gardism. By the 1970s, the circulation and commercialization of these gestures had rendered them devoid of avant-gardist status. Postmodernism served as cultural accomplice of hyper-capitalism without socially transformative intent or possibility.

Postmodernism in Sociology of Organizations

Sociology responded to postmodernism and poststructuralism in ambivalent ways. For many analysts, postmodernism irrevocably deepens the crisis in sociology, and reveals the unavoidable decline of classical sociological notions. It furthers the decomposition of modernity and indicates the need for new forms of thought and social practice beyond it. Interestingly, as I have argued in earlier chapters, some of the key challenges to classical sociology, especially with regard to its notions of society maintaining a central unifying principle of rationality, came from organizational sociology, as well as from functionalism. But organizational analysis responded with a pragmatic turn to strategic action, especially on the part of management actors. For many organizational sociologists, the cultural turn directs attention to myriad cultural phenomena and processes for which a postmodern deconstructionist methodology yields fruitful analysis. Postmodernist ideas in organizational analysis have, for the most part, been utilized by neo-rational strategic management theorists. But the initial interest in postmodernism was launched by critical organizational analysts most of whom were associated with sociological forms of analysis and critical of the managerial hegemony apparent in organizational analysis from the mid-20th century.

Although poststructuralism and postmodernism attracted much interest in cultural and social analysis, many sociologists in both the United States and Europe have been hesitant to embrace poststructuralist cultural discourse apparently on the basis that the theories are largely literary and under-attentive to matters of social structure and organization. There were some important early exceptions, including Wexler (1983), Aronowitz (1981), Morgan (1986) and Brown (1989) who endeavoured to draw the new literary criticism and poststructuralist philosophy into sociological theory. For some sociologists, the rhetoric of poststructuralism, for instance of 'subject-positions' and 'enactment', represented an unnecessary reinvention of the familiar vocabulary of status and role (on this point see Calhoun 1994). Similarly the literary turn of new French theory adopted by many cultural theorists was often ignorant of long-standing critiques of modernity and modernism. Some critics argue that much of the prominence of the cultural turn has, in part, been at the expense of sociological theory (Calhoun 1994, Giddens 1982, Mouzelis 1995). There has been a tendency to ignore sociological theory, or to reject it all as ineluctably positivist or functionalist. In the process, many of the developments in sociological thought both contesting its dominant paradigm and forging significant developments in social theory have been overlooked.

Many similar ideas to that of poststructuralism are found in the socio-logical psychological work of the interactionists, including the symbolic interactionists such as Mead, Goffman and Hughes, and object relations theorists of psychoanalysis, notably Karen Horney and Eriksen, as well as Vygotsky and Lacan.[7] For these diverse theorists, the so-called Cartesian cogito was rarely accepted as the singular modern category of self. Moreover, feminist theorists once again point out that feminist thought had prefigured many of the criticisms of Western logocentrism elaborated by Derrida, and had challenged assertions of universal objectivity deter-mined by an inherent masculinist bias. Nancy Fraser points out that the rise of interest in cultural studies in theories of identity and difference (such as race, gay and lesbian and communalist interests) akin to that of the feminist project are vitally important to the over-socialized socio-logical analysis that had previously prevailed. But, she adds, a shift too far toward cultural analysis and an ignoring of social institutional processes is equally unhelpful (Fraser 1997).

For many theorists adopting postmodern conceptions, the rejection of Enlightenment humanism and essentialism is especially important. Although this challenge was clearly prefigured in Althusser, and some-what in the symbolic interactionists and role theorists, it was welcomed by many for its apparent release from the 'naturalizing' discourses of moder-nity, in which persons were positioned and subjugated by their biology, their inheritance, their class and functional role in a rational social system. For many theorists, the disruptive possibilities of postmodern thought pose a potential emancipation from subjectification by rationalizing modernity. Feminist organizational analysts have typically welcomed the postmodern cultural turn. It provides a rich source of theoretical validation of much feminist criticism formulated in earlier decades. Now, a longer-standing feminist disruption of particular, masculinist, Euro-centred points of view projected as universal reasoned norms is supported by particular interpretations of a complex philosophy of deconstruction of Western metaphysics and an anti-humanist critical genealogy of historically specific cultural practices. The poststructuralism of Derrida and the later Foucault, in particular, enables an emancipatory opening both for the constructions of the critique of normative, essential notions, and for the reconstruction of gender and sexuality, and the valuing of difference. An emphasis on incompleteness, fragmentation and contradiction enables practices of individual identity and difference to interrupt established power relations, to subvert, invert, deconstruct and reconfigure according to conditions that are always in flux and open to possibility. By implicitly retaining or recovering an acting subject, as Foucault's later work does, these theorists seek possibilities for a counter-normalizing, political movement.

But other theorists point out that Foucault and Derrida conceive the identity-making subject as either the product of signifying inscriptions with little space for effectivity and creative action, or as abstracted from any kind of sociality at all. Postmodernist philosophy of deconstruction and undecidability makes it impossible to proceed to any form of collective political practice or any kind of social recomposition that is not already undone (Calhoun 1995, Kellner 1989a, Touraine 1995, Wexler 1996b). Postmodernism is ineluctably part of the degradation of modernity and modern thought in its dead-end, private resistance without sociality. Its uses for social theory and sociology are patently misguided. Moreover, some theorists argue that the conventional, one-sided, understanding of modernity is retained in the postmodern attack (Calhoun 1995, Touraine 1995). The equation of modernity with unmitigated instrumental rationality is mistaken and a misrepresentation of both the Enlightenment and modernity. Depicting modernity as a monolithic totality of rationalization allows a distortion of modernity's social and cultural complexity to triumph. Importantly in Touraine's view (1995) modernity's rationalization was continuously contested by the idea of the Subject – of subjectivation, and by non-(rationally) modern dimensions of religion, affect and libido which Freud had much earlier pointed out.

But the theories of Foucault and Derrida – and more extremely of Baudrillard – which portend an implosion of the very social with which sociologists have long been occupied, have attracted much interest in an unconfident, crisis-ridden sociology. The appeal of postmodernism and cultural studies to many sociologists indicates a wider disaffection with the crisis in modern thought that its defenders, with deepening awareness, endeavour to address.

In organization studies the notions of classical sociology, in which society is conceived as a central system of institutional and behavioural regulation (Touraine 1995), were already being challenged by the mid-20th century. But the two major paths of response to those challenges, one toward neo-rational strategic organizational management theory and the other toward an organization science, converged in their adherence to an ideological agenda of control, function maintenance and managerial problem-solving. It was against these prevailing trajectories that critical organizational analysts were pitted. After the 1960s many critical analysts had become increasingly disillusioned with the Marxist-inspired criticism of modern critical theory. For these critical analysts of organization, notably Burrell (1988), Cooper and Burrell (1988), Power (1990), Clegg (1990), Hassard and Pym (1994), Hassard and Parker (1993), Reed and Hughes (1992), Clegg, Hardy, and Nord (1996), as well as many others through the 1980s and 1990s, postmodernism offered a way out of the modern crisis, and academic intrication with totalizing technocratic rationality. Although differing often widely from each other, these writers saw in postmodernism a significant break with both modern conventional organization practices and theories, and the long-standing critiques of political economy, structure and capitalist relations of power of earlier generations of critics. The global expansion of unmitigated capitalist organizational forms and a new privileging of the market defied modern criticism, and indeed implicated all aspects of modernity. The postmodern disruption to modern philosophical categories and scientific methods, from the privileged, universalized notions of reason, truth, progress and humanism, to the positivist epistemologies and certainties of modern social science (although these latter critiques had been thoroughly elaborated by an earlier generation of Frankfurt School theorists), launched challenges and opportunities in organizational analysis that the modernist frameworks and agenda had foreclosed.

In many circles of organizational analysis, the notion of the postmodern is currently posed as the vanguard of organizational criticism. With its pragmatic versions now filtering usefully into mainstream organizational analysis, it is gaining growing legitimacy in the field. It has reinvigorated a cultural analytical approach to organizations most demonstrably, and attracts feminists seeking new ways of analysing organizational problematics and human relations therein. At the same time postmodernism has attracted the interest of strategic management theorists, consultants and organizational designers for its legitimation of continuous flexibility, flux and non-commitment. The strategic utilization of postmodern theorizations and approaches to practical organization and management issues in contemporary conditions has fuelled a commodification of postmodern ideas serving entrepreneurial advantage.

Amid the diversity of postmodern endeavours in the study of organization, are discernible a number of thematic clusters in which problematics of more characteristically postmodern vein are addressed. Drawing on the poststructuralist linguistic theories of Derrida, some analysts emphasize the construction and represention of knowledge and meaning, and the arbitrariness of claims to truth positions. Depicting organizations as narrative constructions reveals the way in which competing interests in power, control and legitimacy are managed by dominant narratives represented as truth. The deconstruction of these practices enables various practices of organization to be repositioned (e.g. Cooper 1989) and potentially transformed. It opens up possibilities for alternative narratives to contest and reshape the prevailing views and practices of organization. Among the first and exemplary works on these lines was Morgan's (1986) *Images of Organization*. This book creatively invokes metaphorical approaches to analysing organization. In simultaneously inviting consideration of organizations as various metaphors from organism and machine to psychic prison, for instance, Morgan exposes the wide use of selective metaphors of organization long in use in organization and management theory. Narrative approaches in organizational analysis, albeit with a tendency to ignore or discursively dissolve institutional structures, continue to find much appeal for their insights into previously neglected aspects of organizational experience. Many offer fruitful insights and potential applications in organizational practice (e.g. Alvesson and Willmott 1992, Boje et al. 1996, Clegg 1990, Gergen 1992, Grant et al. 1998, Hassard and Parker 1993). But transformative outcomes from their insights and applications, as feminists often note, are difficult to discern.

Many organizational analysts invoke Foucauldian theories to develop critical analyses of organizational practices of power and control, sexuality, identity and discursivity in contemporary organizations which have been under-addressed in modern organization analysis and criticism (e.g. Clegg 1990, du Gay 1996, Hearn et al. 1989, Jermier et al. 1994, Sewell and Wilkinson 1992). Contributions to Hassard and Parker's 1993 collection, for instance, provide excellent illustrations of these pursuits. Importantly, a raft of new feminist criticism of organization practice and theory has developed through a use of the rich sources of Foucault, and to some extent Derrida and Lyotard. Practices of sex and gender within organizations and constructions of subjectivity and self-identity are deconstructed and reinterpreted in various ways (e.g. Diamond and Quinby 1988, Kondo 1990, Martin 1992, Mills and Tancred 1992 and Alvesson and Billing 1997). Calas and Smircich (1996) also address the ways in which sex and gender practices are constructed or ignored by academic analysts of organizations. In much of this work Foucault's genealogical exploration of sexuality is seen as offering both critical deconstructions and new and potentially creative ways of practising sex and gender in organizations. One of the earliest efforts to bring Foucauldian theory to organizational analysis is Kathy Ferguson's (1984) *The Feminist Case against Bureaucracy*, which endeavoured to draw on Foucault's linguistic structuralism while rejecting his elision of resistance by people in everyday life. This selective invocation of Foucault has indeed become a hallmark of most organizational analyses in which postmodernist notions are used. Many analysts find much that is insightful and useful for criticism of various aspects of organizational practice but avoid, or reject, the implications of a closed system of critical theory in which all claims to knowledge, meaning and preferred practice are irresolvably relative and always subject to deconstruction. For many, most obviously feminist theorists, oppositional and disruptive Foucauldian theories are invoked and the project of agentic subjectivity is left either confused or downplayed.

Postmodern organization analysis includes interrogation of many conventional modern notions of power and authority, of bureaucratic rationality, order, efficiency, regulation and legitimation. But most importantly, postmodernism has vastly expanded the role of cultural analysis of organizations. In addition to earlier forms of cultural analysis, such as Deal and Kennedy in the 1970s and 1980s which drew on phenomenological approaches to organizations, myriad studies of diverse cultural practices in organizations are now popular. From emotion and sexuality to storytelling, fantasies, myths, folklore, symbols and linguistics, to ethnicity and tribe, interest in cultural and identity practices has in many instances supplanted interests in structural problematics and political resistance more common in previous decades.

The practical effects of many of the postmodern theorizations circulating within academic organizational commentary are mixed. There has been encouragement in organizational management practice to attend to matters of organizational culture, including the recognition of ethnic and sexual diversity, communicational and value systems and micro-processes within the organization. But the dominant interests of organizational elites practising a neo-rationalist management of production and labour relations have scarcely been affected by these new discourses. Moreover, attention to processes and values associated with organizational change which has utilized theoretical and practical insight from postmodern perspectives and criticisms of organization, has typically turned those insights to existing, unchallenged, managerial imperatives and power relations (e.g. Barry and Elmes 1997, Hatch 1997, Prasad and Prasad 1993). They serve as eminently useful devices for strategic managerial interests and subjectification of organizational employees and clients.

Whether wittingly or not, much of the work invoking postmodernism, even that which adopts a total acceptance of the 'death of the subject' through, as Gephart (1996: 41) expresses it, rejecting 'the myth of human agency', allows management actors, who evidently practise a belief in the endurance of the actor – at least corporate ones – to apply the insights of postmodern analysis to practical problems of organization management. Significantly, in an attempt to move beyond what many see as modernist humanism in autonomous individualism, a 'relational alternative' is posed (e.g. Gergen 1992). For these thinkers, a relational alternative includes teamwork and interpersonal and group identifications in which notions and behaviour associated with self-interested individualism are diminished or surpassed. Relationality, according to Gephart (1996: 43) 'provides a "constellation" wherein structure is not substantively fixed but rather is a shifting cluster of variable aspects or elements'.

While many of those engaging in postmodern interests variously adopt or employ postmodern philosophical commitments, especially those concerning humanism and anti-humanism, there is relatively little application of postmodern approaches to organizational problematics more readily associated with the modernist agenda: structure, hierarchy, class, capital, technology and even globalization. Postmodernism's implosion or denial of the social renders its usefulness for reconsidering structural elements in social and organizational institutions very limited. Moreover, social analysis is rendered redundant in a non-social society, and the nomadic space perceived, by Deleuze and Guattari (1986), in its place. An extreme individualism occupies the non-social space. In this current of individualism the actor, who may be for Deleuze and Guattari a wanderer refusing direction and hierarchy, is more likely reduced to consumer acting in self-interest toward goals of identity construction or consumption. A reduced, or imploded, sociality diminishes the need for attention to 'modernist' problematics of social structure and institution. In either despair, collusion or ambivalence (see Knights 2000 for his recommendation of ambivalence as an 'appropriate position to adopt'), postmodernism in organizational analysis typically displaces or ignores the enduring practices of political economy, of class, exclusion and ecology in favour of identity and recognition.

While an initially critical postmodernism made a welcome disruptive contribution to many modernist impasses and illusions in organizational analysis, postmodernist and poststructuralist approaches were more readily appropriated by an already strategic, neo-rationalist managerial organization theory. Now it is often invoked to avoid or excuse the absence of a substantial rationale for organizational inquiry. Postmodern studies of organization theories and practices has led to a plethora of debates and approaches to organizational analysis that now appears more like the postmodern form, that Huyssen derided: that 'easy post-modernism…of the "anything goes" variety' (Huyssen 1984) in which the postmodern critical intervention has been appropriated for use by strategically enduring elites in organizations. Or it aimlessly meanders on a plane of deconstruction foreclosing recomposition of sociocultural alternatives (e.g. Burrell 1997). A ceaseless deconstruction of the grounds for differentiation of value at the crux of postmodernism has generated the present deregulated, unranked, hypermarket of choice in organizational analysis in which those actors who re-establish differentiations and assert productivist values set the course of action in what is left of society. Now, when it is popular, legitimate and career-enhancing to invoke the postmodern in organization studies, criticism of a liberal reformist inclination to capitalist modes of production and administration poses as, or captures, the once radical and delegitimating postmodern approach to organization theory and practice. The shift away from more conventional modern approaches to understanding and criticizing organizations presents at once the possibility for emancipatory critique and revitalization, and the risk of degenerative, idiosyncratic and incorporated fantasy offering neither critical practice nor ethical principle. A criticism defeated by (post)modernity's continued instrumentalist trajectory, or incorporated as handmaiden to hyper-capitalism's now global expanse, presents as the fate of postmodernism in organizational analysis. As the 21st century begins, critical organizational analysis is in dire need of revitalization and ethical discrimination in theory and practice.

From Impasse to Action

As postmodernism as theoretical innovation wanes, its influence leaves evident traces of new explorations in a disrupted field tentatively seeking regeneration. Conferences on organization studies show a wide range of topics and new problematics being raised by a new generation of organizational researchers which would scarcely have appeared in the field only a decade ago. Diverse organizations operating in rapidly globalizing market environments retain and renew a considerable heritage of modern organizational practice. At the same time they manifest practices in everyday organizational life that are neither typically modern nor disjunctively, chaotically, postmodern. Many of these latter practices are being ignored by established organizational analysts whose imaginative gaze has been dulled by protracted internal academic debates on organization theorizing, or for some, by the immediate gratifications of applied managerial research. An imaginative, sociological gaze upon contemporary organization practices, emergent especially in corporate organizations, is rarely undertaken in current organization analysis. An ironic consequence of postmodern iconoclasm may well be an ill-equipped, ahistorical generation of organization analysts unable to analyse and interpret unexpected (to a modern and postmodern social scientist's eye) manifestations in contemporary organizations.

For postmodern critics, modern criticism failed to significantly influence or counter the trend of hegemonic capitalism and its instrumental rationalities which now permeate all aspects of hyper-organized life. But postmodernism completes that failure to offer a counter-movement to modern degradation and dissolution. Indeed, it inadvertently exacerbates that degradation in its final assault on the idea of the acting subject. Against both of these conditions, new forms of organizational criticism are emerging in the everyday world of production organizations. They pose wholly new challenges to conventional organizational analysis of both modern and postmodern forms and new possibilities for social theory and practice.

Despite the postmodern turn in which systemic domination of displaced and weak subjects presents as an extreme form of functionalism, the organizational sociology that gave way to neo-rational strategic management theory has long been aware of the weak hold of organizational systems and structures. Empirical studies, rather than abstract philosophical propositions, founded these theorizations. It is therefore somewhat extraordinary that a view of organizations as totalizing systems, or even poststructurally, as discursively absent systems, should have become so popular. We can observe in the West a range of contemporary cultural, and social, practices which appear to be contestational to both modern instrumental rationality and to postmodern implosion and self-loss. A careful attention to these goings-on, especially as they arise in the midst of work organizations, reveals some important signs of individual and collective seeking for viable cultural and social alternatives. It appears that the subject-actor is not dead and that she or he acts again in new forms of contest and struggle for the cultural modes of social life, including that in organizations. As well as indicating the historicity of organizational analysis, these practices indicate a drawing on an expanded repository of cultural resources of meaning-making and values which modernity suppressed. These resources, and the new forms of contest associated with them, may pose significant challenges within workplaces and to organizations and social institutions more broadly. The following chapter describes and critically discusses emergent patterns of new forms of criticism in practice in many contemporary corporate organizations.

Notes

1. Critic Anderson (1998) contends that the book's influence was in inverse relation to its intellectual interest: it scarcely excited philosophers outside that Parisian circle at the time. By the 1970s Lyotard was recognizing capitalism, in contrast to Marxism, as 'godless' with 'no respect for any one story' for 'its narrative is about everything and nothing' (Lyotard cited in Anderson 1998: 29). This critical view is raised similarly by others who see in Lyotard's criticism a ready appropriation, or legitimation, of liberal pluralism (e.g. Touraine 1995).

2. For a full discussion on these matters see, for example, Anderson (1998), Best and Kellner (1997), Smart (1983, 1999). In particular, Smart (1999) offers a considered reflection on the thought and influence of 'postmodern in(ter)ventions' and our current contemporary 'facing' of modernity.

3. French structuralist social thought was influenced by the linguistic structuralism of Saussure and Lévi-Strauss among others. In brief, Saussure emphasized the distinction between the signifier and the signified, with the structural relationship between them constituting a linguistic sign. Language is made up of these components. Lévi-Strauss' structuralism extended to other cultural phenomena. Structuralism is also used in functionalist schools of thought with varying similarities to the Marxist formulation.

4. Foucault, who was at one time a member of the French Communist Party, later claims to have 'never been a Marxist' (Foucault, 1988b: 22). He preferred to refuse positioning in any of the major intellectual movements of his day, including psychoanalysis, and expressed an unfamiliarity with many German theorists, including Weber and the Frankfurt School critical theorists.

5. In a recent (August 1999) address to a large public audience in Auckland, New Zealand, Professor Derrida presented a formal lecture entitled 'Forgiving the Unforgivable'. The title and the opening discussion offered some promise of a philosophy beyond a juridical economy of guilt and expiation, and a possible ethic guiding future social practices. And indeed in subsequent conversations I heard that many of those present thought Derrida had offered such: distinct traces of a Judaeo-Christian ethic repackaged for a secular audience. Yet, on the contrary, Derrida had posed the problem and the paradox of the ethic of forgiving the unforgivable (for something can only be forgiven when it is of such gravity that it is unforgivable), but he concluded that without sovereign subject of the traditional or modern sort, not God, nor Reason, nor Man, 'it is impossible!' If the point implied is to embrace the apparent intractability of paradox, a proximity to a familiar – Durkheimian – religious tradition in that appeal is remarkable.

6. Baudrillard's [1977] 1987 book *Oublier Foucault* (New York: Semiotext) argued that Foucault's discourse 'allows no place for the real' as his theory is a mere reflection of the power it seeks to describe and therefore transforms power into a reified objected that cannot be resisted.

7. Jacques Lacan is, of course, a major figure associated with structuralism and poststructuralism. But his influence in sociology and in organizational analysis has been notably less significant than the theorists I have discussed, and his work remains a highly contentious matter for feminists, some of whom see his neo-structuralism as hostile to the emancipation of women's subjectivity (see Nancy Fraser 1997 for further discussion).

6   After Postmodernism

As we move toward a hyper-industrialized society in which large organizations, beyond the realm of production, increasingly dominate most aspects of social life, new conflicts and new sources of action arise. Postmodernism, after critical theory, theorized an implosion of the social, reducing actors to rationally choosing consumers in a marketplace of commodities and identities. A consumption-driven individualism coexists uneasily with subjectification by myriad discourses of power. As production organizations accelerate growth and planetary exploitation and impose new stresses on human workers through increased insecurity, demands for flexibility and congenial conformity to corporate managerial agendas, critical organizational analysis struggles to find alternative horizons beyond discursive opposition. New studies are published every year showing higher rates of employee disaffection, stress, anxiety, depression and absenteeism (ILO Report 2000). Individuals try to devise new ways of coping with or contesting these conditions. Meanwhile, commodity consumption in the West continues to grow. Neo-rational strategic management succeeds in purely instrumental terms for many organizations, but its non-economic costs to humans increase. While a Marxist-influenced political criticism continues in both the academy and in workplace union movements, and neo-modernist theoretical efforts seriously attempt to recover social theory and society from postmodernist decay, organization practices remain both deeply enmeshed in rationalizing modernity, *and* subject to conflicting social forces.

Even as some organizational analysts turn to cultural theory and postmodern ideas, the bulk of organizational theory remains committed to functionalism and continues to grant central importance to control and integration under the guise of liberal affirmation. For some, a modernist realism insists on critical possibilities of a once familiar form. But critical analysis of organizations, still affected by the crisis in modern social thought, and introspectively absorbed, is at risk of not seeing signs of new forms of organizational criticism and renewed imaginary emerging from (conventionally) unexpected sources. Although mainstream forms of sociological inquiry have been aligned with dominant interests in society, and critical theory has come to be associated only with negation, there was always a current of thought claiming sociology and critical theory as representations of social life. Beyond exposition of social process and ideological domination, an aspiration of emancipation in its many meanings, bequeathed from classical social theorists in the wake of the French Revolution, has long been upheld. It is this ethos of sociology that a new sociology rediscovers, and refocuses. It is focused this time not on rationalization, system and order, but on movement, action and multiplicity.

A renewed sociological and critical theoretical gaze seeks signs or possibilities of creative revivification emergent in existing social practices. As Touraine (1988, 1995) theorizes, in privileging a notion of social movement over complex rationalizing system, society is conceived as a contested terrain of social forces. These forces are comprised of subject-actors and institutional forces contesting for control over historicity – 'the set of cultural models a society uses to produce its norms' (Touraine 1995: 38). For Touraine, the idea of society as social movement recognizes that action is not limited to reaction to systemic forces but directed toward the production of social outcomes and new cultural models staking out the rules of social practice. These social relations are always relations of power. But they are practised by actors and institutions which are both determinate and indeterminate – there is no a priori designation of the social agent. In this schema, in which society is conceived as an ensemble of social movements, concrete social movements are not merely individuals or groups of actors with specific grievances and demands within institutions. Social movements are characterized by the degree to which they act upon the prevailing cultural model. This new sociological conception rejects notions of blind forces, of totalizing bureaucratic domination, actorless systems, *and* systemless actors – the latter a preferred notion of an extreme neo-liberal individualism. But it does not deny the critical significance of struggles over accumulation, and of what must still be called class relations, and institutionalized political power.

A new sociology of social movement enables a new critical analysis of organizational practices. This approach discovers not only new forms of critical action and social forces, but new, or at least recomposed, value sources of that action. In the first instance, various activities of resistance to domination and unfreedom, particularly domination dispersed through the governmentality of social institutions and organizations, may reveal a continued, though subjugated, insistence on some forms of delimitation to technocratic excess and anti-life absurdity. Many of us as critical theorists, rejecting postmodernism's defeated conclusions, welcome and are inclined to exaggerate signs of resistance in corporate organizations of the typically modernist political form. At the same time, some draw selectively – even sympathetically – from forms of organization analysis which offer relief from nagging worry about intensified instrumental rationalities and their accelerating destructiveness by focusing on scholastic abstractions, narratology and subjectivity. Postmodernism at least insists on the power of absence: uncertain meanings and contingencies may allow conversations to alter the order of things, although always in undecidable directions.

Notwithstanding the contingencies of organizational practice and the weak hold of centralizing rational systems, modern technical rationalities in economic production have not only succeeded in production but have expanded into most spheres of life. Not surprisingly, postmodern efforts to criticize and alter contemporary organizational practices are both fraught and vociferous, generating indignant opposing camps of so-called neo-modernist critics, liberal and postmodern affirmationists, and post-modern critics. Many defend their theories and agendas by assertions of incommensurability and thinly veiled intimations of superior, or simply winning, difference. A critical sociology of social movement enables us to move beyond these impoverished positions. It inspires a new imagination, and enables a new scrutiny and interpretive analysis of contemporary practices in social and organizational life which our conventional modern and postmodern lenses are unprepared to see. Postmodernism has at least made the break with old modes of thought and the many tendencies to interpret postindustrial phenomena in modern industrial language.

My observations of people currently living and working in organizations invite deeper reflections on, and interrogation of, our social practices of work and organization, and their role in making history. We may find in these practices signs that a new critical organizational analysis and practice has already begun.

A close observation of life in contemporary organizations and work-places detects a sort of 'revolt from within' the technocratic, strategically bureaucratic organization, and the exclusive scientific humanism we typically consider totalizing and hegemonic. Against expert discourse, ordinary people, it seems, are wanting something more and other than is offered by rationalizing modernity, and its costs. Despite their formation over generations in the West as industrialized and bureaucratized producers and as commodity consumers, and as increasingly detraditionalized individuals, many people now are experimenting with a variety of alternative meaning-making activities and value orientations. In the broader culture of Western societies there are many signs of these activities which include experimenting with diverse religious, spiritual and body practices. These activities are often described as 'New Age' explorations. They include interests in Eastern and pagan religions, mysticism, divination, magic and soul-seeking, as well as various alternatives to

Western science and medicine such as acupuncture, mind/body therapies, homeopathy, naturopathy and spirituality. These tendencies have recently gained academic attention in the work of, for example, Heelas (1996), Lewis and Melton (1992), Roof (1993), Wexler (1996b) and Wuthnow (1998). A considerable popular literature is now widely available. Of course, there have always been insubordinate and antinomian alternative world-views, spiritualities and lifestyles on the social fringes of norma- tive society, from the 17th century Ranters to mid-20th century hippies. Every century has many examples of religious, mystical and conscious- ness-altering explorations. Moreover, the content of most of what we currently call New Age explorations is very old, and has certainly been much in evidence throughout the 20th century and not just its final years. Hence, it is not new at all. But the expanding popularity of these acti- vities among many people who invoke the New Age term validates the retention of the term for analytical use for the time being. I do wish to argue, however, that what is new about these New Age explorations, alternative meaning-making and counter-scientifically rational practices, is that they are being practised within production organizations and working life. These highly instrumentally rationalized arenas once emi- nently typified rationalizing modernity, and coercively discouraged counter-rational contestation. At the same time, the instrumental ration- ality singularly privileged in production organizations withdrew from a substantive rationality concerned with ends and values.

Within contemporary corporate organizations in Western societies many individuals and some groups of employees are overtly expressing their interests in alternative, and competing, rationalities. They speak of pursuing 'higher' values, of seeking spiritual sensibilities, and valuing higher authorities, contrary to those conventionally legitimately practised. In many instances, these new orientations and demands meet a new toler- ance, even encouragement by management. The expression and expan- sion of these counter-modern, counter-scientifically rational practices in the workplace are empowered, in large part, by a growing influence of broader contestations to modernity, including postmodern cultural forms of identity interests, consumer choice and consumer saturation. A diverse disaffection with modern instrumental rationality emerges among the for- merly compliant. Other contributing factors to this turn of interest among rational organizational producers are those resulting from considerable organizational changes over the last decade or two in which, even in highly successful organizations, long-serving, productive employees in good standing with their companies have been laid off. These people, often highly skilled, well-paid, and accustomed to a relative degree of self-effectiveness and directedness in their professional-technical lives, find themselves precipitated into major life reassessments and 'soul-searching' as a result. Personally experiencing the impersonal application of instrumental rationality – especially in the form of sophisticated technological developments which enable growth with fewer workers – displaced workers and their insecure neighbours now raise questions once silenced with the systematic defeat of the labour movement.

A growing literature addresses the personal effects of organizational change. But, with some exceptions, it does so typically from the managerial vantage point which seeks to manage the effects of these organizational changes and redirect the reassessments of organizational work now occurring. Moreover, there is a burgeoning management literature addressing spirituality at work. My research in organizations among highly skilled and professional corporate employees presents findings which, only a decade ago, would have been unexpected and sceptically rejected by a conventional modern social science. The presumption, following Weber's prediction, that modern organizational employees are characteristically scientifically and economically rational and secular and well adapted to the bureaucratic rational calculability and efficiency of production organization, must now scarcely be taken for granted.

In contrast to the forms of contestation evident in modern organizations, such as those arising from the institutions of profession and occupation – in which professional and class assertions pose challenges to incorporation – I observe different forms of demands in which those of a rational economic and political type are put into abeyance. The new demands are for alternative sources and expressions of value, meaning and self-identity. They appeal to a re-enchantment, and even transcendence, of disenchanted, overly-rationalized, organizational working life. Drawing from a range of repositories of knowledge and historical practice especially religion and spirituality, a diverse 'New Age'[1] movement attracts once rationally disciplined organizational workers. It offers a repertoire of re-enchantment activities and beliefs and a polytheism of sacralizing and alternative meaning practices.

These explorations of alternative rationalities, new sources of meaning-making and 'resacralization', especially in their New Age experimental manifestations, are typically ignored or dismissed by a conventional sociological approach. For some, these activities are frivolous and fleeting or politically reactionary moments of little social or analytical importance (e.g. Wallerstein 1998). Organizational analysis similarly displays a remarkable silence about such activities even as management and business practice manifestly encounters, and readily responds to, this turn. A growing number of management theorists and commentators (e.g. Barrett 1998, Briskin 1996, Lewin and Regine 2000, Mitroff and Denton 1999, Canfield et al. 1999), and popular business publications, do not hesitate to recognize the importance of soul-seeking interests. Dismissing these activities as whimsical New Age obscurantism, or as peculiar to a never secularized United States of America, is mistaken.

This chapter describes and critically explores some of these contemporary practices of people at work in organizations. These particular practices, which are increasingly commonly observable among a diverse range of people but notably among middle-class professionals or white-collar workers in Western detraditionalized societies, may have wholly unexpected implications for work and organizational practice, and may pose deep challenges for conventional organizational analysis. The current intensification of the commodification of virtually all dimensions of social and personal life generates opposition and counter practice. Notwithstanding the prevalence of modern secular humanism, religious practices appear again, as Durkheim predicted, as mutations or reassembled bricolage in contemporary life. Their new iteration may indicate not only the limits of rational system but a return of the actor-subject appealing against the rational organizational order of things.

A New Age Comes to Work

In a social context of vast changes in technology, production, market and financial exchange, corporate organizations strategically endeavour to redesign organizational structures and cultures which enable rapid response to altering environmental conditions, especially those of flux and uncertainty. Organizations confront complex paradoxes resulting from the globalizing intensification of economic and technological rationalities, and their counter-practices of localization and communalism, as well as competing interests in self-identity and individualism. Obstacles to the ubiquitous requirement to expand production and consumption now appear not only from expected external environmental sources and traditionally unionized workplaces, but from within the non-unionized corporate organization's highly paid, highly trained and organizationally identified professional middle-class employees. Scarcely articulated, non-economic disaffection generates criticism and demands in counterpoint to the acute productivism of hyper-capitalism.

Corporate organizations since the 1980s have institutionalized the successful implementation of isomorphic programmes of organizational cost-cutting, restructuring and cultural reformation. A popular practice has been the design and installation of organizational cultures which promise employees compensatory, participatory, familial and team workplaces. Debate over the role and efficacy of team cultures in production organizations continues. Among a number of benefits to many parties there are controversial, psychological effects and outcomes of engineered team cultures (e.g. Casey 1995, Kunda 1992, Sinclair 1992). Incorporating affective and relational needs into organizational cultures of production endeavours to stimulate communalist identity and belonging and sustain psychological rudiments of productive and ever more innovative activity. These programmes have typically met with mixed reception: they are popular among business leaders and managers, criticized by some labour leaders and organizational analysts, and ambivalently accepted by many employees.

One of the outcomes of these interventions has been an increased yet flexible instrumentality in the treatment of employees. For instance, greater use of short-term contract employment, increased management expectations of geographic mobility and job flexibility among employees, and expectations of high employee commitment, long hours of work, few pay increases and an acceptance of insecurity and uncertainty, are now commonplace. While many employees have endeavoured to accept these imposed changes there is also opposition to intensified objectification and utility. In particular, assertions of contestational, individualized self-interest and privatized resistance are evident. These behaviours are evident, for instance, in demands among highly paid executives for improvements to their conditions and benefits and in diminished organizational loyalties, and in efforts to protect a growing assertion of self-interests against organizational imposition or appropriation. These behaviours do not necessarily indicate resistance to particular organizational or production activities and rationalities so much as a heightened individualism in a strategic, self-interested response. But this individualism itself is a source of opposition to totalizing organizational tendencies in which individual interests as well as collective cultural interests are incorporated into the flexible instrumentality of the new-style organizational cultures. These strategies are especially evident in de-unionized corporate organizations.

Many organizational employees, notably but not only professional and highly skilled and valued ones, are seeking ways to resist, oppose or escape the self-identity erosion and meaning-making crisis consequent of intensified corporatization in unconventional ways. Corporate organizations are responding with sophisticated strategic managerial adeptness to the needs and impulses of persistently disenchanted, dispirited and distracted employees. After generations of modernity's rationalization and secularization there are signs of expressive interests officially subjugated by, if not eliminated from, rational organizational life. Employees at all levels in organizations are seeking new forms of spiritual interests and sources of inner meaning in an effort to transcend what some report as the 'emptiness' of the workplace. In response, corporate organizations are permitting initiatives or providing programmes on spirituality at work. From the World Bank, Ford, Nike, Apple, Aetna and Shell Oil to break-fast cereal and telecommunications companies, a growing number of corporate organizations are now offering programmes of corporate renewal that both recall the rites of traditional religion, and reflect and accommodate contemporary laicized religious, and affective, sentiment. In addition to bringing one's mind and body to work in service of the organization one is now permitted, if not required, in a growing number of organizations to bring heart and soul as well.

Research Data

My long-standing interest in the relations of social institutions, self-creation and social action oriented and stimulated my research into current practices of organizational and working life in Western societies. The research, from which selected data is reported below, focused on questions concerning the effects of immense changes in organizational and work practices, especially technological, structural and cultural changes. In particular, I inquired into the effects of these changes on workers' experiences of work and its place in their lives: their responses, meaning making, and courses of action. My research drew on a number of sources: firsthand observation of organization and management practices; organization practitioner, popular and emerging academic literature; and interviews and observations among employees and former employees in the United Kingdom, the United States, Sweden, Germany, Italy, Australia and New Zealand. Most of the observation and interviews took place among employees in medium to large-size organizations including finance institutions such as banks and insurance companies, pharmaceutical, telecommunications, public relations and consulting companies and research laboratories. Most of my organizational observations were carried out while visiting organizations for the purpose of interviewing persons who had already agreed to my visit and interview.

Firsthand data was gathered from many informal and formal interviews during 1995–2000. In addition to employed persons, data was gathered from those describing themselves as unemployed, not-working, and self-employed. Most of my respondents were found through word of mouth connections, or collegial referrals (especially from banks with near-global operations and sites, and international university associates), and others by spontaneous conversations at likely gatherings. My semi-structured questions sought data on respondents' experiences, reflections, expectations, wishes, values, meaning constructions and general concerns on matters to do with organizations and work. Excerpts from the interviews cited below use pseudonyms and their locations are disguised.

The data that came to light from observation drew my attention to what I term 're-enchantment'. The emergence and variety of expression of this phenomenon quickly sharpened my research gaze and agenda. My subsequent research interviews followed more closely questions around respondents' interests in alternative meaning-making explorations. My research continued in other gatherings of people talking about work, such as conferences and seminars on spirituality at work, organizational and professional ethics, and ecology and organizations. Literary sources addressing these matters are readily available in university and public libraries, bookstores, and various corporate waiting rooms. Information on 'spirituality at work', 'business and consciousness' and related consultancies, conferences and gatherings is available on the Internet, in practitioner-focused management and labour journals and magazines, popular culture publications, workplace, student and New-Age-style gatherings.

The discussion in this chapter on selections of my research findings and representative literature focuses on particular aspects of these complex trends. It describes some of these new practices of organizational work and forms of critical organizational analysis. The following chapter provides an interpretive sociological analysis, but I disclaim any attempt to offer a substantive cross-cultural discussion or to address many national differences in organizational practices, and personal value and self-identity formation. Although my data is drawn from across Western societies, all my respondents spoke English and my literature sources were predominantly in English. Moreover, my interest was in patterns of similarities of interests among 'modern' people, and emergent trends and social movement, in contemporary practices of corporate organization around the globe. As patterns of postmodernity, postindustrialism and globalization have affected the West (and the rest), so too may patterns emerge of social movements toward self and social revitalization.

Spirituality at Work

The emergence of current forms of spirituality at work finds expression among individual employees as well as in deliberate corporate sponsorship and encouragement of spiritual sensitivities. As the New Age, 'unchurched' (Wuthnow 1998) spiritual explorations appeal first to the individual, my narrative follows the same path. Organizational initiatives and responses are discussed subsequently. This section describes expressions of spirituality and quasi-religious divination practices which I have observed and listened to among organizational employees. As well as these new forms of spiritual exploration gaining attention and approval by management some employees, of course, retain an older form of religious faith and practice such as Judaism or Christianity. But in quintessentially modern organizations such practices are relegated to private life and are officially omitted or denied effectivity in the prevailing rational practices of bureaucratic and professional work. Those retaining adherence to established faith traditions, as observers have noted, were required 'to check their souls at the door when they came to work'. For the unchurched spiritual explorers, however, a confidence and zealousness in their seeking inspires new demands on the corporate organizational workplace, including the freedom to explore various New Age activities. Many of these explorations present an idiosyncratic cobbling together of fragments of religious and spiritual traditions, as well as magic and mystery traditions. My observations noted an apparently more overt display of unconventional religious interest than displays of affiliation to established religions. Except among new non-Western immigrants to the West who retain and occasionally assert displays of religious identity (Sikh, Muslim, Hindu), I observed that adherents to traditional Western Judaism and Christianity (except fundamentalists) were usually more circumspect in their display. There was little such hesitation on the part of the New Age spirituality seekers.

Through the course of my roving observations of organizational workplaces in a number of countries, I have observed various new forms of self-expressiveness, meaning-making and spirituality to that which I noticed in earlier years, and that which has typically been reported in ethnographies of organizational life. Moreover, these new tendencies compete with the continued display of expected modernist resistance in pay disputes, political contestations, humour and quiet dissent (including, for instance, hours spent perusing the Internet for fun or escape). Prominent among the new forms of expression are displays of decorative or devotional symbols, in addition to the usual signs of personalization of workspace such as photographs and plants, depicting spiritual sentiments. I have observed, for example, crystals, Native American 'dreamcatchers' and statuettes of the Buddha displayed, often together, in corporate cubicles. I have also seen pictures of Sai Baba, Yoga gurus and Hindu goddesses displayed, as well as artifacts of pagan traditions, alchemy and Wicca (the term practitioners prefer to witchcraft). My comments to the cubicle occupants about these items have invariably elicited a warm response and typically a tendency to authoritatively explain their significance and veracity. Initial conversations lead to discussions about, as one respondent put it: 'the need to feed the soul at work, to allow the soul to find expression here, and to help me stay in touch with what really matters…'.

The need 'to feed the soul at work' was expressed in many stories of bringing spiritual interests 'out in the open' at work. Megan is a manager in a marketing division of a pharmaceutical company in which she had worked for more than 13 years. She reported that her interests in spirituality became more important to her after she 'went through a really awful time in this company a few years ago'. 'We had been going through all these restructurings and changes in the way the company was being managed, and where we wanted to be….A lot of people I knew lost their jobs. I had to relocate to this city to keep my job in the company, and there were a lot of problems with that….There were a lot of things that I didn't like that were happening, and I guess you could say, it was a crisis. It sure was for me!… I got really stressed out and I had to make some changes, and, well, I started to look at things and decide what was really important. I started doing yoga…I realized I wanted to bring more of my spirit to work…and to make my work and this company more sensitive to more spiritual things. It's like we've got to become a company that values our souls, and not just what we do for the market, and like the bottom line, and get aggravated by that.'

Echoing Megan's expressed interests is John, a management consultant who has worked for several years consulting to organizations in the process of introducing new financial and information systems. John explained that his experiences in his work and the problems he repeatedly encountered in different organizations drew him to 'thinking about leadership'. 'I started to move toward management coaching as part of my consulting work. And from there I started to see that there were so many things, invisible things, just missing from how we're used to managing people and processes in organizations. The same old problems would come up, and we'd do the same thing, even though the game, like the technologies and markets, was changing so fast, and that's what we'd be supposed to be managing….So I found myself getting interested in something I'd read about soul, about listening to the soul, my soul, other people's souls, at work. People somehow perform better when their soul is in what they do…'.

In response to my question, what does it mean to bring soul to work? John explained: 'It means that you encourage people to bring their real values out in the open, you build more open communication and spiritual awareness. You listen to each other, really listen, and you build compassionate leadership by caring and listening, and a strong sense of purpose and community….It means that you start getting in touch with your own soul, your real purpose in life.'

Another respondent, Kerry, suggested: 'it means you value your whole person, and you really connect with one another. And it means more personal responsibility and not blaming everyone else or the organization for all the stuff that happens...I've found that, you know...caring about my soul, it's like you start thinking about what it's all about, and what you want, and kind of what's really right...'.

For Matt, a corporate consultant, who has 'thought long and hard about this', bringing the soul to work enables 'amazing changes in the organization and in individuals'. He explains: 'Getting in touch with the source of creativity unleashes human potential, fosters innovation, expresses talent, brilliance and genius, and increases moral and ethical behaviour and sense of integrity.' It also enables business to 'take its rightful place' in society. 'The idea flow from the human spirit is unlimited. All you have to do is tap into it.' At the same time, for Matt, spirituality's purpose 'is not to serve work, but work's purpose is to serve spirituality'. 'That is a real shift in our point of view...and that's the question employees should be asking of themselves: how can this company, and my work here, serve my spirit?'

Similarly sharing this view, Camilla believes that 'we should be bringing the soul and spirit to the forefront in our organizations'. In her address to a workshop on spirituality at work, Camilla encouraged participants to 'get in touch with the soul through elemental things'. 'Work when it is a devotion and not a compulsion leads to new expressions of self. Learning to speak earth, air, fire and water in organizations will change them fundamentally, and bring whole new dimensions to work.' The participants in the workshop, who were mostly professional middle-class employees, attentively took notes and asked sympathetic questions. In my conversations with them I heard various ways in which they construed their own meanings of the call 'to speak earth, air, fire and water' as a way to transform their working lives and their organizational workplaces. The common element was a mystical one, an interpretation and seeking of divine or sacred meaning to the business of their daily work and its ends.

Paul, a senior executive explains: 'we need to do something serious about the soul being marginalized in organizations. We need a wake up call. We need to start coming home to ourselves. When we allow soul to be expressed and nurtured in the workplace we learn to understand the world differently – not as a fragmented place of irreconcilable differences, but see the world relationally, holistically, collectively, as flowing motion.'

For Jan, a finance manager, bringing soul to work means, 'quite a turn around of the way we've always done things....It's about making work serve the soul, serve the spirit within us. If the organization can't lead from soul and allow people to have soul at work it's an unhealthy place to be. People won't do this for much longer, they want to be where their soul is nurtured and valued, and where others seek that too. A spiritual transformation of organizations is seriously needed.'

Another illustration, but one expressing more tentativeness and some ambivalence about soulfulness at work, comes from Nik, who currently works in technological product development. For Nik, 'I've worked in a few companies…and even in Australia and Europe they all do things the same way…we all work on the same things. This product we're developing now, it's like what we did at X Co. six years ago…same systems and ways….It makes you wonder…I like the money, but it's not everything. There's other things, and whether you call it soul or spirit or feelings, if you start focusing on them…maybe I would want to do things differently. Like here, in T Co. we could be doing things better if we paid attention to other things. I guess like being sensitive to soul things….We are supposed to recycle the pallets, but we don't actually do that. It's terrible. But it's just the way it is. If it costs the company, they won't do it.'

Among employees wanting to explore spirituality at work I have witnessed some of the ways in which their various expressions are put into practice. A number have developed personal ways of practising meditation, yoga and quiet time out at work. In addition, a number of companies now provide quiet rooms, meditation times, and some managers openly speak of 'soul moments'. As well as these gentle arts I have witnessed an interest in other forms of spirit-seeking, magic and divination occurring in organizations. I have observed a range of people including human resources managers, social and natural scientists, educationists, and organizational consultants individually using tarot cards. On one occasion I observed this happening in the tea-room of a research laboratory. Colleagues variously looked on, joined in, or took the cards away for private use. Others have reported 'listening to their angels', participating in 'dream workshops', pursuing 'journeys of shamanic healing' and attending company-sponsored workshops on these arts. I have listened to reports from highly skilled corporate employees on their consulting fortune-tellers, astrologers, numerologists and spirit guides in order to gain knowledge to discern direction and aid decision-making in their work and in their lives. I have witnessed senior managers encourage employees in reading self-discovery and spiritual literature, and company-fund middle managers' participation in mind/body spiritual and personal growth programmes. Managers and their consultants, often at very expensive seminars, invoke and advocate the language of openness to alternative or competing rationalities. At first glance this 'openness' presents an apparently ironic contradiction to encouragement of the practice of conventional rationalities of production. It adds further complexity to the usual management tasks of managing counter-rationalities and errant affectivity, and facilitating production.

The invocation of spirituality and, as one CEO put it, 'the L-word' (love), is apparently no longer considered a threatening competing rationality. It is instead regarded by those actively encouraging these sensibilities as an 'energy source' increasingly vital to organizational production. Some of these activities are taken up as part of a newer cultural sensitivity to employees from diverse cultural backgrounds. I have observed, for instance, organization executives and employees partaking in pre-modern tribal rites and prayers on the premises of highly modern, technologically advanced business and administrative organizations (for example in the opening of a new building or the 'blessing' of a new enterprise).[2] But many of these activities arise out of diverse forms of spiritual exploration which makes use of popular, or marginal or hybridized forms of cultural practices drawn from virtually anywhere around the globe. A growing interest in an ancient Chinese divination practice of Feng Shui in regard to 'energy flows' and auspicious alignments with the fields of energy is readily observable. Magazines from architecture to management frequently carry stories on the design and arrangement of living and working spaces according to the precepts of Feng Shui. Examples of these interests can be found from Helsinki to Los Angeles, London, Bangkok and Sydney. A recent book, *Feng Shui at Work* (King 1999), promises to 'increase good fortune and luck in business and the workplace'. Organizational consultants include these arts in a repertoire of alternative organizational advice offered to diverse corporate clients in private companies and public organizations, and employees discuss these ideas over coffee breaks.

Spiritual and divination practices include a considerable range of activities which practitioners may or may not submit to some form of regulation through adherence to a group or association of similar practitioners. One of the favoured, entirely unregulated, practices of New Age explorers is the art of 'aura reading' of one's companions or associates. Tara holds an MBA degree and works in a public relations and consulting company. She reported that she and some of her colleagues were proficient, as she puts it, in 'reading the aura of the person we're with'. She and some of her co-workers had taken a course in this art and now put it to use for their compnay. 'It's hard to explain. Basically, it's about getting a reading of the person from the light or heat around them…'. 'We do this with clients or with people wanting to work for our company. I think we're pretty good at it…. You can tell by the colour and shape of the aura if they'll be suitable for us.' While my informant laughed at that point, expecting a sceptical, if unspoken response, she later added more seriously that: 'It has worked for us and I don't see why we shouldn't use these things if they help....You might be surprised, but in firms like ours with a lot of creative people and a lot of competition out there that a lot of people are doing these sorts of things....We have to be open, and we say that we encourage out-of-the-box thinking. And I believe that it works.'

Another illustration of New Age spiritual seeking among persons employed as rational modern producers is provided by Derek, a senior medical scientist employed in a prominent research institute in Europe. Over a long lunch interview with me Derek reported (initially to my considerable surprise as my questions had been entirely unrelated) his deeply held spiritual beliefs. Derek reported 'a journey of life-changing experiences' through his following the wisdom of a non-denominational spiritual figure. This figure invokes the name of a Hebrew prophet and claims to be an ancient spirit guide. He prophesies and offers edifying life guidance through the entranced body of a former computer scientist on the American west coast. His followers record and disseminate his trance-delivered talks and wisdom to a widely dispersed audience. According to my informant, the inspiration from this mysterious prophet which he believes guides his life necessarily carries over into his research work. He believes that he is 'more intuitive...more sensitive to the mysteries of life'. At the time of my meeting with him another similarly believing microbiologist confessed a similar influence of this prophet guide in his research work. They gave me details of electronic discussion groups, journals and conferences in the United States and Europe in which scientists inclined toward such paranormal and parascientific interests discussed their explorations. Furthermore both men assured me that while their interests were admittedly 'unusual' they were a recognized dimension of the 'new sciences,'[3] especially the 'new physics' and 'new biology'.

Another illustration of current forms of exploration which draws on ancient arts comes from an economist employed in a London bank. Geoff, self-presenting with the expected accoutrements of a corporate banker, invited further conversation with me. In the course of conversation Geoff reported his practice of 'playing with the numbers' (numerology) and consulting a nearby fortune-teller 'for a bit of help!' in his personal life and professional work. Apparently, in the same London banking district there are fortune-tellers and numerologists practising their arts among a steady clientele of professional rationalists in formally secular organizations. Again, there was laughter in the conversation in which he reported this aspect of his interests, but a non-judgmental response on my part elicited further similar disclosures and reports of other colleagues and associates engaging in various, usually unspoken, alternative, counter-rational explorations. Like Geoff, Ron works in the London financial district. On the trading floor dealing in rapid financial transactions, Ron feels that some combinations of numbers such as dates or stocks are 'auspicious'. He reports that his experience has been that when he pays attention to his feelings about the numbers he makes better financial decisions. He believes that there is a 'higher power' guiding his judgements.

Stories such as these expressing interest in spirit guides, magic and other-worldliness, from formally educated, highly trained professional corporate employees accompanied the passing occasional admissions from other informants that they were, for instance 'brought up Presbyterian, but I've left all that behind me now'. Or, 'I'm a recovering Catholic…'. Similarly, others remarked about affiliation with conventional Church religion that 'nobody really talks about Church attendance around here. I don't think that's what people are into any more.' Moreover, I have listened to employees discussing with bemusement one of their colleagues who openly practises his Jewish faith. The point here is that organizational employees indicating adherence to traditional religious affiliations meet the expected modernist, secularist disparagement. But among those experimenting with New Age practices of meaning-making or resacralization admission is not difficult to elicit or witness. In many instances it is assertively pronounced. The risk of being considered weird or 'flaky' by one's colleagues is surprisingly disregarded.

A number of respondents who expressed dismissive views about conventional religions, including fundamentalism, had no hesitation in admitting to their own interests in New Age spirituality, in angels, crystals and Hindu goddesses, and in the use of homeopathic and naturopathic remedies, or partaking in company-offered classes in yoga, 'massage therapy' or transcendental meditation. Breda, a former teacher and currently a senior administrative officer, informed me that she always uses alternative medicines and therapies, and consults her various sets of tarot cards for spiritual, emotional and organizational decision-making guidance. She has received financial support from her managing director to attend workshops on bringing new forms of spirituality to the workplace.

My observations to date indicate that explorations of New-Age-style spirituality and counter-rationalities are found unevenly among men and women. While I have observed, and others reported (Canfield et al. 1999, Heelas 1996, 2000, Roof 1993, Wuthnow 1998), that the 'baby-boomers' aged in their 40s and 50s are leading this turn to spirituality, I also witness a number of younger men and women in their 20s and 30s entering these discussion and explorations. A particular aspect of the New Age explorations, that of magic and Wicca, currently growing in popularity (witness the shelves of books now available in many bookstores on the subject), appears to be more prominently practised by younger women.

For example Astrid, a young woman with a college degree working as an administrative officer in a large insurance company, illustrates an interest increasingly readily found among younger women in and out of employed work. Astrid reports that she is 'training in the arts of Wicca'. She attends a small workshop led by an experienced witch which, she explains, 'is a bit like an apprenticeship'. She says that she feels 'very drawn to Wicca' and learning its arts 'gives a great deal of meaning' to her life in general, and also to her working life. According to Astrid she is able to practise her arts in the workplace and with (unsuspecting) clients. She assured the interviewer that she, and her sister witches, only practise good spells and divination for good purposes. But she is aware that disclosing her identity as a witch and the practising of her craft – although there are shops from Glastonbury to Sydney in which one can buy one's supplies – does raise 'a lot of misunderstanding and sometimes fear' among her co-workers. But others come to her for advice based on her divination usually for dealing with relationship problems, including those at the workplace. Her manager, who was aware of Astrid's interests, was reluctant to comment, but did indicate a tolerance of the activities as long as 'there's no harm done'.

More commonly, and modestly, practised are the simply sensory-affective sensibilities of aromatherapy and meditative or relaxing music in the offices or cubicles of diverse organizational employees in many countries. I have observed that as candles or open flames are typically prohibited (except, it appears, in Sweden) electric oil-burning devices for heating essential oils or incense solids are popular. Preference for olfactory pleasures and their relaxing or transcendence-inducing qualities are apparently more common among women employees – for whom it may even be more tolerated as a 'female thing'. But men use relaxing music in their workplaces too. Moreover, efforts to practise meditation or other relaxation-seeking arts, such as yoga or Tai Chi or 'music therapy', are reported among corporate employees, especially those who have offices with doors. For workers entirely unable to personalize their shared workspaces some resort to more simple practices of re-enchantment, or at least pleasure. For example, immigrant Pacific Island women working as supermarket checkout operators and packers in New Zealand cities regularly adorn their hair with bold hibiscus flowers to delight and enchant, at least, each other. Many young workers do their utmost to express alternative, nonconformist self-identities in their styles of clothing, linguistic innovation and assertions of value.

These examples illustrate a range of exploratory practices from minor attempts to restore elements of human affective sensibility and personalize routinized, rationalized organizational life, to more serious interests in the validity of alternative meanings and rationalities divined through counter-modern beliefs. From a conventional analytical vantage point this turn to mysticism and gnosticism could be dismissed as idiosyncratic and frivolous, and of little relevance to the continued business of rational organizational affairs. If these spiritual pursuits bespeak a critical disaffection with conventional rational organizations, their individualism in expression and apparent intent undermines any current of political effectivity. Employee seeking of the spiritual world while at work might also be readily dismissed as a neurotic desire or desperate impulse to make meaning in a condition of institutionalized compartmentalization of self and rationalized alienation. Such pathological conditions among workers is not new and conventional individual psychological treatments might effectively manage such maladaptation. If it were not for the considerable interest shown by increasing numbers of organizations, and the burgeoning popular management literature and conferences addressing these same matters, such conventional modern analytical responses might more readily suffice.

Organizational Responses: Joining the 'New Age'

The 1990s saw a proliferation of management and organization texts and applications in workplaces that expound various new theories on how to gain strategic advantage through restructured, culturally reformed organizations and employees. These activities are not new. But the content and direction of the latest among the corporate cultural design programmes indicate a new trend. The programmes currently extolled by organization culturalists and management motivators now overtly encompass the utilization of religio-affective impulses and non-economic and non-scientific rationalities emerging among even the mainstream professional middle class. Religious and affective dimensions of human experience so long omitted from the rational institutions of production and work are, it appears, now welcome. As *Business Week* (November 1999) observes: 'Today, a spiritual revival is sweeping across Corporate America as executives of all stripes are mixing mysticism into their management, importing into office corridors the lessons usually doled out in churches, temples and mosques.'

As part of a burgeoning New Age literature, a new management literature targeted at corporate executives as well as middle-ranking employees in the English-speaking West proliferates. From the emotional appeal of titles such as: *Getting Employees to Fall in Love with Your Company* (Harris 1996), *Heart at Work* (Canfield and Millar, 1996), and *The Living Company* (de Geus 1997) to the more soothingly spiritual *Chicken Soup for the Soul at Work* (Canfield et al. 1999). *The Stirring of Soul at Work* (Briskin 1996) and *Liberating the Corporate Soul* (Barrett 1998), to the more mystical *True Work: The Sacred Dimensions of Earning a Living* (Toms and Toms 1998), *Zen at Work* (Kaye 1996), and *The Corporate Mystic* (Hendricks and Ludeman, 1997), a stirring of interest in activities conventionally excluded from management practice and organizational analysis is widely evident. Moreover, in addition to popular publications, prominent organizational academics, such as the European writer Charles Handy in his 1997 book, *The Hungry Spirit: Beyond Capitalism – A Quest for Purpose in the Modern World*, and Mitroff and Denton's *A Spiritual Audit of Corporate America* (1999) are similarly exploring and advocating the incorporation of spiritual and 'post-capitalist' values in the workplace.

Ian Mitroff and Elizabeth Denton's *A Spiritual Audit of Corporate America* addresses what the authors identify as a 'spiritual impoverishment' in corporate organizations today. The book, which includes an empirical study of executives and managers, explores the effect of spirituality, and the lack of it, on organizations. In their preface the authors state that they believe the field of organization science 'has failed to produce fundamental and long-standing changes in the vast body of organizations' (p. xiii). Organization science 'must no longer avoid analysing, understanding, and treating organizations as spiritual entities' (p. xiii). Defining spirituality as the 'search for meaning, purpose, wholeness and integration in one's life' the authors find that 'workers are searching for non-religious, non-denominational ways of fostering spirituality in the workplace' (p. xiii). They argue that 'unless organizations learn to harness the whole person and the immense spiritual energy that is at the core of each person, they will not be able to produce world-class products and services. Unlike reengineering, Total Quality Management, and other methods, spirituality is not a fad or a gimmick. People are hungry not only to express their souls but also to further the development of their innermost selves' (p. xvi).

The book endeavours to offer useful models of spirituality in the workplace in order to seek 'a far deeper transformation of organizations than has ever been dreamed of'. High commitment and involvement on the part of both management and employees is required, the authors point out, but spiritual enrichment will reap great benefits for all parties. As the book's jacket summarizes: 'spirituality is one of the most important determinants of organizational performance. People who are spiritually involved achieve better results. In fact, spirituality may well be the ultimate competitive advantage' over other organizations.

Sharing many similar perspectives with Mitroff and Denton is Roger Lewin and Birute Regine's 2000 book, *The Soul at Work*. For Lewin and Regine, 'a wind of change is blowing through the business world, bringing with it a new hope and a potential for a deep human resonance within organizations, which we all seek deep in our hearts' (Lewin and Regine 2000: 15). This shift in the world of business is one 'where valuing people and relationships is not just a good or espoused idea, but a conscious management action that has a positive outcome on the economic bottom line…by genuinely caring about people in the workplace, the bottom line often benefits as well' (ibid.: 14). The authors argue that there 'continues to be a denial in the business mind, a stark omission of the importance of people and valuing them for not only the revenues they bring in, but simply as human beings…when people are treated as replaceable parts, as objects of control, are taught to be compliant, are used as fuel for the existing system…inevitably you are going to have an organization that is fraught with frustration, anger, and isolation, which ultimately is detrimental to the business' (ibid.: 22).

The antidote to this condition, the authors argue, is the recognition of people and organizations as complex adaptive systems in which interconnectedness and meaningful engagement are vital. Recognizing the 'soul at work' points to 'future horizons and challenges for a different way of working' (ibid.: 26). In bringing a complexity science thesis to organizations the authors claim that: 'how we interact and the kinds of relationships we form has everything to do with what kind of culture emerges…with the emergence of creativity, productivity, and innovation'. They add that: 'When more interactions are care-full rather than care-less in an organization, a community of care and connection develops, creating a space for the soul at work to emerge' (ibid.: 26). Lewin and Regine explain their notion of the soul at work as ' a *double entendre*: it is at once the individual's soul being allowed to be present in the workplace; and it is the emergence of a collective soul of the organization' (p. 26). If organizations through their leaders and employees develop a conscious effort to change into relationships of 'care-connections' (ibid.: 316–330), the authors contend, complex systemic relationships of soul extend to connections with the living environment. Their final chapter offers a brief comment on the need to include ecological environmental issues in the organizational relationship.

Ideas along these lines, especially those of complexity science, are found in a number of 'new science' publications such as the *New Scientist* and the *Journal of Noetic Sciences*, and also in business publications such as *Harvard Business Review, Business Week* and the *New Statesman*. They comprise a significant focus in contemporary discussions about organizations, business and management. They reflect a continued belief in systems theories adding something of a mystical sensorium to the functioning of the complex system.

Charles Handy's book, which also addresses many of these ideas about changing organizational relationships and values, endeavours to bring the discussion to a more societal level of analysis. For Handy in *The Hungry Spirit: Beyond Capitalism – A Quest for Purpose in the Modern World* (1997), the quest is not only for organizations with more soul and humanity, but for a 'decent society' to be restored through a restoration of individual remoralized responsibility. Handy recognizes the cynicism, burnout and instrumentality of relationships which are commonplace in contemporary organizations. The irresponsibilty of *laissez-faire* capitalism has left many people in organizations watchful for only their own self-interest, having discarded values of working together with others for common value-driven ends. For Handy, 'Capitalism needs to be reinterpreted to make it decent, and companies, which are the key institutions of capitalism, need to be rethought' (Handy 1997: 151). Handy's rethinking proposes that organizations need to see themselves as 'communities not properties' and to see 'their people as citizens', and that they must understand that they 'need an implicit license to operate in their societies, where they are citizens too' (ibid.: 153). Handy argues for a reinstitution of values of responsibility, trust, community relationships, loyalty and commitment. He argues for a humanistic reinvention of capitalism with, this time, a theory of limits against an 'undiluted ideology of self-interest' (ibid.: 264). This, for Handy, will redress the systemic errors of an unchecked capitalism which has triumphed in recent decades. The book, intended for a popular business management as well as academic business school readership, offers a number of new value statements intended to be applicable in organizations, as well as inspirational stories of accomplishment and respirited transformations. In the latter sense, and interspersed with religious metaphor and aphorism, it shares the agenda of a growing range of programmes and courses offered to a disenchanted organizational workforce. It also indicates a growing current of thought among intellectuals which favours a (re)turn to community for sources of morality and belongingness as society breaks down (e.g. Bellah et al. 1996, Etzioni 1994).

Examples of management and organizational consulting firms (operating in the United States, Europe, South America, Australasia and South Africa) offering training seminars and courses in, for example:

'Spirituality in the Workplace', 'The Inner Life of Business', 'Igniting Purpose and Spirit at Work', 'The Transformed Organization' are readily found. Many are advertised on the Internet and in popular management and business magazines. The impulse for these new consultancy offerings arises from the perceived need for organizations to address their values and cultures of relationships and purpose. Like the illustrations from the literature selections above, one consultancy company explains the summative rationale for their spirituality programmes: 'Spiritual consulting and training honors the whole of each person within the whole of the company so individual and corporate needs and goals are honored and fulfilled.' A Hollyhock Spirit and Business Conference in the United States in 1998 promoted its purpose as seeking to encourage 'business as a vehicle for social change and integrating spirituality and business'.

At an international 'Spirituality in the Workplace' conference in Canada in 1998, the Chairman of Aetna International gave a keynote address on 'The Dollars and Sense of Spirituality in the Workplace' in which he encouraged companies to make space for the spiritual needs of employees. Such attention would simultaneously reap dividends in the conventional manner for the company. A now well known International Conference on Business and Consciousness meets annually in Mexico. In partnership with the Business Spirit Journal Online this has sparked other conferences all around the world. Spirit at Work conferences in New Zealand and Australia in 2000 sought to 'build workplaces that capture the hearts of those who work within them, where...spiritual awareness and interconnectedness...are explored to enhance life and uplift organizational synergy and productivity'.

Moreover, a number of very large corporate organizations including IBM, Xerox, AT&T, Nike, Forbes, Apple, Pepsico, General Electric and others, fund in-house or off-site employee participation in retreats which include yoga, meditation, mind-body work and the like. Establishments in several countries offer regular programmes of 'corporate yoga' to companies and individual corporate executives. Yoga, which often includes chanting to Hindu deities, is selectively adapted to corporate consumer needs. During my attendance at a yoga class for corporate employees I listened to the teacher instruct: 'Focus on your body and the energy; let your mind go.... Listen to your breathing and feel the echo of your heartbeat. Attend to what feelings come up for you, just let them be... then gently exhale them free....Feel the cosmic energy around you, in you, through you....Feel yourself as flow' (Corporate Yoga Class 1999).

Business Week (November 1999) reports that in addition to yoga, shamanic healing and divination, and Native-American-style quests for meaning, soul and truth, prayer meetings and the study of sacred texts of the Talmud, the Bible and the Bhagavad Gita are offered in companies such as Deloitte and Touche, Xerox and Pizza Hut. My own research has found similar quests practised in public organizations, pharmaceutical companies and prisons. These illustrations of corporate involvement in non-traditional activities of this nature, the literature appearing on managers' desks (and in their MBA curricula), and the expressions of spiritual seeking and experimentation with counter-scientific rationalities among professional organizational employees, suggest an apparent convergence of interest between a significant number of employees and organizations in alternative, non-modern, rationalities. For employees these pursuits are undertaken for personal interests in enhancing well-being and developing knowledge or consciousness that are precluded by their performance of rational, scientific, professional roles and identities. Their activities are responses to an experience of lack in overly rationalized, instrumentalized, dispirited and constrictive workplaces. They indicate efforts, initially at re-enchantment, and potentially at revitalization of their lives at work. As technological developments – especially in information and communication – in organizational work in recent years have blurred boundaries between at-work and not-at-work life, the encroachment of organizational rationalities into all aspects of the life-world, long feared by critical theorists, may seem irresistible. But in defence of the life-world, or in pursuit of self-identity, New Age seekers confront technocratic rationalities with an unexpected counter-rational opposition in spiritualization.

Conventional religious sensibilities were expected to be kept out of modern industrial organizations as an exclusive instrumental rationality in production organizations was singularly privileged. But in contemporary conditions a monological instrumental rationality and economic ideology of one-sided modernity now meets a counter-force it unintendedly helped generate. Informational capitalism, simultaneity of exchange and boundary collapse expose organizational rationalities – which were always fragile – to forces and demands in the wider cultural sphere. New oppositional voices and alternative practices fuelled by a cultural and identity turn contest the stakes of organizational and working life. They compete with, or circumvent, more typical modern contestations in political and economic demands. They indicate new sources from which critical impulses may become constitutive social action – a point I discuss further in the next chapter.

But the organizational interest in these spiritual activities raises many criticisms. At first glance, the corporate organization allows, or encourages, some of these counter-scientifically rational practices to the extent that they may be applied to the conventional rationalities of organizational production and profitability under changing conditions of an informated, networked global economy. The appropriation and application of current New Age interests in popular culture to encourage more spirited and devoted employees in service of established organizational ends is simply a cost-effective production incentive and employee-motivator in highly competitive markets. These interests may be interpreted as corporate commodification of neo-religiosity that captures and utilizes affective and spiritual impulses among disaffected employees. In the mid-20th century the ideal type of corporate employee was a dedicated professional, scientifically and economically rational, publicly secular, emotionally repressed individual (Drucker [1946] 1960, Whyte 1956). In the 1980s and 1990s the desirable employee was the familial, caring, team participant (Casey 1995) who had relinquished strong occupational and professional identificatory bonds. As the new century begins, it is the mystic and the votary.

But notwithstanding the emphatic incorporative response to employees seeking mystical meaningfulness, this current of interest is a complex one, with many unmanageable features and directions. Many organizational leaders and managers are themselves personally exploring some of these new interests, whether it is in the form of entranced gurus conveying wisdoms over the Internet, attending Business and Consciousness or Spirituality at Work conferences or reading the recent books by Charles Handy or Alan Briskin or Lewin and Regine on the plane or train. Their interest may simultaneously indicate a disaffection shared with middle-ranking employees with the impoverishment of a monological capitalism, as it does for the authors of the books discussed above, and which has more typically been expressed by left critics of capitalism of the industrial era.

Moreover, there are other aspects to the organizational benevolence and toleration, even encouragement, of religio-affective interests among employees. The movement toward organizational change in which aspirations of corporate citizenship and relational networks of 'trust and loyalty', as Handy (1997) puts it, in which the employee is valued as a 'whole person' with 'soul' in service of organizational production is a timely shift. The encouragement of affective and spiritualizing organizational sensitivities, though generally accepted and oftentimes popular, encounters forces and impulses which may be more seriously opposed to intensified postindustrial work in contemporary conditions.

Career Moves: A Practical Criticism

While corporate organizations and many of their employees seek soulful and affective re-enchantment of soulless workplaces a number of others, usually but not only those more established in once typical organizational professional careers, act on their soulful impulses and make more radical career moves. They leave, or dramatically alter their relationships with, the world of organizational work. The central career locus of modern society, in the late 20th century in the West for women as well as men, in the world of work demonstrated the hold of modernity's assertion that we are what we do. This assertion has by no means given way, but it is now newly challenged by diverse emergent cultural movements – as well as by postindustrial technological and organizational practices which render human work (as industrially defined) less central to production.

Current academic investigations (e.g. Beck 2000, Casey 2000, Gorz 1999, MacKinnon 1997, Rifkin 2000) and reports from a growing body of anecdotal, journalistic and company sources (Ansley 2000, Caudron 1996, Ehrenreich 1995, Laabs 1996) indicate that another important pattern is emerging in relations of production. People from a wide range of working life backgrounds in Western societies are acting in ways which suggest that the modern societal privileging of work as ultimate *raison d'être* and of self and social value is being challenged and altered. A number of people are endeavouring to alter their relations to work – as conventionally practised[4] – and to employing organizations. My observations of these developments suggest that they take the form of several clusters of trends which we might designate as trends toward 'downshifting', intermittent work, non-work, work-refusal and work-transformation. (They include, too, persons forcibly excluded from participation in paid work – a sector for which discussion must be deferred in this book.) Evidence for these trends is drawn from my own firsthand data, from data reported in academic investigations, and considerable secondary sources in journalistic articles and popular publications. These matters are complex and controversial, and they require a comprehensive analytical consideration. For my purposes here, a brief discussion focuses only on those persons who are downshifting or opting out of organizational work.

An emergent trend toward altered relationships to production organizations and work as conventionally practised encompasses people in, or formerly and potentially in, relatively secure relations to work and employing organizations. Many professional and highly skilled workers in technological, financial, managerial and other well-paid positions in large organizations or secure professions are experiencing or seeking new relationships to work and employing organizations. For such middle-class, white-collar, overworked personnel in the West the new relationship they seek is one in which they might actively, of their own volition, find 'more meaningful' lives. These people, regarded by their employing organizations as valued human resources, typically hold high-status positions in successful organizations. Yet they are wanting to alter their involvement, and the character of that involvement, in their work. They report that they want more than the benefits and costs of work and organization currently normatively practised. They express interest in various seekings of 'voluntary simplicity', 'spiritual growth', personal development, creativity, ethics, ecology and relationships. Many but not all of them are in the 35–50 + age bracket. Most have worked hard and devotedly in organizations but are disillusioned with the personal results even if financial prosperity is welcomed. They want, as they say, 'to do what I'd rather be doing'. As Tom (a former data analyst) expressed it: 'Now I do what I used to spend all year working for – a couple of weeks' vacation to do what I'd rather be doing.' Tom is an example of a number of financially secure people who have deliberately 'downshifted' or opted out of regular participation in modern organizational work and routinized work-compulsion and accepted a reduced financial income in so doing.

Alan, a former corporate executive reports: 'For 25 years I've devoted myself to work and it's been hard yakka, you know....Well, now I've given up those 12 hour days – it's over. I don't know exactly where things will go, but I'm out of there for good now. We've bought this property up here [in the countryside] and it's got all these old roses on it...I've never felt better, we're thriving on not working!...It's like we've done this big reassesment: did I really want to continue that work-driven way of life for the sake of what, a new car, or something? I feel there's other things in life I've been missing out on, and well, I want to find out what that is...already we're finding things here among these old roses. It's kind of spiritual as well as beautiful.'

A similar view is expressed by another former executive. Dan, in his late 40s, has left a career in a multinational company. He reports: 'I've worked in seven or eight countries, and travelled to many others for meetings and disputes. I spent 12 hours a day in the office, as well as working on the plane to New York or Bangkok or London...it was always aggressive – putting up proposals, tearing them up, everyone always on the make. Waiting in airport lounges working and forgetting where you were....It's like you were supposed to be a machine...you didn't take notice of your stress levels, they were like very high, but it wasn't cool to be stressed. A couple of years ago I decided that there must be a better way of life...how did all this happen?'

Dan has chosen a 'downshifted' life supported by some consulting work of his choosing, and a portfolio of investments. He is able 'to do a hell of a lot of sailing' and pursue interests long precluded by his former corporate life. He reports that the quality of his life has 'improved enormously' as he has become newly aware of his relationships and his 'real needs'.

Like Dan, Peter, a former senior manager for a telecommunications company has similarly 'downshifted': 'Since leaving the company rat race there's been a tremendous sense of release. It feels that I'm being me...not what other people want me to be. My wife's much happier too. It's like without realizing it it's what we've wanted for a long time. Working for N Corp was one very long mistake...I just wish I'd seen it earlier. I can't imagine going back....Some of our friends can't really understand it. A lot of people worry about the money if they retire early. But I say it's not retirement, it's just not working!' Peter and his wife, aged in their 50s, have chosen to relocate to a country village and to 'live well on less'.

A former corporate lawyer has emigrated from her home country to find a quieter, more environmentally sustainable lifestyle. Sue reports: 'I've seen women in their 20s and 30s under enormous pressure. They think it's what women with careers and families just have to expect. They don't seem to consider that it's the way their companies operate that puts all this stuff on them. And the men just shrug and if you ask them they say well they've had it too – they've missed their kids' sports games and birthdays and stuff like that and it's put strain on their marriages but nobody else cared. So if the women [in corporate work] are complaining, you have to ask them what did they expect?

'I think the alternatives just have to be explored. You have to ask yourself if being in the fast-paced corporate environment is really good for you. I probably thought I could make a difference as a woman, but now I just think I want a better life – spiritually and emotionally...and also get back more in touch with the natural environment. It's like we've got to re-evaluate things and what we're doing to the environment.'

For May, another downshifter and now non-worker, the shift in her working life occurred 'quite suddenly, really'. 'I came home from work one day and looked at my husband. I actually noticed that he looked dreadful, and realized that I did too. So it's like I said "enough"... this is enough. Let's stop doing this. I'd been working at my career, we both had been, for so long even...when the children were young. But suddenly it seemed no longer relevant. It was like something dawned on me...you could say it was a spiritual moment. It was a release...and I knew it was going to be our new life.'

May and her husband have meagre savings, but with a mortgage-free house and 'plenty of energy' they have, May reports, adjusted to a 'dramatically lower income'. After three years of downshifting and not working (in organizational work), May says that: 'we know we've made the right choice. Our spiritual and emotional lives feel like they have never been better'.

One further illustration is offered by Terry, a university-educated man in his mid-30s with a school-age child. Terry reports that he is no longer in regular organizational work, nor in regular self-employment. He laughs as he tells me his now firmly held views about organizational work. 'This is how I see it, and how I want it – I call it the "royalty structure" – a nice passive income for very little work. And lots of do-what-you-want leisure. That's definitely what I want.... I've worked my guts out over the years for a few [electronics and computing] companies here and abroad, and they're all the same....Now they think casual Fridays are going to cut it! Well, not for me. I've got a lot of other things to live for, and I'll work now and then when I need to for some money. And you know, I'm not the only one doing this kind of thing [intermittent work], and I think more people should wake up to it. Why should the royals get it, get out of working all the time?'

My research indicates that among more financially secure, or at least financially self-sustainable, people an option to deliberately 'downshift' or reject regular participation in modern organizational work and a culture of routinized work-compulsion is increasingly attractive. Among current organizational employees the fantasy of doing so, and knowing of someone who has, is frequently reported. For companies reliant on the expertise of ostensibly highly valued knowledge workers, the expressed interests and activities of these growingly disaffected people pose challenges to the conventional uses of humans in organizations. Companies are increasingly aware of these trends among high-achieving people. As *Fortune* magazine puts it a 'profound reassessment, a rethinking' (December 1999) is taking place among high-achieving employees, and organizations must make efforts to accommodate the emotional and spiritual interests of their workers.

Of course, many millions of people around the world are forced into intermittent work or unemployment. Their stories and the social analysis of such involuntary exclusion from work-based society demands attention and requires another book. The important works of Beck (2000) and Castells (1997, 1998), for example, have begun this task. For the moment, in my account, those privileged with relative economic security, and probably class histories and cultural capital which encourage self-assertion and bourgeois opposition to capitalism, are the focus of my analytic attention. Not having experienced the collective defeat of working-class workers and movements, the professional middle class, or the individualized remnants of that class, presents sources of opposition and demand-setting that may develop into social action.

The seeking of self-creation or meaning-making through re-enchantment, spirituality and mysticism coincides with the business turn to consciousness. Together they suggest more momentous implications for organizations and work as conventionally practised in rationalized modernity. The turn to re-enchantment and the expression of individualized efforts to respond strategically to organizational imperatives and market commodification indicate a move, contrary to modern political responses and systemic truncation, of spirited human action. These people are striving for the conditions of more satisfying, emancipatory lives. They do not want to be the resources of powerful others' utility. Beyond subjectification and alienation, the subject-actor returns. The postindustrial actor draws on a variety of cultural modes, and contests and raises new demands of the current dominant social institutions. He or she strives to remake the order of things social.

Notes

1. A full discussion of the New Age movement is found, for example, in Paul Heelas' (1996) excellent study. An interpretive discussion is beyond my task here, but it is important to note that what are currently called 'New Age' explorations may be found throughout Western history, including throughout the 20th century in which modern rationalities and secularization were highly favoured. Moreover, there are signs of revived fundamentalist religious traditions which arise concurrently with the New Age, detraditionalized, movements.

2. I have observed that these activities even offer opportunities for some corporate employees to develop particular 'professional' expertise in these knowledges and practices. Most especially there is considerable scope for employees from ethnic minority backgrounds to draw on and embellish their traditional knowledge in spiritual practices and apply them to contemporary organizational cultures. I have witnessed corporate organizational decision-making being influenced by the serious insistence of employees from ethnic minorities that the planned action would fail because their divination practice had

so predicted. Spiritual mystification and alternative rationalities contribute a new source not only of self-identity in the workplace but of power and control.

3. An article in the *New Scientist*, 165 (2226) 19 February 2000 notes (p. 47) that 'magic is making a comeback' and that its reappearance joins that of mysticism, which has had a long history of episodic influence in science.

4. Work as conventionally practised in the modern industrial West refers to work that is paid for, socially valued, and typically engaged in over time in the form of an occupational job or jobs, trade, profession or 'vocation'. Unpaid, though socially valued, work (e.g. childcare), personal work and socially illegitimate work (e.g. crime) are not included.

7   Revitalization

Against instrumental reason, which a distorted, one-sided modernity privileged and which apparently triumphs in a globalizing capitalist world, can we meaningfully pose a return of the subject-actor as a *social* force? Are the practices described in the previous chapter signs of reawakened subject-actors, emerging again in the sites of production – after the virtual defeat of modern political and industrial forms of opposition – contesting, negotiating and remaking the social? Or are they, more crudely, a manifestation of heightened individualism demanding further consumer choice in modes of idiosyncratic identity construction? Are these stirrings of disaffection or of soul merely a private retreat, another iteration of quietism, which has long appealed as a defence of the life-world against encroaching instrumental rationalities? Are they, therefore, benignly tolerated, readily contained and strategically managed by rationalizing institutions of organization and market? The many questions raised by the spiritualizing practices described in the previous chapter require a careful response.

The manifest efforts in seeking expressions of self-identity, of spirituality, emotionality and meaningfulness occurring in organizational workplaces are signs of a wider cultural reaction against the totalizing ideology of modern, and postindustrial, productivism. The reduction of humans and their potentialities to instrumental resources as organizational producers and consumers is, in these new ways, being challenged from within, and beyond, the organizational sphere. Re-enchantment of one's own life at work is a new, and in the first instance non-political (that is, in the usual modern understanding of political expression), counter-practice. Of course, whether or not such interests lead to organizational transformations, and in what directions, is too soon to say. For the moment, these subject-actor interests and efforts of counter-practice appear predominantly as acts of individuals. But these individuals are readily forming groups and Internet fora for support and sojourn, and some seek new forms of community and political organization. At the same time, however, reinvigorated traditional identity and communalist movements are active everywhere. Are there ways in which a revivification of charisma, charm and soul might inspire both personal and social transformation beyond rationalizing modernity? Or is a warring of restored traditional gods, as Weber predicted, in a non-social communalist regression on the horizon? To try to address these questions and pose an interpretive analysis of these matters I wish to recall and reconsider our sociological views on religion.

Religion

Modern sociology predominantly accepted the view, most famously enunciated by Weber, that processes of societal modernization entail progressive rationalization in all spheres of life. Rationalization of the traditional domains of sacred and ordinary breaks down the hold of religious social order. The rise of *Gesellschaft* displaces *Gemeinschaft*, and a subject with free will emerges to make individual choices regarding traditional social organization and obligatory social ties. For Weber, secularization laicizes and disperses religion and its meaning-making repository, into a private realm of individual need and choice. Indeed, Weber's prognosis is succinctly expressed in his renowned lecture, 'Science as a Vocation':

> The fate of our age, with its characteristic rationalization and intellectualization, and above all the disenchantment of the world, is that the ultimate, most sublime values have withdrawn from public life, either into the transcendental realm of mystical life or into the brotherhood of immediate personal relationships between individuals. (Weber [1918] 1989: 30)

For Weber, and for most other theorists throughout modernity, including its famous critics, Nietzsche and Freud, secularization and rationalization are inevitable. As science develops reasoned explanation for the formerly inexplicable, religion is rendered less credible. By the mid-20th century modernization had achieved, at least in the view of that generation of social theorists, near completion of secularization and wide acceptance of rational social organization. At the forefront of social rationalization were the institutions of economy and production. The modern industrial and administrative bureaucracy, Weber theorized, epitomized rational, scientific, efficiency and order. The bureaucratic ideal of rational organization had no place for irrational religious sentiment, or sublime questions.

But there was always within sociology – especially Durkheimian sociology – a view that recognizes a continuing role for religion, even as rationalization expands. For Durkheim, who believed that 'there is something eternal in religion which is destined to survive' (Durkheim [1915]

1965: 474), modernization entails a transmutation of forms of religious and collective life rather than total secularization and individualization.[1] In the Durkheimian view, the persistence of the sacred (that which is set apart as ultimate from the ordinary/profane) in both religious and non-religious manifestations and in new forms in modern society demonstrates a dialectical relationship between secularization and sacralization. Against the Weberian tradition's over-emphasis on instrumental rationality and assumed secularization as characteristic of modern societalization, sociologists drawing on the Durkheimian tradition argue that the decline in traditional religion in modern culture and the plurality of metanarratives of meaning and choices of identity in postmodern culture represent a laicization of the sacred rather than an eradication of the sacred.[2] A renewed interest in religion in anthropological and sociological work (e.g. Alexander 1988, Csordas 1994, Roof 1993, Thompson 1990, Wexler 1996b, Wuthnow 1998) expresses similar Durkheimian perspectives. Of course Weber, too, recognized the phenomenon of charisma and the seminal role of unconscious elements as counter-forces to rationalization, and alternative sources of meaning and value in modern society.

Close observation of contemporary conditions in Western societies suggests at the very least that the metanarrative of progressive rationalization and emancipation from traditional and religious forms can no longer be assumed as a singular trajectory – if indeed it ever was. Modern institutions are currently immensely challenged from a variety of sources which (as discussed in earlier chapters) include challenges posed by critical and anti-modern philosophies, as well as communalist assertions of difference, and marketized individualism. Moreover, the social effects of many of modern capitalism's technological products, most dramatically the Internet, bring unexpected juxtapositions. The development of the Internet, and the ways in which it is used, breaks through many conventions of modern scientific and social theory. A fragmentation and pluralization of meaning systems at once evidence of and enabled by high-tech individualism has generated, among other things, a laicization of the sacred as well as, and distinct from, secularization. Postindustrial technologies are being used to recompose personal and communal worlds broken up by extreme rationalization and postmodern disjunctures.

The diverse range of sacralizing and meaning-making practices grasped under the term 'New Age' (for want of a better term) practices presents evidence in most arenas of contemporary cultural life. Notwithstanding their diversity analysts interpret the New Age as, for Heelas (1996), 'an internalized form of religiosity…it is at heart all about Self-spirituality…about developing a new consciousness'; as a project of 'revitalization of the experience of organic, bodily being' (Wexler 1996a), and as 'spiritual seeking...outside established religious institutions' (Wuthnow 1998), and as explorations of alternatives to hyper-industrialized social practices.

Desecularizing impulses include the uses of the laicization of the sacred which present in the diversity and idiosyncrasy of expressions of spirituality or sacralization (Csordas 1994, Heelas 1996, Roof 1993, Wuthnow 1998). They are accompanied by, though distinguishable from, a revivification of traditional cultural, ethnic and religious communalism which similarly exerts an influence on the seeking of spirituality and other competing rationalities in organizational life. The renewed seeking of traditional cultural communalism is undoubtedly a salient aspect of contemporary counter-modern practices with immense implications. But my attention in this exploration is confined to the influence of 'unchurched spiritualities' (Wuthnow 1998), laicized religious expression (including magic) and individualized self-expression in contemporary organizations. Revived traditional and other forms of cultural communalism and communitarianism are set aside for the time being. Their importance requires a substantive analytic discussion which I must defer. But I do want to note that the laicized, unchurched, detraditionalized explorations actually pose, in the first instance, a counter-movement to fundamentalism and communalism – even as they pose direct challenges to modern progressive rationalization and secularization. Of course, the directions in which these unchurched mystics may go is unclear, and could certainly degrade into instrumentality or identity as individualism. I want to suggest that these explorations by detraditionalized moderns are signs of the subject-actor endeavouring to create rather than consume an individual self-experience. I return to this discussion momentarily.

Critical sociology, like functionalism, has tended to overestimate the system integration and totality of society and organization, and notions of a system without actors – or a non-social realm of strategizing consumers – are often now resignedly accepted. But the evidence, once again from production organizational practice, shows up the contested and always limited rationality of social systems – and simultaneously, the competition between instrumental rational achievements and cultural and identity demands. Managerial organization theory, long practically cognizant of this daily arena of fragility and contest, seeks, predictably, a rational, strategic response. An instrumentally rational response to counter-rational sparks and unmanageable flights of fancy and spirit allows a liberal accommodation and even encouragement of some of these new meaning-making activities. Let us first consider a strategic management view of these activities.

A Managed Re-enchantment?

Organizations, both sociological and management organizational analysts know, operate in complex competitive environments that include an increasing plurality of meaning and value among ethnically diverse employees and potential employees. In much of the West, and even in the pre-eminently rational world of work and organizational production, it is clear that not everyone is willing to conform to the 'one best way' as defined by the West, and so long assumed to be the inevitable consequence of rationalizing modernity and the universal seductions of capitalist consumption. Both disaffected modern Westerners and persons from non-Western cultural traditions raise new demands of the organizations in which they now meet, even virtually, to work. Accordingly, many of the new deliberate efforts on the part of both employees (including former employees) and management to encourage affective and spiritual practices at work which mutually serve employee-self and organizational interests may be seen as efforts to restore elements of human being that have been systematically subjugated and repressed in typically alienated modern production processes and relations. Organizations through the 1980s and 1990s widely practised programmes which encouraged a restoration of affective and sensual sensibilities through the establishment of familial and 'caring' organizations. And they achieved demonstrable results. Notwithstanding the practical ends which these (managed) sensitivities to emotional needs and expression served in maintaining organizational production, the 'caring company' programmes have generally been well received by employees and managers. Even as downsizing ruptures the organizational family, such realities are compensated somewhat by a more adept, emotionally expressive and rhetorically accommodatory corporate culture.

But the underlying contradictions of an espoused integrative corporate culture and the instrumental rationality unwaveringly privileged in the reductive utilization of humans in organizational production persist. Once again, organizational workers, especially those who are well-paid and highly skilled, raise further demands. For many employees, choosing to seek a spiritual world while at work bespeaks an effort to make meaning in the midst of, or to transcend, the apparently intractable contradictions and emptiness of everyday organizational life even as they expend their labour and expertise for organizational goals in intensely competitive markets. An organizational response to this movement in matching those quests with organizational programmes offering affirmative spiritual and affective sensibilities among employees is a sophisticated, postmodern, organizational strategy. Extending the success of the 1980s and 1990s emotionally intelligent and organizationally identified employee into an encouragement now of the 'corporate mystic' accompanies and enables further organizational use of strategically managed corporate human resources. Simultaneously presenting as sensitive and accommodating to dispirited and disaffected employees the new programmes enable the organization to respond quickly to its environment, by enabling a super-flexible human resource management practice that may downsize, restructure, reorganize and relocate with little traditional opposition.

Mystical, soulful employees take responsibility for their own karmic experiences in organizational participation. Corporate mystics, according to their designers and advocates Hendricks and Ludeman (1997), 'have a respect and even fondness for change....At times they may have unpleasant feelings about the directions of change, but they are careful not to let those feelings limit their ability to respond'. Corporate mystics have a 'type of discipline that makes them flexible and adaptable rather than rigid'. They represent the ideal postindustrial employee.

Encouraging soulful, mystical equanimity as a corporate cultural value both appeals to dispirited, overworked and potentially downshifting employees, and endeavours to rekindle their devotion and service to their work and organization in increasingly precarious global conditions. The potential freedoms offered by a managed desecularization to jaded employees whose professional identity and sources of motivation and value in their work performance have been eroded or truncated by corporate instrumental saturation are, management intends, harnessed and utilized by the corporation.

Companies encouraging spirituality or consciousness-seeking at work display smart, strategic, business intent. Their spiritual programmes accomplish an incorporation of yet further sources of employee energies in the service of conventional production and profitability goals. Moreover, this strategy is forward-looking beyond the technological innovation which dominated the 1980s and 1990s. It represents a *strategic* pursuit of a post-technology consciousness.

A sociological analysis framed in established conventions of sociological thought adds another perspective to the interpretive effort. A modern, evolutionist sociological view, upholding the Weberian expectation of increasing rationalization and secularization, would argue that an expansion of secularization encompasses processes of laicization of the sacred. Laicization retains a privileged notion of the sacred while loosening or breaking ties to religious institutions which traditionally regulate and legitimize forms and expression of the sacred. But laicization inevitably leads to further secularization, or marginalization of the deinstitutionalized religious. In this view, the current interest displayed by some people, including economically rational employees, in spirituality is an expression of individual taste and consumer choice, rather than a movement of desecularization. As rationally choosing agents people may experiment with diverse choices of self-identity constituents now available on a global market. These actions of choice include consumption of the identity-making products currently packaged as New Age spirituality. However, a modern sociological view would also point out that there is potential in these activities for a revival of communalist cultural and identity forms which threaten modern societal organization. Recalling a functionalist orientation, this analytic view would argue, in accord with the managerial view, that the accommodatory and appropriative responses by organizations to these cultural product choices indicates an adept organizational strategy in managing counter-organizational rationalities and disorder while maintaining flexible cohesion and retention of efficient producer employees. An incorporation and commodification, rather than an eradication, of competing interests, including the diversely (laicized) religious, into organization production goals is a sign of flexible, highly adaptable postmodern, postindustrial capitalism.

Sharing the defining conventions of modern social thought, although offering a trenchant criticism of monological instrumental rationality and anti-humanism, a critical theory analysis of these new organizational cultural practices offers another view. A classical Frankfurt School interpretation of these activities sees them as further manifestation of a mystification of worker alienation and domination by ideological corporate organizational interests. Moreover, bringing spirit and soul to the workplace as currently advocated in many corporate organizations inclines to an absurd and potentially socially dangerous desecularization. Even though the soul-seeking and mystical interests of employees may indicate efforts toward de-alienation and emancipation of technologized selves at work, and a defence of the life-world, spiritual pursuits ineluctably indicate a false consciousness – a substitution of rationalization ideologies by neo-traditionalist religious ideologies of domination, or other-worldly flights of fancy. The deliberate effort to restore (or construct) domains of ordinary and sacred from which the non-instrumental life-world might be defended is a romantic delusion.

The organization's part in endeavouring to diminish or obscure objectification at work through encouraging employees to take responsibility for spiritualizing and fun-filling their workplaces, represents a capitalist organizational strategy to mystify awareness of the hyper-capitalist intensification of rational instrumentality *and* its crisis in contemporary society. The corporate appropriation and commodification of spiritual interests toward conventional organizational goals as well as hyper-modern productivist rationalities circumvents generative efforts at re-enchantment, dealienation and self-creation in the workplace. These efforts must be pursued, if such possibilities are not already foreclosed, by *reasoned* political action. The complexities of organizational practice in uncertain global environments encourage the use of these activities, promoted as humanistic restoration and revaluing, to obscure and mitigate the intensification and generalization of totalizing instrumental rationality in modern institutions, and the dispersion and dissolution engendered by postmodern dedifferentiation and self-loss.

A further interpretation is offered by a postmodern deconstructionist reading. In such a view, the idiosyncratic spiritualities, mysticism and laicization of former ecclesiastical privileges of sacralization now presenting in organizational life as in society may be seen as a further pluralization of self-identity and social constituents. This pluralization is enabled by an erasure of boundaries, an implosion of universalist social theories, and a condition of free-floating cultural rudiments of symbol, language and sign. The impermanence and erasure of discursively constructed boundaries renders self and social constructions matters of choice or chance within discursively determined conditions. From Foucault – at least in his earlier phase – we might see these self-identity pursuits through spirituality as indicative of remnants of modern subjectivity in which the ideology of subjecthood mystifies its actual political subjugation and elision. Rational organizational systems allow the pursuit of spiritualized self-identity interests while simultaneously maintaining power/knowledge relations of subjugation and discipline. A romantic charm compensates for a pessimistic realism of systemic domination and discursive normalization.

Moreover, drawing on Derrida and Lyotard a postmodern analysis points out that there can be no certain notions or values of the sacred, the profane, the self and the other, nor of systemic rationalities of economy and organization. These matters are fluid, undecidable, contingencies of everyday life in which meaning is always partially and fleetingly constructed and continuously deconstructed. Participation in corporate organizations, as in any other activity, generates sites of positionings and contestation. The aspirations of subject-actors and their experimentations with spiritualities yield multiple micro-narratives among those of rational production organization. There is no reliable way of knowing whether these narratives have political intent or are the playful products of advertising. The managerial response in encouraging or permitting spiritualization in everyday organizational activity rightly recognizes bounded rationality. It is an eminently strategic, contingent and optimal response to postmodern uncertainty.

We can observe that postmodern cultural practices of multiplicity, of pastiche reconstructions and reconfigurations of the elements of self-identity drawn idiosyncratically from the fragments of old traditions, the formerly exotic, the technologically new, the magical and the scientific, are being enacted in the everyday sites of corporate workplaces. These activities manifest a postmodern condition. But postmodern theoretical approaches (at their best) attest only to the potential for reconstitutions and altered relationships made possible by a postmodern cultural turn. Postmodernism as mode of analysis circumvents the modern critical problem of structure and system, action and change. Its elision of subject-actor agency concedes a hyper-modern organizational structural dominance of employee subjects. In its definitive rejection of the modern project of the subject as an ideological humanism, postmodernism offers only fracture, dispersion and absence in its place.

Postmodernism exacerbates the failure of Frankfurt School criticism to significantly influence or counter the trajectory of the 'semi-modernity', in Touraine's term, of technocratic rationalization. But postmodernism not only fails to conceive of a counter-movement to modern degradation – other than identity pursuits (which are themselves a fragmentation of culture) – it inadvertently facilitates and legitimizes the distortion and degradation of modernity in self and social dissolution. Postmodernism's insistence that modernity's deep flaws are irreparable exclusively within its own terms is a compelling indictment influentially expressed not only by Nietzsche but by more contemporary anti-humanist, anti-modernist thinkers such as Foucault and Derrida. Yet in posing only an incessant deconstruction of those terms a liberation from modernity's one-sided monologue is scarcely enabled. Even as Foucault in his later years sought possibilities for the subject in creating a self-project, as Taylor (1989) describes it, of interiority, consciousness, individuality and relationality, his effort was shadowed by a deep suspicion of modern humanist subjectivity – which for him always accomplished subjectification. Postmodernism more generally refuses a subject-actor capable of sustained and purposeful action in a constant contest over the cultural stakes of society.

The turn to the cultural sphere in critical theory from the Frankfurt School to Foucault has been a vital move in enabling a break with social systems theories and structuralism. But the linguistic abstraction and refusal of all spectres of modernity in postmodernism has foreclosed a re-visioning of the social. The unmasking of the exclusive humanism and privileged subject to reveal an anti-humanist subjectification since the Enlightenment most especially has been a powerful, but ultimately ungenerative, accomplishment. From the Frankfurt School to postmodernism the conflation of the idea of the subject with subjectification has been remarkably accepted in the academy. The despair of the loss of a subject-self engendered by extreme modern instrumental rationalization is understandable. The Frankfurt School theorists, Foucault, and other post-modern theorists, wrote in a period in which they could see no effective oppositional actors and in which the old social movements had been dramatically defeated and converted into apparatuses of power. All efforts to create subject-self against the forces of both instrumental rationality and tradition are ultimately defeated by a postmodernism offering no way out of a degraded, instrumentally petrified modernity. As postmodernism disperses in a nomadic wandering, critical social theory seeks now a renaissance of emancipatory possibility. It seeks resources for the revitalization of human life in sustainable relation with the planet beyond rationalizing modernity and postmodernism.

Re-enchantment: A New Critical Practice

After postmodernism, a critical social analysis of organizations searches widely among the knowledges and events in social history and the diverse mass cultural rudiments now available. It might draw anew, as some theorists are already doing (Touraine 1995, Wexler 1996b) on elements of a classical sociological heritage while moving beyond taken for granted frames of modern social science. As Foucault in his later life searched Greek antiquity for sources of ethics outside those of the Judeo-Christian heritage, critical theory now revisits and reconsiders a vast range of possible resources for analysis and action. A renewed drawing on Durkheim's sociological interpretation of religion reconsiders a secular rationalized interpretation of re-enchantment and mysticism, and offers another point of view. Durkheim, like Weber, observed through the 19th century the path of secularization and rationalization which accompanied and was constituent of the establishment of modern industrial society. As secularization, albeit unevenly, normalized, sacralization as social meaning-making and social bonding found expression elsewhere. For Weber, modern secularization did not eradicate the sacred, rather it simultaneously replaced and incorporated the sacred as rationality, science, technology and production. The reification of science and technology competed with the reification of the nation-state as the new gods of Olympus, as well as competing with a lingering traditional *Geist* religiosity. For Weber, as for Marx, privileging *substantive* rationality – as the rationalization of the traditionally sacred – signified an historical advance.

For Durkheim, though, sacralization is not found in rationalization. Durkheim, like Freud (and also Weber), sought to understand the unconscious sources of social life. For all of Durkheim's well-known emphasis on positive social science, his search for the foundations of social energy and meaning-making took him outside of rational science. For Durkheim, the collective energy of religious experience is the core of social life. The rationalization of all spheres of life, including those core elements, in both secular institutions and in frozen religious institutions, produces the mechanical petrification elaborated by Weber. Religion provides a reciprocal flow of energy between individual and collective life. In its energy it is a creative social force. The experience of fusion and ecstasy, which is the essence of primitive religion, is a source for the renewal of society. In prophetic tone Durkheim asserts:

> The old gods are growing old or already dead....A day will come when our societies will know again those hours of creative effervescence, in the course of which new ideas arise and new formulae are found which serve...as a guide to humanity. (Durkheim [1915] 1965: 475)

For Durkheim, the religious experience of transcendence of fragmented individual consciousness which modernity has produced will inspire a social consciousness, and will aspire to 'higher justice' that existing formulae do not satisfy. Humanity through social action is capable of inventing 'new gospels' and 'orders of things social'.

Drawing a Durkheimian view to the current expressions of interest in religious sentiment, mystical experience and higher value seeking, which have typically been excluded from modern rationalized social practices and political conceptions, suggests an alternative interpretation of secularization. The neo-religious turn indicates a dialectical turn of resacralization, and of new designations of the sacred, in contemporary secularized society. The activities of unchurched spirituality seekers represent an impulse to recreate a social sphere of 'warmth' and creative energy in place of cold, 'deadened civilization'.

Contemporary iterations of the laicization of sacred and of religious expression – in both the formal theist traditions and of the atheist neo-religiosity of god-substitutes – represent an emancipation of individuals from both mechanical petrification and repressive traditions and communities. Deinstitutionalization generates diverse, plural arenas for signification and expression. The workplace, which under official modern aspirations was thoroughly rational, secular (and dispirited), is now another arena of resacralizing signification as well as individual identity expression. The electric, spiritualizing and alternative meaning-making practices currently evident in Western culture are brought to the workplace as 'effervescent' expressions, for Durkheim, of cultural resacralization. Employees in organizations exploring new sources, elements, and configurations of identity, meaning and value outside those of the conventionally modern, may utilize these resources to channel 'effervescent' energy into self and socially creative social practices. A restoration of domains of the sacred as a privileged domain and unassailable by totalizing, dedifferentiating technocratic rationalities is potentially a domain, not only of re-enchantment and play, but of resistance, freedom and cultural politics. The social relations of production in everyday life, if this effervescent, charismatic turn sparks collective appeal, may be transformed through a deep religio-cultural renewal.

Corporate organizations pursuing their conventional goals and maintaining strategically bureaucratic forms retain a tendency toward domination and governmentality. But the totality of these practices, as we have established, is by no means complete nor well defended against now diverse forces of contestation, including spirituality. The deepening malaise of industrial and postindustrial production recognized by traditional left critics as alienation, and by organizational leaders as disaffection, is a condition, and site, of conflict and re-creation. Employee efforts at re-enchantment are seeds of criticism which hold potential for transformation. The organizational interest in desecularization at work is an effort to rechannel disruptive, effervescent, energy (or 'holy sparks' in Wexler's 1996b metaphor) back toward rational organizational ends. But for employees seeking spiritual expressive practices in the workplace the interest is scarcely so singular. For some, of course, spiritualization may be added to an emotional attachment to the organization. A closer identification with the corporate organization may provide a stronger defence against uncertainty, ambivalence and anxiety. But for others, the effort to practise diverse or idiosyncratic spiritualities and to express alternative communalist self-identities represents a potentially disruptive and creative counter-practice. The corporate organizational move to utilize, manipulate, contain and incorporate emerging impulses and demands from dispirited, disaffected highly skilled employees manifests efforts to pre-empt the potential of these impulses – that are more widely evident in other social counter-practices such as communalism and fundamentalism – to more seriously disrupt the meta-rationality and exclusive humanism of capitalist production and economy.

Productivist-consumer society predicated on heightened individualistic interests and impulse also fuels demands for greater opportunities for other forms of self-interest, self-directedness and chosen relationality with others. That same heightened bourgeois individualism and self-interest may ironically propel a shift away from acceptance of instrumental and economic rationalities dominating cultural and social life. The new corporate benevolence, toleration and encouragement of religio-affective interests among employees is *both* a strategic neo-rationalist managerial response, and simultaneously a recognition of the limits and fragmentation of instrumental rationality. As my data shows, instrumentally rational organizations, separated from a realm of ends which are not defined solely in productivist terms, confront emergent tendencies – among, if not the proletariat, a demanding bourgeoisie – of new forms of social and organizational criticism.

As leaders of the business world already know,[3] the coming decades of the 21st century will be about consciousness. The information technology drive of recent decades must be superseded by the application of consciousness already being pursued by diverse New Age seekers and others of a mystical inclination. A growing number of people, it seems, are seeking self in ways unprescribed by either rationalizing modernity or received tradition. Against productivism, a movement for a liberatory alternative struggles to emerge.

On another level, the question of the apparent revival of paganism (and neo-gnostic expressions) in Western countries (after centuries of its repression and survival as a subordinate religious discourse) to which many of the new spiritual seekings refer, is sociologically interesting. In the first instance, the interest in paganism, especially evident in northern Europe, indicates the wide variety of historical and cultural resources available for reconstitution in self and social projects. A return to elemental sources of meaning-making and action, as Weber and Durkheim recognized, now being practised among unchurched and formally unreligious people, indicates a revival of primitive, or primal, religious sacralization. For many, it is a place to start. A neo-pagan rejection of modernity's desecration of earth gods finds a postmodern expression in contemporary deep ecology movements.

Toward Revitalization

Postindustrial, postmodern capitalist conditions generate new tensions, as well as heightening tensions which were relatively managed or contained under the cultural dominance of modernity. The expansion of rationalizing modernity achieved, as so many theorists have elaborated, modern systems of governmentality and normalization. Although always contested by some, detraditionalization and secularization won the modern day. Now, however, technological, hyper-modern society encounters new opposing impulses toward desecularization and recomposed traditions. Simultaneously disruptive of a monological rationalization and of established religious institutions, the criticisms and demands posed by the spiritual seekers at work indicate new potential sources of social revitalization. The organizational effort to capture and manage these impulses and demands through utilizing respiritualization for instrumental organizational goals continues a modern rationalization of traditional religious forms and the subjugation of their remnants. Moreover, it indicates the efforts of economic institutions to reinstitutionalize and normalize, just as traditional religious institutions have typically done, the 'charismatic movements' of change, renewal and subjective experience. The risk of unmanageability and disintegrative energy requires an institutional reintegrative response. As New Age explorers seek other-worldly realms of knowledge and meaning, expert scientific knowledge must compete with 'spiritual wisdom'.

Rationalizing modernity and its exhaustive utilization of all life forms and planetary resources for productivist consumptionist ends now meets a crisis beyond modernist or traditionalist opposition. Hyper (or post) modernity fragments modern social systems, and its advanced technologies effect a globalization of networks of information generation and exchange. In these conditions many sociologists and social theorists despair of possibilities for justice and participatory democratic life and see authoritarianism and extreme forms of social exclusion on the horizon. But as well as heightened individualism and invasive marketization, possibilities for new configurations of oppositional and demand-setting movements open up. Our reflexivity has exposed a one-sided modernity and found it gravely wanting. But our reflections have also drawn attention to subjugated emancipatory elements and currents of modernity. Among those currents, a heritage of Renaissance humanism (which was conceived as non-autonomous and relational)[4] is revealed and made available for recovery and as a resource. The dissolution of institutionalized practices of the sacred – of ultimate meaning and value – generates reconstitutive, resacralizing explorations. An effervescence stirred up by a fragmenting modernity arises between the fragments in ways rarely available under traditional and modern institutions favouring rigidity, repression and order, or – for opponents – revolution sweeping away all of the past. A growing disenchantment with the gods of modernity potentially heralds a revitalization of human social life which includes a renewed recognition of non-modern sensibilities and their possibilities.

Re-enchantment is an early first expression of an effort toward renegotiating and reconstituting ultimate values and cultural aspirations. A reconstitution of the realm of ends, of ultimate value, requires in a Durkheimian view, a recognition of the debasement of sacralization in rationalizing modernity. The elevation of instrumental rationality abstracted from substantive ends results in a debasement and elision of sacralization. Culturally establishing a differentiation between sacred and profane is, for Durkheim, a fundamental and enduring human practice. While a reassertion of differentiation restores dualism, it is not a dualism which insists on the modern autonomy of separate spheres. Rather, in Touraine's (1995) view, dualisms are constituent of a society conceived as dynamic social ensemble. The eclipse or implosion of these dualities results in either the hypertrophic dominance of one, as modernity achieved, or the dissolution of the possibilities enabled by their recognition and delimitation, as postmodern implosion portends. A revitalization of social relations does not require an erasure of boundaries but their dynamic reconstitution and a renewed attention to their possibility and limit, as Touraine (1995) and Melucci (1996) demonstrate.

Efforts toward a renewed constitution of sacred and profane – ultimate and ordinary – are evident in organizational life; in the sites where their dedifferentiation has been most evident. Once again, the nature of the cultural stakes by which society constitutes itself are struggled over. The commodified corporate mysticism now offered to employees after the corporate team-family indicates one aspect of this struggle. Most especially, it indicates a strategic response to the demand for soul-sensitive, spiritual values expressed by over-rationalized employees now newly contesting the ultimate values of productivism in organizational practice. While this strategic rational response continues to singularly privilege instrumental rationality and the commodification of human beings as economic resources with a flexible postmodern character, the spiritualized opposition among employees risks corruption by a productivist appropriation. The deliberate design of 'corporate mystics' exactly demonstrates that corruption.

Still, even as the corporate capture of a re-enchantment and spiritual turn makes these energies available for use by a strategic neo-rational management, such energies also defy manageability. Their unreasoned sources provide these actions with a potential for counter-practice which modern forms of political resistance do not grasp. Employees spiritually questioning the *modus operandi* of contemporary production organizations are using their dissident spiritualizing practices and 'charisma' toward new demand-setting in organizational life. Dissident spiritualization and resistance to subjectification and self-dissolution by hyper-capitalist technocratic instrumentality, now aided by selected postmodern cultural practices in organizations, is a new action in a contested field of forces in which organizations are formed and reformed.

But the impulses of re-enchantment, spiritualization and sacralization have another side. The revival of primitive religious expression (and debased forms of mysticism), and even the apparently harmless soul-seeking among the middle classes, might lead just as readily to fanatical repression and destruction as to emancipatory revitalization. The turn to spirituality practices carries potential for social good and bad. Unleashed religious or erotic energy may quickly turn to violence and destruction. The new actions fuelled by spiritual electricity, as Durkheim put it, may spark fundamentalism and fascist communalism in many forms. Vivid images of recent and present campaigns of systematically implemented policies born of collective irrationalities, from the Holocaust and 'ethnic cleansing' to armies of child soldiers and mass cult suicides, come all too readily to mind. When fanatical irrationalism joins with instrumental rationalities and technologies the results are spectacularly horrific.

Rapprochement

How might we respond to the fears and forces of totalitarianism and fanaticism of which we are well aware? Can these forces – which lurk in the shadows of rationalization as much as of religion – be limited or indeed overcome, after modernity's failure to do so starkly reminds? The charismatic turn to unchurched religion in order to resacralize and reconstitute ultimate, collective, values arises from a critical exhaustion with instrumental production and consumption rationalities. It indicates, as I have explained, a potentially creative, recomposing social force. For Weber, though, while recognizing religion as a source of social energy, a wariness of unrationalized experience cools a Durkheimian passionate interpretation. For Weber, famously concerned with the mechanical petrification of dispirited bureaucracy, charisma does indeed pose a counter-force to economic and instrumental rationality (a counter-force he sought despite his prognosis for modern industrial society). But Weber considered that the active turn to mysticism (which he noted in his own time) which charisma often inspires, leads to an inner-worldly asceticism which is hostile to economy. A quietism that does not act in the world of production waits for grace, and accepts the secular structure.

Weber did recognize, as Wexler points out, the tendency of mysticism to emphasize unity and ecstasy which 'contains an ethical demand...in the direction of universal brotherhood' (Weber cited in Wexler 1996b: 68), but this recognition did not inspire him to imagine a popular pursuit of 'religious brotherliness'. Instead, Weber thought there was little opportunity for such other-worldly pursuits for most people in everyday modern life, in which 'the vocational workaday life, asceticism's ghost, leaves hardly any room' for the cultivation of acosmic brotherhood' (ibid.). Those few able to pursue inner-worldly mysticism and contemplation may experience religious ecstasy, but more effectively, the spirit of religious asceticism – the secularization of Protestantism – fuels the rationalization and intellectualization of capitalist civilization.

Wexler, however, re-examines asceticism and mysticism. He poses very different possibilities for a socially aware mysticism. For Wexler, respiritualization practices are part of a 'much broader mass cultural tendency...toward inner worldly mysticism in the religious foundation of a new age' (1996b: 157). Wexler argues that Weber's inner-worldly ascetism as the cultural foundation of bureaucratized, rationalized modern society, is transmuting to an inner-worldly mystical orientation. This signifies a different outlook for the inner-worldly in which the private, quiet and ascetic inner-worldly turns to a contemplative and outward-looking orientation. It signals a cultural and social transformation. For Wexler, this emergent social ethic is generally integrated in the apparatus of postindustrial capitalism, as much of my data confirms. But the effects of this turn contest the cultural stakes from which society constitutes itself. A very different range of potential sociocultural movements and forces emerges on the cultural horizon.

A mysticism that is socially interested – unlike Weber's inner-worldly asceticism which eschews economy – for Wexler, 'goes beyond a symbolic reintegration of communities toward a socially transformative ethic' (ibid.: 157). A social, inner-worldly mysticism acts in the world from community building to ecology. Its demands in organizational productive practice may effect change negotiated with a management – which is one complex of actors with a set of demands – among other negotiating actors.

Yet notwithstanding Wexler's hopeful mysticism – a mysticism which may inspire a new cultural foundation for social transformation – the risks of religious or erotic fanaticism and the appeal of asceticism in its rationalized intensification remain. Modernity's long history of tendencies to debase rationality into instrumentalism and culture into identity, as Touraine argues, render the risks associated with wild religion, and its communalist tendency, considerable. In order to avoid the risks of fanaticism and rational productivism, the heightened consciousness of religious subjectivity needs to find a *rapprochement* with rationality in ways that harness these forces for social generativity.

For Touraine, the only possible recourse against rational destructiveness, repression and fanaticism is the idea of the subject. Even as so many critical intellectuals from the Frankfurt School onwards have rejected an idea of the subject, for its identification with reason and normalization, I draw directly on Touraine (1995, 1996) to refute that idea. The subject must not, and cannot, be reduced to rationalization. Most importantly, the reduction of modernity to rationalization is mistaken: 'Modernity has two faces and they gaze at one another: *rationalization* and *subjectivation*' (Touraine 1995: 205). The concealed half of modernity brings 'the emergence of the human subject as freedom and creation' (ibid.). It is this subject who is able to act and to create. It is not a product of power, nor reduced to a rationally choosing economic agent, nor identity construct.

For Touraine (1996: 297), the subject is 'born of a double refusal'. 'The subject constitutes itself in and by a dual conflict – a conflict with communalization on the one hand, and the instrumentalization of personal and collective life on the other.' The subject-actor is formed in a struggle against rationality degraded to instrumentalism, and against communal totalitarianism. The process of subjectivation – by which one becomes a subject – is achieved through 'an individual's will to act and to be recognized as an actor' (Touraine 1995: 207). Subject-actors construct personal self-projects through the events of their lives and strive to create spaces for autonomy and freedom. Even as the individual constructs its individuation against the world of commodities and the world of community, it succeeds in its individuation as it unites instrumental rationality and collective identity. Touraine's subject and its process of *subjectivation* is clearly differentiated from *subjectification*, which is at the heart of Foucault's criticism of the subject; and from naive individualism that does not recognize social determinants or that dissolves the subject into the rationality of economic choices. For Touraine, the subject is always a 'dissident' idea. It is an ethical demand which enables us to resist authoritarian and unjust power.

The subject-actor we now conceive, following Touraine, is a far cry from the subject as reason, as economically rational actor or as communalist identification. But, importantly, I want to propose, this creative acting subject, which is not reason, does not refuse the mystical elements of subjectivation. Indeed, these elements may heighten individual and historical consciousness and appeal to a conscience opposing authoritarian powers. It is the subject which must ensure that religion in a recomposed society becomes not a communitarian bond, or neo-traditionalist repression, but an appeal to consciousness, and Erasmian criticism.

Although there is much disputation in feminist thought on the idea of the subject, many feminists similarly call for a recomposition of the world through the action of relational, attached subjects. They call for a reconciliation between reason and affect, including spirit and eros, and a creative, emancipatory departure from the masculinist dualism in which these categories are rendered oppositional and unequal. This oppositional dualism is still widely upheld in social thought even as postindustrial society reveals its redundancy. Nancy Fraser's (1997: 5) advocacy of a critical theory that is 'bivalent', which integrates the social and the cultural, the economic and the discursive, still maintains a differentiation. But it is a conciliatory dualism, in my reading, which allows a recognition of difference that is not designated a priori but which may also be institutionally determinant. Subject-actors and social institutions constitute a dynamic social field in which antagonism and struggle, cooperation and solidarity, recompose the world.

The current of spiritual explorations, and the criticism and demands made according to those interests, among organizational employees, reveals, I propose, signs of persons striving for subjectivation. Their efforts of soul-seeking, spirituality and sensual re-enchantments are efforts toward freedom. These various expressions of self-creation, which include attention to spiritual and bodily well-being and personal development, and which oppose monological rationalization, seek simultaneously new significations of value ends. In this sense, their elements of individualism and narcissism may be drawn toward the necessarily collective action of resacralization – of ultimate value setting. A most remarkable aspect of this turn to spiritual self-pursuits, which are part of a wider cultural turn, is that they are being expressed and demanded in the world of organizational work – a world in which dominant elites, most famously since Taylorism, and productivist ideologies have prohibited creative and personal interests divergent from instrumentally rational ends. The presence of these new spiritual oppositions and demands, and the strategic managerial response, manifest postindustrial dynamics of strategy, struggle and cultural possibility. They clearly show the crisis in instrumental rationalities in practice, as they do the redundancy of lingering functionalist ideological images of society and organization.

Identity appeals and individual expressivism constitute a social struggle, at least in their defensive character. But for these actions to become a politically effective, socially recomposing, social movement they must move beyond defensive particularism of individualized interests, assertions of difference, or other-worldly mysticism. The social calls outlined in both Wexler's socially interested mysticism, or Touraine's 'labor of democracy', are necessarily accomplishments of subjects reaching beyond their subjective spiritual experiential interests and the narcissism attendant on neophytes or communalists. The subject's social task, which is also the subject's personal task, is the call to act to recompose the world in which both extremes of rationalization, including hyper-individualism, and communalism are resisted. A recomposition on the basis of a combination between instrumentality and identity demands both an ethic of recognition of other subjects and responsibility for the conditions of subjectivation. This demand of the subject is a moral one.

As the philosophers Ricoeur and Levinas (and Buber before them) respectively theorize, the subject-self is a relational one. It requires the recognition of the other to be itself. For Ricoeur, 'otherness is constitutive of selfhood. Oneself as Another suggests…that the selfhood of oneself implies otherness to such an intimate degree that one cannot be thought of without the other…that one passes into the other' (Ricoeur 1992: 3). For Levinas, an intersubjective relationship of love or friendship and an 'ethic of a priori responsibility' (1996) constitute self–other relations. Recognizing the other, and hence all others, as subjects requires, for Levinas, a reciprocal respect for institutional rules which guarantee the right of each to become and act as subject.

Unchurched spiritualization and resacralization is simultaneously an expression of protest and opposition to both the institutional religion of church and temple, and to reified instrumental rationality. As practised in organizational life, these oppositional actions are also rapidly strengthening into demand-setting movements of cultural change and social recomposition. Subjectivation must constantly be alert to the twin tendencies by which it is shadowed: toward debasement of its drive for freedom and its drive for relational identity. Ricoeur and Levinas' mystical ethics of love and social responsibility, as non-modern as they are, hold a key to the revitalization the New Age protesters seek.

The spiritual, soul-seeking movement among many organizational employees encounters some resistance in production organizations. But the resistance and derision these interests would have faced only a decade ago have, in my observation, presented only weakly. Conversely, organizational leaders show a remarkable openness to these possibilities of change, even as they reveal the organization's vulnerability in the field of culturally contested relations from which organizational relationships are socially composed. In some instances the absence of designated leaders or gurus among many New Age seekers at work and the counter-institutional character of many of these activities, thus far, render their appearance somewhat innocuous or their practitioners individually negotiable. But there are worrying signs too of communalist movements with strong neo-traditional leaders politically mobilizing identity aspirations around the globe. My very general observations of these latter matters require empirical substantiation and closer analytic interpretation beyond what I have attempted here.

But from my data among individual seekers of this new spiritualized criticism of organizational life, there appear some elements of a *rapprochement* between subjugated emancipatory elements of modernity – of relational selves – and, after the postmodern breaking up of modernity's dominant technologized rationalities, a recomposed substantive rationality. In organizations the changes sought by spiritual-seeking employees, in my observation, are not the destructive revolutionary calls of an earlier modern social movement. These spiritual seekers speak of ethical practices and new relations between self and other, of ecological relations between humans and other life forms on the planet we share. Emerging ethical subject-actors resisting the excess of instrumental rationalities, and fundamentalist religious, ethnic and communalist fanaticism, act to bring about a revitalization and recomposition of the world.

I have offered in this book a reflexive sociology and a critical analysis of organizations from their representation in modern discourses to their postmodern dispersion, and now beyond. Following Touraine, my sociology proposes a reorientation of social analysis of organizations away from a concept of system or of strategic action, to one which sees the social ensemble as an arena of contest, movement and historicity. This conception casts a new light on organizational practices. It recognizes that even as organizations do form complex systems of production, they do so in a context of dynamic forces of actors and institutions. A new view of social movement brings to light new actors, *postindustrial* actors, who are people making their lives in, and against, the world of organizational work. Actors who are both – yet never completely – rational and relationally attached – to identity, spirit, affect, eros and other – labour and create in the context of social institutions other historical actors have put in place. In taking seriously the manifest efforts of many workers in contemporary organizations in the West to explore cultural rudiments and possibilities beyond rationalizing modernity and productivism, I invite their consideration as resources for self and social transformation which modern social science and organizational practices have precluded or repressed. Reading them as neither neurotically desperate delusions nor as already incorporated weak politics, I see these activities on the shop floor as efforts to criticize, revitalize and transform. A critical analysis of organizations following and interpreting existing social struggles in always conflictual and dynamic social fields, encourages a rethinking and recomposition of organizations, and of critical social analysis and practice more generally.

Notes

1. Simmel, too, developed a thesis along these lines, and Weber himself showed much evidence of neither welcoming the trajectory of modern societal rationalization, nor of accepting its intractable inevitability and total disenchantment. See Weber [1904–05] 1958, [1918] 1989.

2. Laicization is used in this text to refer to practices in which established ecclesiastical orders and officers have been withdrawn and dispersed and in which 'lay' and 'unchurched' persons variously retain, appropriate or reconstruct formerly clericalized rites and knowledges of the sacred.

3. Martin Rutte, United-States-based organizational consultant and author, reported at a Spirit at Work conference in New Zealand (October 2000) that a McKinsey and Co. executive participating in the Mexico Business and Consciousness Conference in 1999 expressed his view that 'the coming decades of the 21st century will be about consciousness'. The information technology drive of recent decades must be superseded by the application of consciousness, the executive announced. Business organizations must capture the movement toward consciousness presenting in gatherings such as the Mexico conference.

4. Importantly, Charles Taylor and Stephen Toulmin, for instance, emphasize the importance of the Erasmian tradition in Renaissance humanism. Toulmin (1990: 23–25) points out that the humane, relational and religious humanism of Erasmus and Montaigne was rejected in the counter-Renaissance that prevailed in the modernity we know. Taylor argues that the Erasmian tradition was 'still alive and fighting' (1989: 249) even as the 17th century was dominated by the rise of empiricism. For the Erasmians, 'the spirit of true Religion is of a more free, noble, ingenuous and generous nature...it thaws all frozen affections...makes the soul... free' (ibid.).

References

Adorno, Theodor (1950) *The Authoritarian Personality*, New York: Harper.

Aglietta, Michel (1979) *A Theory of Capitalist Regulation – The United States Experience*, London: New Left Books.

Alexander, Jeffrey C. (ed.) (1988) *Durkheimian Sociology and Cultural Studies*, New York: Cambridge University Press.

Althusser, Louis (1970) *For Marx*, New York: Vintage Books.

Althusser, Louis and Balibar, Etienne (1970) *Reading Capital*, trans. Ben Brewster), London: New Left Books.

Alvesson, Mats (1990) 'Organization: From Substance to Image', *Organization Studies*, 11(3): 373–394.

Alvesson, Mats (1993) *Cultural Perspectives on Organisations*, Cambridge: Cambridge University Press.

Alvesson, Mats and Billing, Yvonne (1997) *Understanding Gender and Organizations*, London: Sage.

Alvesson, Mats and Deetz, Stanley (1996) 'Critical Theory and Postmodernism Approaches to Organizational Studies', in Clegg, S., Hardy, C. and Nord, W. (eds), *Handbook of Organization Studies*, London: Sage.

Alvesson, Mats and Willmott, Hugh (eds) (1992) *Critical Management Studies*, London: Sage.

Anderson, Perry (1976) *Considerations on Western Marxism*, London: New Left Books.

Anderson, Perry (1998) *The Origins of Postmodernity*, London and New York: Verso.

Ansley, Bruce (2000) 'Just the Job', *Listener*, 29 January: 16–20.

Arato, Andrew and Gebhardt, Eike (1982) *The Essential Frankfurt School Reader*, New York: Continuum.

Aron, Raymond (1967a) *Main Currents in Sociological Thought 1: Comte, Montesquieu, Marx, Tocqueville*, Harmondsworth, UK: Penguin Books.

Aron, Raymond (1967b) *Main Currents in Sociological Thought 2: Pareto, Weber, Durkheim*, Harmondsworth, UK: Penguin Books.

Aronowitz, Stanley (1981) *The Crisis in Historical Materialism*, New York: Praeger.

Aronowitz, Stanley and DiFazio, William (1994) *The Jobless Future*, Minneapolis: University of Minnesota Press.

Baldamus, W. (1961) *Efficiency and Effort*, London: Tavistock.

Baran, Paul and Sweezy, Paul (1966) *Monopoly Capital*, New York: Free Press.

Barker, J.R. (1993) 'Tightening the Iron Cage: Concertive Control in Self-managing Teams', *Administrative Science Quarterly*, 38: 408–437.

Barnard, Chester [1938] (1964) *The Functions of the Executive*, Cambridge, MA: Harvard University Press.

Barrett, Richard (1998) *Liberating the Corporate Soul: Building a Visionary Organization*, Boston, MA: Butterworth-Heinemann.

Barry, D. and Elmes, M. (1997) 'Strategy Retold: Toward a Narrative View of Strategic Discourse', *Academy of Management Review*, 22 (2): 429–452.

Baudrillard, Jean (1975) *The Mirror of Production*, St Louis: Telos Press.

Baudrillard, Jean [1977] (1987) *Oblier Foucault*, New York: Semiotext.

Baudrillard, Jean [1981] (1988) 'For a Critique of the Political Economy of the Sign', in Poster, Mark (ed.) *Jean Baudrillard: Selected Writings*, Stanford, CA: Stanford University Press.

Baudrillard, Jean (1983) *Simulations*, New York: Semiotext(e).

Baum, Howell S. (1987) *The Invisible Bureaucracy*, New York: Oxford University Press.

Bauman, Zygmunt (1991) *Modernity and Ambivalence*, Cambridge: Polity Press.

Bauman, Zygmunt (1992) *Intimations of Postmodernity*, London: Routledge.

Bauman, Zygmunt (1993) *Postmodern Ethics*, London: Routledge.

Bauman, Zygmunt (1997) *Postmodernity and its Discontents*, New York: New York University Press.

Beck, Ulrich (1992) *Risk Society: Toward a New Modernity*, London: Sage.

Beck, Ulrich (1997) *The Reinvention of Politics: Rethinking Modernity in the Global Social Order*, trans. Mark Ritter, Cambridge: Polity Press.

Beck, Ulrich (2000) *The Brave New World of Work*, trans. Patrick Camiller, Cambridge: Polity Press.

Beck, U., Giddens, A. and Lash, S. (1994) *Reflexive Modernization: Politics, Tradition and Aesthetics in the Modern Social Order*, Stanford, CA: Stanford University Press.

Bell, Daniel (1976) *The Cultural Contradictions of Capitalism*, New York: Basic Books.

Bellah, Robert (ed.) (1973) *Emile Durkheim: on Morality and Society*, Chicago: University of Chicago Press.

Bellah, Robert, Madsen, R., Sullivan, W.M., Swidler, A. and Tipton, S.M. (1996) *Habits of the Heart*, Berkeley, CA: University of California Press.

Bendix, Reinhard [1956] (1974) *Work and Authority in Industry*, Berkeley, CA: University of California Press.

Benhabib, Seyla and Cornell, Drucilla (eds) (1987) *Feminism as Critique*, Minneapolis: University of Minnesota Press.

Benhabib, Seyla, Butler, Judith, Cornell, Drucilla and Fraser, Nancy (1994) *Feminist Contentions: A Philosophical Exchange*, New York: Routledge.

Berger, Peter [1963] (1972) 'Invitation to Sociology: A Humanistic Perspective',selection reprinted in Glass, John F. and Staude, John R. (eds), *Humanistic Society: Today's Challenge to Sociology*, Pacific Palisades, CA: Goodyear.

Berger, P. and Neuhaus, R. (1970) *Movement and Revolution*, New York: Doubleday Anchor.

Best, Steven and Kellner, Douglas (1997) *The Postmodern Turn*, New York: Guilford Press.

Bittner, E. (1967) 'The Police on Skid Row: A Study of Peace Keeping', *American Sociological Review*, 32(5): 699–715.

Black, M. (ed.) (1961) *The Social Theories of Talcott Parsons*, Englewood Cliffs, NJ: Prentice-Hall.

Blau, Peter (1955) *The Dynamics of Bureaucracy*, Chicago: University of Chicago Press.

Blau, P. and Scott, W.R. (1962) *Formal Organizations*, San Francisco, CA: Chandler.

Blauner, R. (1964) *Alienation, Freedom and Technology*, Chicago: University of Chicago Press.

Block, Fred (1990) *Postindustrial Possibilities: A Critique of Economic Discourse*, Berkeley, CA: University of California Press.

Boje, M. David (1995) 'Stories of the Story-telling Organization: A Postmodern Analysis of Disney as "Tamara-land"', *Academy of Management Journal*, 38(4): 997–1035.

Boje, M. David, Gephard, Robert P. and Thatchenkery, T.J. (eds) (1996) *Postmodern Management and Organization Theory*, London: Sage.

Bottomore, T.B. (ed.) (1964) *Karl Marx: Early Writings*, New York: McGraw-Hill.

Bottomore, T.B. (1975) *Sociology as Social Criticism*, London: Allen and Unwin.

Boulding, Kenneth (1966) *The Impact of the Social Sciences*, New Brunswick, NJ: Rutgers University Press.

Bourdieu, Pierre (1977) *Outline of a Theory of Action*, Cambridge: Cambridge University Press.

Bourdieu, Pierre (1988) *Homo Academicus*, trans. by Peter Collier, Stanford, CA: Stanford University Press.

Bourdieu, Pierre (1992) *An Invitation to Reflexive Sociology*, Cambridge: Polity Press.

Braverman, H. (1974) *Labor and Monopoly Capitalism*, New York: Monthly Review Press.

Brech, E. (1948) *Organization: The Framework of Management*, New York: Collier Macmillan.

Briskin, Alan (1996) *The Stirring of Soul at Work*, San Francisco: Jossey-Bass.

Brown, J.A.C. (1954) *The Social Psychology of Industry*, New York: Viking Penguin.

Brown, R.H. (1989) *Social Science as Civic Discourse*, Chicago: University of Chicago Press.

Brown, Richard Harvey (1995) *Postmodern Representations: Truth, Power, and Mimesis in the Human Sciences and Public Culture*, Urbana: University of Illinois Press.

Burawoy, Michael (1985) *The Politics of Production*, New York: Verso.

Burrell, Gibson (1988) 'Modernism, Postmodernism and Organizational Analysis 2: The Contribution of Michel Foucault', *Organization Studies*, 9(2): 221–235.

Burrell, Gibson (1993) 'Eco and the Bunnyman', in Hassard, John and Parker, Martin (eds), *Postmodernism and Organizations*, London: Sage.

Burrell, Gibson (1997) *Pandemonium: Toward a Retro Organization Theory*, London: Sage.

Burrell, Gibson and Morgan, Gareth (1979) *Sociological Paradigms and Organisational Analysis: Elements of the Sociology of Corporate Life*, London: Heinemann.

Butler, Judith (1990) *Gender Trouble: Feminism and the Subversion of Identity*, New York: Routledge.

Calas, Marta B. and Smircich, Linda (1992) 'Rewriting Gender into Organizational Theorizing: Directions from Feminist Perspectives', in Reed, Mike and Hughes, Mike (eds), *Rethinking Organization*, London: Sage.

Calas, Marta B. and Smircich, Linda (1996) 'From the Women's Point of View: Feminist Approaches to Organization Studies', in Clegg, Stewart R., Hardy, Cynthia and Nord, Walter R. (eds), *Handbook of Organization Studies*, London: Sage.

Calhoun, Craig (ed.) (1994) *Social Theory and the Politics of Identity*, Oxford UK and Cambridge, MA: Blackwell.

Calhoun, Craig (1995) *Critical Social Theory: Culture, History, and the Challenge of Difference*, Oxford, UK and Cambridge, MA: Blackwell.

Callinicos, A. (1989) *Against Postmodernism: A Marxist Critique*, Cambridge: Polity Press.

Canfield, J. and Millar, J. (1996) *Heart at Work*, New York: McGraw-Hill.

Canfield, J., Hansen, M. V., Rogerson, M., Rutte, M. and Claus, T. (1999) *Chicken Soup for the Soul at Work*, Deerfield, FL: Health Communications.

Caplow, Theodore (1964) *Principles of Organization*, New York: Harcourt Brace.

Carey, A. (1965) 'The Hawthorne Studies: a Radical Criticism', *American Sociological Review*, 32: 403–416.

Carr, Adrian (1998) 'Identity, Compliance and Dissent in Organizations: A Psychoanalytic Perspective', *Organization*, 5(1): 81–99.

Casey, Catherine (1995) *Work, Self and Society: After Industrialism*, London and New York: Routledge.

Casey, Catherine (2000) 'Work, Non-Work, and Re-Sacralizing Self', *Social Compass*, 47(4): 571–587.

Castells, Manuel (1996) *The Rise of the Network Society (The Information Age: Economy, Society and Culture Vol. 1)*, Oxford: Blackwell.

Castells, Manuel (1997) *The Power of Identity: The Rise of the Network Society (The Information Age: Economy, Society and Culture Vol. 2)*, Oxford: Blackwell.

Castells, Manuel (1998) *End of Millennium: The Rise of the Network Society (The Information Age: Economy, Society and Culture Vol. 3)*, Oxford: Blackwell.

Caudron, Shari (1996) 'Downshifting Yourself', *Industry Week*, 245(10): 126–130.

Child, John (ed.) (1973) *Man and Organization*, London: Allen and Unwin.

Chomsky, Noam (1969) *American Power and the New Mandarins*, New York: Penguin.

Cicourel, A.V. (1964) *Methods and Measurement in Sociology*, New York: Free Press.

Clegg, Stewart (1975) *Power, Rule and Domination*, London: Routledge and Kegan Paul.

Clegg, Stewart (1990) *Modern Organizations: Organization Studies in the Postmodern World*, London: Sage.

Clegg, Stewart R. and Dunkerley, D. (1980) *Organization, Class and Control*, London: Routledge and Kegan Paul.

Clegg, Stewart R., Hardy, Cynthia and Nord, Walter R. (eds) (1996) *Handbook of Organization Studies*, London: Sage.

Cohen, Percy (1968) *Modern Social Theory*, London: Heinemann.

Comte, Auguste [1855] (1974) *The Positive Philosophy*, trans. and ed. Harriet Martineau, New York: AMS Press.

Cooper, R. (1989) 'Modernism, Postmodernism and Organizational Analysis 3: The Case of Jacques Derrida', *Organization Studies*, 10(4): 479–502.

Cooper, R. and Burrell, G. (1988) 'Modernism, Postmodernism and Organizational Analysis', *Organization Studies*, 9(1): 91–112.

Coser, Lewis A. (1956) *The Functions of Social Conflict*, London: Routledge.

Crozier, Michael (1964) *The Bureaucratic Phenomenon*, Chicago: University of Chicago Press.

Csordas, Thomas, J. (ed.) (1994) *Embodiment and Experience: The Existential Ground of Culture and Self*, Cambridge: Cambridge University Press.

Culler, Jonathan (1979) 'Jacques Derrida', in Surrock, John (ed.), *Structuralism and Since: From Lévi-Strauss to Derrida*, Oxford: Oxford University Press.

Czarniawska-Joerges, Barbara (1996) *Narrating the Organization: Dramas of Institutional Identity*, Chicago: University of Chicago Press.

Czarniawska, Barbara (1998) 'Who is Afraid of Incommensurability', *Organization*, 5(2): 273–275.

Daft, Richard (1996) *Organization Theory and Design*, Minneapolis, MI: West.

Dahrendorf, Ralph (1959) *Class and Class Conflict in Industrial Society*, London: Routledge.

Darwin, Charles [1859] (1968) *The Origin of the Species* edited by J. W. Burrow, Harmondswort, UK: Penguin.

de Gues, Arie (1997) *The Living Company*, Boston, MA: Harvard Business School.

Deleuze, Gilles and Guattari, Felix (1986) *Nomadology*, New York: Semiotext(e).

Derrida, Jacques [1972] (1982) *Positions*, Chicago: University of Chicago Press.

Derrida, Jacques (1978) *Writing and Difference*, London and New York: Routledge.

Derrida, Jacques (1994) *Spectres of Marx*, London and New York: Routledge.

Diamond, Irene and Quinby, Lee (eds) (1988) *Foucault and Feminism: Reflections on Resistance*, Boston, MA: Northeastern University Press.

Donaldson, Lex (1985) *In Defence of Organization Theory*, Cambridge: Cambridge University Press.

Donaldson, Lex (1995) *Anti-management American Theories of Organization*, Cambridge: Cambridge University Press.

Donaldson, Lex (1998) 'The Myth of Paradigm Incommensurability in Management Studies: Comments by an Integrationist', *Organization*, 5(2): 267–272.

Drucker, P. [1946] (1960) *The Concept of the Corporation*, Boston, MA: Beacon Press.

Drucker, Peter (1993) *Post-Capitalist Society*, New York: Harper Collins.

du Gay, Paul (1996) *Consumption and Identity at Work*, London: Sage.

du Gay, Paul (2000) *In Praise of Bureaucracy*, London: Sage.

Durkheim, Emile [1893] (1964) *The Division of Labour in Society* (introduction by Lewis Coser), New York: Free Press.

Durkheim, Emile (ed.) [1895] (1972) *The Rules of the Sociological Method*: extracts in Giddens, Anthony, *Durkheim: Selected Writings*, Cambridge and New York: Cambridge University Press.

Durkheim, Emile [1915] (1965) *The Elementary Forms of Religious Life*, trans. J.W. Swain, New York: Free Press.

Edwards, Richard (1979) *Contested Terrain*, New York: Basic Books.

Eggertsson, T. (1990) *Economic Behaviour and Institutions*, Cambridge: Cambridge University Press.

Ehrenreich, Barbara (1995) 'In Search of a Simpler Life', *Working Woman*, 20(12): 26–29.

Eisenstadt, S.N. and Curelaru, M. (1976) *The Forms of Sociology: Paradigms and Crises*, New York: Wiley.

Eisenstein, Hester (1983) *Contemporary Feminist Thought*, Boston, MA: G.K. Hall.

Eldridge, J.E.T. (1971) *Sociology and Industrial Life*, London: Nelson.

Eldridge, J.E.T. and Crombie, A.D. (1974) *A Sociology of Organizations*, London: Allen and Unwin.

Emery, F. and Trist, E. (1960) 'Socio Technical Systems', *Management Sciences Models and Techniques*, 5: 83–91.

Epstein, Cynthia Fuchs (1970) *Woman's Place: Options and Limits in Women's Careers*, Berkeley, CA: University of California Press.

Etzioni, Amitai (1968) *The Active Society*, New York: Free Press.

Etzioni, Amatai (ed.) (1970) *Complex Organizations: A Sociological Reader*, New York: Holt, Rinehart and Winston.

Etzioni, Amatai (1975) *A Comparative Analysis of Complex Organizations*, New York: Free Press.

Etzioni, Amitai (1994) *The Spirit of Community: the Reinvention of American Society*, New York: Simon and Schuster.

Feibleman, J. and Friend, J.W. (1969) 'The Structure and Function of Organization', in Emery, F.E. (ed.), *Systems Thinking*, New York: Penguin. pp. 30–55.

Ferguson, Kathy (1984) *The Feminist Case against Bureaucracy*, Philadelphia: Temple University Press.

Fineman, Stephen (ed.) (1993) *Emotion in Organizations*, London: Sage.

Fineman, Stephen and Gabriel, Yiannis (1996) *Experiencing Organizations*, London: Sage.

Fischer, F. and Siriani, C. (1994) *Critical Studies in Organization and Bureaucracy*, Philadelphia: Temple University Press.

Flax, Jane (1989) 'Postmodernism and Gender Relations in Feminist Theory', in Mason, Micheline, O'Barr, Jean, Westphal-Wihl, Sara and Myer, Mary (eds),

Feminist Theory in Practice and Process, Chicago: University of Chicago Press.

Foster, Hal (ed.) (1985) *Postmodern Culture*, London: Pluto Press.

Foucault, Michel (1972) *The Archaeology of Knowledge*, London: Tavistock.

Foucault, Michel (1973) *The Order of Things*, New York: Vintage Books.

Foucault, Michel (1975) *Discipline and Punish: The Birth of the Prison*, New York: Vintage Books.

Foucault, Michel (1980a) *Power/Knowledge: Selected Interviews and Other Writings 1972–1977*, ed. Colin Gordon, New York: Pantheon.

Foucault, Michel (1980b) 'Two Lectures', in *Power/Knowledge*.

Foucault, Michel (1980c) 'The History of Sexuality', in *Power/Knowledge*.

Foucault, Michel (1980d) 'Power and Strategies', in *Power/Knowledge*.

Foucault, Michel (1980e) 'Body/Power', in *Power/Knowledge*.

Foucault, Michel (1983) 'Preface' to Deleuze, Gilles and Guattari, Felix, *Anti-Oedipus: Capitalism and Schizophrenia*, London: Athlone Press.

Foucault, Michel (1988a) *Care of the Self: The History of Sexuality, Vol. 3*, trans. Robert Hurley, New York: Vintage Books.

Foucault, Michel (1988b) *Technologies of the Self*, ed. L. Martin, H. Gutman and P. Hutton, Amherst: University of Massachusetts Press.

Fox, Alan (1971) *Industrial Sociology and Industrial Relations*, London: Colin Macmillan.

Fox, Mary Frank and Hesse-Biber, Sharlene (1984) *Women at Work*, Palo Alto, CA: Mayfield.

Fraser, Nancy (1989) *Unruly Practices: Power, Discourse, and Gender in Contemporary Social Theory*, Minneapolis: University of Minnesota Press.

Fraser, Nancy (1997) *Justice Interruptus: Critical Reflections on the 'Post-socialist' Condition*, New York and London: Routledge.

Freud, Sigmund [1922] (1973) 'Beyond the Pleasure Principle', in *Standard Edition of the Complete Psychological Works of Sigmund Freud*, Vol. XVIII, London: Hogarth Press.

Friedman, Andrew (1977) *Industry and Labour*, London: Macmillan.

Friedmann, G. (1955) *Industrial Society*, New York: Free Press.

Fromm, Erich [1941] (1965) *Escape from Freedom*, New York: Farrar and Rinehart.

Fromm, Erich (1955) *The Sane Society*, New York: Holt, Rinehart and Winston.

Fromm, Erich (1961) *Man for Himself*, New York: Holt, Rinehart and Winston.

Fromm, Erich (1964) 'Foreword' to Bottomore, T.B. (ed.), *Karl Marx: Early Writings*, New York: McGraw-Hill.

Fuss, Diana (1989) *Essentially Speaking: Feminism, Nature and Difference*, New York: Routledge.

Gabriel, Yiannis (1991) 'Organizations and their Discontents: a Psychoanalytic Contribution to the Study of Corporate Culture', *Journal of Applied Behavioural Science*, 27: 318–336.

Gabriel, Yiannis (2000) *Storytelling in Organizations*, Oxford: Oxford University Press.

Gane, Mike (ed.) (1986) *Towards a Critique of Foucault*, New York: Routledge and Kegan Paul.

Gane, Mike (1991) *Baudrillard: Critical and Fatal Theory*, London: Routledge.

Gane, Mike (ed.) (1992) *The Radical Sociology of Durkheim and Mauss*, London: Routledge.

Gane, Mike (ed.) (1993) *Baudrillard Live: Selected Interviews*, London: Routledge.

Gardner, B. (1945) *Human Relations in Industry*, Chicago: R.P. Irwin, Inc.

Garson, Barbara (1988) *The Electronic Sweatshop: How Computers are Transforming the Office of the Future into the Factory of the Past*, New York: Simon and Schuster.

Gephart, Robert (1996) 'Management, Social Issues, and the Postmodern Era', in Boje, M. David, Gephard, Robert P. and Thatchenkery, T.J. (eds), *Postmodern Management and Organization Theory*, London: Sage.

Gergen, Kenneth (1992) 'Organization Theory in the Postmodern Era', in Reed, Michael and Hughes, Michael (eds), *Rethinking Organizations: New Directions in Organizational Analysis*, London: Sage.

Giddens, Anthony (ed.) (1972) *Emile Durkheim: Selected Writings*, Cambridge and New York: Cambridge University Press.

Giddens, Anthony (1973) *The Class Structure of the Advanced Societies*, London: Hutchinson.

Giddens, Anthony (1976) 'Introduction' to Weber, Max (1958) *The Protestant Ethic and The Spirit of Capitalism*, New York: Scribner.

Giddens, Anthony (1982) *Profiles and Critiques in Social Theory*, London: Macmillan Press.

Giddens, Anthony (1996) *In Defence of Sociology: Essays, Interpretation and Rejoinders*, Cambridge: Cambridge University Press.

Glass, John F. and Staude, John R. (eds) (1972) *Humanistic Society: Today's Challenge to Sociology*, Pacific Palisades, CA: Goodyear.

Goffman, Erving (1959) *The Presentation of Self in Everyday Life*, New York: Doubleday.

Goffman, Erving (1967) *Interaction Ritual*, New York: Doubleday Anchor.

Goldthorpe, J.H. (1968) *The Affluent Worker: Industrial Attitudes and Behaviour*, Cambridge: Cambridge University Press.

Gorz, André (1989) *Critique of Economic Reason*, London and New York: Verso.

Gorz, André (1999) *Reclaiming Work: Beyond the Wage-Based Society*, Cambridge: Polity Press.

Gouldner, Alvin (1954a) *Patterns of Industrial Bureaucracy*, New York: Free Press.

Gouldner, Alvin (1954b) *Wildcat Strike*, London: Routledge and Kegan Paul.

Gouldner, Alvin, W. (1959) 'Organizational Analysis', in Merton, K.A., Broom, L. and Cottrell, L. (eds), *Sociology Today*, New York: Basic Books. pp. 400–428.

Gouldner, Alvin W. (1970) *The Coming Crisis of Western Sociology*, London: Heinemann.

Gouldner, Alvin (1979) *The Future of Intellectuals and the Rise of the New Class*, New York: Seabury.

Gramsci, Antonio [1935] (1971) 'Americanism and Fordism', in *Selections from the Prison Notebooks of Antonio Gramsci*, ed. Quintin Hoare and Geoffrey Nowell Smith, London: Lawrence and Wishart.

Grant, David, Keenoy, Tom and Oswick, Cliff (eds) (1998) *Discourse and Organization*, London: Sage.

Habermas, Jürgen (1975) *Legitimation Crisis*, Boston, MA: Beacon Press.

Habermas, Jürgen (1981) 'Modernity versus Postmodernity', *New German Critique*, 22 Winter: 3–14.

Habermas, Jürgen (1984) *Knowledge and Human Interests* (trans. Jeremy Shapiro), Boston, MA: Beacon Press.

Habermas, Jürgen (1987) *The Philosophical Discourses of Modernity*, Boston, MA: MIT Press.

Hamilton, Peter (ed.) (1990) *Emile Durkheim: a Critical Assessment*, London: Routledge.

Handy, Charles (1997) *The Hungry Spirit: Beyond Capitalism – A Quest for Purpose in the Modern World*, London: Hutchinson.

Harding, Sandra (1986) *The Science Question in Feminism*, Ithaca, NY: Cornell University Press.

Harris, Jim (1996) *Getting Employees to Fall in Love with Your Company*, New York: Amacom.

Hartmann, Heidi (ed.) (1987) *Computer Chips and Paper Clips: Technology and Women's Employment*, Washington, DC: National Academy Press.

Hartsock, Nancy (1983) *Money, Sex, and Power*, New York: Longman.

Hartsock, Nancy (1990) 'Foucault on Power: A Theory for Women?' in Nicholson, Linda (ed.), *Feminism/Postmodernism*, New York: Routledge.

Harvey, David (1989) *The Condition of Postmodernity*, Oxford: Blackwell.

Hassard, John (1993) *Sociology and Organization Theory: Positivism, Paradigms, and Postmodernity*, Cambridge: Cambridge University Press.

Hassard, John and Parker, Martin (eds) (1993) *Postmodernism and Organizations*, London: Sage.

Hassard, John and Pym, D. (eds) (1994) *Towards a New Theory of Organizations*, London and New York: Routledge.

Hatch, Mary Jo (1997) *Organization Theory: Modern, Symbolic and Postmodern Perspectives*, New York: Oxford University Press.

Hearn, J., Sheppard, D.L., Tancred-Sheriff, P. and Burrell, G. (eds) (1989) *The Sexuality of Organization*, London: Sage.

Heelas, Paul (1996) *The New Age Movement*, Oxford: Blackwell.

Held, David (1980) *Introduction to Critical Theory: Horkheimer to Habermas*, Berkeley, CA: University of California Press.

Hemple, Carl G. (1959) 'The Logic of Functional Analysis', in Gross, L. (ed.), *Symposium on Sociological Theory*, New York: Harper, pp. 271–302.

Hendricks, Gay and Ludeman, Kate (1997) *The Corporate Mystic*, New York: Bantam.

Hirschhorn, Larry (1988) *The Workplace Within: Psychodynamics of Organizational Life*, Cambridge, MA: MIT Press.

Hochschild, Arlie (1983) *The Managed Heart: Commercialization of Human Feeling*, Berkeley, CA: University of California Press.

Hochschild, Arlie (1989) *The Second Shift*, New York: Avon Books.

Horkheimer, Max [1947] (1974) *Eclipse of Reason*, New York: Seabury Press.

Horkheimer, Max (1972) 'Authority and the Family', in *Critical Theory: Selected Essays*, New York: Continuum.

Horkheimer, Max (1972) 'Traditional and Critical Theory', in *Critical Theory: Selected Essays* (trans. Matthew J. O'Connell), New York: Herder and Herder.

Horkheimer, Max and Adorno, Theodor [1947] (1972) *The Dialectic of Enlightenment*, New York: Herder and Herder.

Horowitz, Irving (ed.) (1965) *The New Sociology: Essays in Social Science and Social Theory in Honor of C. Wright Mills*, New York: Oxford University Press.

Hughes, E.C. (1958) *Men and their Work*, Illinois: Free Press.

Huyssen, Andreas (1984) 'Mapping the Postmodern', *New German Critique*, 33: 5–52.

International Labour Organization (2000) *Mental Health in the Workplace Report*, Geneva: ILO.

Jaggar, Allison (1983) *Feminist Politics and Human Nature*, Totowa, NJ: Rowman and Allanheld.

Jameson, Fredric (1981) *The Political Unconscious*, New York: Cornell University Press.

Jameson, Fredric (1984a) 'The Politics of Theory: Ideological Positions in the Postmodern Debate', *New German Critique*, 32: 53–65.

Jameson, Fredric (1984b) 'Postmodernism, or the Cultural Logic of Late Capitalism', *New Left Review*, 146, July/August: 52–92.

Jaques, E. (1976) *A General Theory of Bureaucracy*, London: Heinemann.

Jermier, J., Knights, D. and Nord, W. (eds) (1994) *Resistance and Power in Organizations*, London: Routledge.

Jones, Gareth R. (1997) *Organizational Theory: Text and Cases*, Reading, MA: Addison-Wesley.

Kanter, Rosabeth Moss (1977) *Men and Women of the Corporation*, New York: Basic Books.

Kaye, Les (1996) *Zen at Work*, New York: Crown Trade Paperbacks.

Keller, Evelyn Fox (1984) *Reflections on Gender and Science*, New Haven, CT and London: Yale University Press.

Kellner, Douglas (1989a) *Jean Baudrillard: From Marxism to Postmodernism and Beyond*, Cambridge: Polity Press.

Kellner, Douglas (1989b) *Critical Theory, Marxism and Modernity*, Cambridge: Polity Press.

Kerr, Clark and Fisher, L.H. (1957) 'Plant Sociology: The Elite and the Aborigines', in Komarovsky, M. (ed.), *Common Frontiers in the Social Sciences*, Glencoe, IL: Free Press.

Kessler-Harris, Alice (1981) *Women Have Always Worked: An Historical Overview*, New York: Feminist Press.

King, Carol Soucek (1999) *Feng Shui at Work*, Glen Cove, NY: PBC International.

Knights, David (2000) 'Autonomy Retentiveness! Problems and Prospects for a Post-Humanist Feminism', *Journal of Management Inquiry*, 9(2): 173–185.

Knights, David and Willmott, Hugh (eds) (1986) *Gender and the Labour Process*, Aldershot: Gower Press.

Knights, David and Willmott, Hugh (eds) (1990) *Labour Process Theory*, London: Macmillan.

Kommarovsky, M. (ed.) (1957) *Common Frontiers of the Social Sciences*, Glencoe, IL: Free Press.

Kondo, Dorinne K. (1990) *Crafting Selves: Power, Gender and Discourse of Identity in a Japanese Workplace*, Chicago: University of Chicago Press.

Kristeva, Julian (1980) *Desire in Language: a Semiotic Approach to Literature and Art*, New York: Columbia University Press.

Kunda, Gideon (1992) *Engineering Culture: Control and Commitment in a High-Tech Corporation*, Philadelphia: Temple University Press.

Kundsen, Ruth B (ed.) (1974) *Women and Success: The Anatomy of Achievement*, New York: Morrow.

Laabs, Jennifer J. (1996) 'Downshifters: Workers are Scaling Back', *Personnel Journal*, 75(3): 62–76.

LaBier, Douglas (1986) *Modern Madness: The Hidden Link between Work and Emotional Life*, New York: Simon and Schuster.

Landsberger, H.A. (1958) *Hawthorne Revisited*, Ithaca, NY: Cornell University Press.

Lash, Scott (1999) *Another Modernity, a Different Rationality*, Oxford: Blackwell.

Lash, Scott and Urry, John (1987) *The End of Organized Capitalism*, Madison, WI: University of Wisconsin Press.

Lash, Scott and Urry, John (1994) *Economies of Space and Time*, London: Sage.

Latour, Bruno (1993) *We Have Never Been Modern*, Cambridge, MA: Harvard University Press.

Lawrence, P. and Lorsch, J. (1967) *Organization and Environment*, Cambridge, MA: Harvard University Press.

Lazarsfeld, P.F. and Thielens, W. (1958) *The Academic Mind: Social Scientists in a Time of Crisis*, Glencoe, IL: Free Press.

Lemert, Charles (1995) *Sociology after the Crisis*, Boulder, CO and Oxford, UK: Westview Press.

Lenin, Vladimir [1902] (1963) *What Is To Be Done?* Oxford: Clarendon Press.

Levinas, Emmanuel (1996) *Basic Philosophical Writings*, ed. Adriaan Peperzak, Simon Critchley and Robert Bernasconi, Bloomington, IN: Indiana University Press.

Levine, Donald, N. (1995) *Visions of the Sociological Tradition*, Chicago and London: University of Chicago Press.

Lewin, Roger and Regine, Birute (2000) *The Soul at Work*, New York: Simon and Schuster.

Lewis, James and Melton, J.G. (eds) (1992) *Perspectives on the New Age*, New York: State University of New York Press.

Lindley, David (1993) *The End of Physics*, New York: Basic Books.

Lipset, S.M., Trow, M.A. and Coleman, J.S. (1956) *Union Democracy*, Glencoe, IL: Free Press.

Litterer, Joseph (ed.) (1969) *Organizations: Structure and Behavior*, New York: Basic Books.

Littler, Craig (1982) *The Development of the Labour Process in Capitalist Societies*, London: Heinemann.

Lockwood, David (1956) 'Some Remarks on the "Social System"', *British Journal of Sociology*, 7(2): 134–145.

Lukács, Georg [1923] (1971) *History and Class Consciousness*, Cambridge, MA: MIT Press.

Luxemburg, Rosa [1904] (1972) 'The Role of the Organization in Revolutionary Activity', in Looker, R. (ed.), *Rosa Luxemburg, Selected Political Writings*, London: Jonathan Cape.

Lyotard, Jean-François (1984) *The Postmodern Condition: A Report on Knowledge*, Minneapolis: University of Minnesota Press.

Maccoby, Michael (1976) *The Gamesman*, New York: Simon and Schuster.

MacKinnon, Catherine (1979) *Sexual Harassment of Working Women*, New Haven, CT: Yale University Press.

MacKinnon, Virginia (1997) 'Working at Making Ends Meet: Formal Income and Informal Economy in a New Zealand Community', MA thesis, University of Auckland.

Mandel, Ernest (1978) *Late Capitalism*, London: Verso.

March, James G. (ed.) (1965) *Handbook of Organisations*, New York: Rand McNally.

March, J. and Simon, H.A. [1958] (1961) *Organizations*, Chichester: John Wiley.

Marcuse, Herbert (1962) *Eros and Civilization*, New York: Vintage Books.

Marcuse, Herbert (1965) *One-Dimensional Man*, New York: Abacus.

Martin, Joanne (1992) *Cultures in Organizations: Three Perspectives*, New York: Oxford University Press.

Marx, Karl [1844a] (1978) *The Economic and Philosophic Manuscripts of 1844*, in Tucker, Robert (ed.), *The Marx-Engels Reader*, New York: W.W. Norton.

Marx, Karl [1844b] (1978) 'Contribution to the Critique of Hegel's Theory of Right', in Tucker, Robert (ed.) *The Marx-Engels Reader*, New York: W.W. Norton.

Marx, Karl [1846] (1978) *The German Ideology*, in Tucker, Robert (ed.), *The Marx-Engels Reader*, New York: W.W. Norton.

Marx, Karl [1859] (1978) Preface to *A Contribution to the Critique of Political Economy*, in Tucker, Robert (ed.), *The Marx-Engels Reader*, New York: W.W. Norton.

Marx, Karl [1867] (1978) *Capital*, in Tucker, Robert (ed.) *The Marx-Engels Reader*, New York: W.W. Norton.

Maslow, A.H. (1968) *Toward a Psychology of Being*, New York: Von Nostrand.

Massie, J.L. (1965) 'Management Theory', in March, J. (ed.), *The Handbook of Organizations*, Chicago: Rand McNally.

Mayo, Elton (1933) *The Human Problems of an Industrial Civilisation*, New York: Macmillan.

McKinley, William and Mone, Mark (1998) 'The Re-construction of Organization Studies: Wrestling with Incommensurability', *Organization*, 5(2): 169–189.

Mead, George Herbert (1934) *Mind, Self, and Society*, Chicago and London: University of Chicago Press.

Melucci, Alberto (1996) *The Playing Self: Person and Meaning in the Planetary Society*, Cambridge: Cambridge University Press.

Merleau-Ponty, Maurice (1973) *Adventures of Dialectic*, Evanston, IL: Northwestern University Press.

Merton, Robert K. [1949] (1968) 'Manifest and Latent Functions', in *Social Theory and Structure*, New York: Free Press.

Merton, Robert K. (1959) 'Notes on Problem-Finding in Sociology', in Merton, R.K., Broom, L. and Cottrell, L.S. (eds), *Sociology Today*, New York: Basic Books.

Merton, Robert K. (1975) 'Structural Analysis in Sociology', in Blau, Peter M. (ed.), *Approaches to the Study of Social Structure*, New York: Free Press.

Michels, Robert [1915] (1958) *Political Parties*, New York: Free Press.

Miliband, Ralph (1977) *Marxism and Politics*, London: Oxford University Press.

Mill, John S. [1843] (1988) *The Logic of the Moral Sciences*, La Salle, IL: Open Court.

Mill, John S. [1861] (1976) *Utilitarianism, Liberty and Considerations on Representative Government*, London: J.M Dent.

Miller, E. and Rice, A.K. (1967) *Systems of Organization: The Control of Task and Sentient Systems*, London: Tavistock.

Mills, C. Wright (1956) *White Collar*, New York: Basic Books.

Mills, C. Wright (1959) *The Sociological Imagination*, New York: Oxford University Press.

Mills, Albert and Tancred, Peta (eds) (1992) *Gendering Organizational Analysis*, Newbury Park, CA: Sage.

Mitroff, Ian and Denton, Elizabeth (1999) *A Spiritual Audit of Corporate America*, San Francisco: Jossey-Bass.

Morgan, Gareth (1986) *Images of Organization*, London: Sage.

Mouzelis, Nicos (1967) *Organization and Bureaucracy*, London: Routledge and Kegan Paul.

Mouzelis, Nicos (1975) 'Introduction to the 1975 Edition' of Mouzelis (1967) *Organization and Bureaucracy*, London: Routledge and Kegan Paul.

Mouzelis, Nicos (1995) *Sociological Theory: What Went Wrong?* London and New York: Routledge.

Nicholson, Linda (ed.) (1990) *Feminism/Postmodernism*, New York and London: Routledge.

Nisbet, Robert (1967) *The Sociological Tradition*, London: Heinemann.

Nisbet, Robert (1974) *The Sociology of Emile Durkheim*, New York: Oxford University Press.

O'Conner, James (1973) *The Fiscal Crisis of the State*, New York: St Martin's.

Offe, Claus (1985) *Disorganised Capitalism*, Cambridge: Polity Press.

Offe, Claus (1996) *Modernity and the State*, Cambridge: Polity Press.

Offe, Claus and Ronge, Volkner (1975) 'Theses on the Theory of the State', *New German Critique*, 6 Fall: 137–148.

Parsons, Talcott [1937] (1968) *The Structure of Social Action*, New York: Free Press.

Parsons, Talcott (1951) *The Social System*, New York: Free Press.

Parsons, Talcott (1956) 'Suggestions for a Sociological Approach to the Theory of Organizations', *Administrative Science Quarterly*, 1: 67–85.

Parsons, Talcott (1960) *Structure and Process in Modern Societies*, Glencoe, IL: Free Press.

Parsons, Talcott [1960] (1969) 'Some Ingredients of a General Theory of Formal Organization', in Litterer, Joseph (ed.), *Organizations: Structure and Behavior*, New York: Basic Books. pp. 197–213.

Perrow, Charles (1972) *Complex Organizations: A Critical Essay*, Glencoe, IL: Free Press.

Pickering, W.S.F. and Martins, H. (eds) (1994) *Debating Durkheim*, London: Routledge.

Piore, Michael and Sabel, Charles (1984) *The Second Industrial Divide: Possibilities for Prosperity*, New York: Basic Books.

Poster, Mark (ed.) (1988) *Jean Baudrillard: Selected Writings*, Stanford, CA: Stanford University Press.

Poulantzas, Nicos (1973) *Political Power and Social Classes*, London: New Left Books.

Powell, W.W. and DiMaggio, P.G. (eds) (1991) *The New Institutionalism in Organizational Analysis*, Chicago: University of Chicago Press.

Power, M. (1990) 'Modernism, Postmodernism and Organization', in Hassard, J. and Pym, D. (eds), *The Theory and Philosophy of Organizations*, London: Routledge.

Prasad, Anshuman and Prasad, Pushkala (1993) 'Reconceptualizing Alienation in Management Inquiry', *Journal of Management Inquiry*, 2(2): 169–183.

Pugh, D. (1966) 'Modern Organization Theory', *Psychological Bulletin*, 66(4): 235–251.

Reed, Michael (1985) *Redirections in Organization Analysis*, London: Tavistock.

Reed, Michael (1992) *The Sociology of Organizations: Themes, Perspectives, Prospects*, London: Harvester Wheatsheaf.

Reed, Michael and Hughes, Michael (eds) (1992) *Rethinking Organizations: New Directions in Organizational Analysis*, London: Sage.

Rex, John (1961) *Key Problems in Social Theory*, London: Routledge and Kegan Paul.

Rice, A.K. (1958) *Productivity and Social Organization*, London: Tavistock.

Ricoeur, Paul (1992) *Oneself as Another*, trans. Kathleen Blaney, Chicago: University of Chicago Press.

Rifkin, Jeremy (1996) *The End of Work*, New York: Putnam.

Rifkin, Jeremy (2000) *The Age of Access*, New York: Tarcher/Putnam.

Ritzer, George (1992) *Classical Sociological Theory*, New York: McGraw-Hill.

Robbins, Stephen and Barnwell, Neil (1998) *Organisation Theory*, New Jersey: Prentice Hall.

Roethlisberger, Fritz J. and Dickson, William J. (1939) *Management and the Worker*, Cambridge, MA: Harvard University Press.

Rogers, Carl (1961) *On Becoming a Person*, Boston: Houghton Mifflin.

Roof, Wade Clark (1993) *A Generation of Seekers*, San Francisco: Harper Collins.

Rossi, Alice (1974) *The Feminist Papers: From Adams to de Beauvoir*, New York: Bantam.

Rouleau, Linda and Clegg, Stewart (1992) 'Postmodernism and Postmodernity in Organization Analysis', *Journal of Change Management*, 5(1): 8–25.

Rowlinson, Michael (1997) *Organizations and Institutions*, London: Macmillan.

Runciman, W.G. (ed.) (1989) *Weber: Selections in Translations*, trans. Eric Matthews, Cambridge: Cambridge University Press.

Sabine, George H. (1961) *A History of Political Theory*, 3rd edn, London: George C. Harrap.

Salaman, Graeme (1979) *Work Organizations, Resistance and Control*, London: Longman.

Salaman, Graeme (1981) *Class and the Corporation*, London: Fontana.

Scherer, Andreas (1998) 'Pluralism and Incommensurability in Strategic Management and Organization Theory: A Problem in Search of a Solution', *Organization*, 5: 147–168.

Schutz, Alfred [1932] (1967) *The Phenomenology of the Social World*, Evanston, IL: Northwestern University Press.

Schwartz, Howard S. (1990) *Narcissistic Processes and Corporate Decay*, New York: New York University Press.

Scott, William G. (1963) 'Organization Theory: An Overview and an Appraisal', in Litterer, Joseph (ed.), *Organizations: Structure and Behavior*, New York: Wiley.

Selznick, Philip [1948] (1969) 'Foundations of the Theory of Organization', in Litterer, Joseph (ed.), *Organizations: Structure and Behavior*, New York: Wiley.

Selznick Philip (1949) *TVA and the Grassroots*, Berkeley, CA: University of California Press.

Senge, Peter (1990) *The Fifth Discipline: The Art and Practice of the Learning Organization*, New York: Random House.

Sewell, G. and Wilkinson, B. (1992) 'Someone to Watch Over Me: Surveillance, Discipline and the Just-in-time Labour Process', *Sociology*, 26(2): 271–298.

Silverman, David (1970) *The Theory of Organizations: A Sociological Framework*, London: Heinemann.

Simmel, Georg [1903] (1971) 'The Metropolis and Mental Life', in *Georg Simmel on Individuality and Social Forms*, Levine, Donald N. (ed.) Chicago: University of Chicago Press.

Simon, Herbert [1945] (1976) *Administrative Behavior*, New York: Macmillan.

Sinclair, A. (1992) 'The Tyranny of a Team Ideology', *Organization Studies*, 13(4): 611–626.

Smart, Barry (1983) *Foucault, Marxism and Critique*, London: Routledge and Kegan Paul.

Smart, Barry (1993) *Postmodernity*, London and New York: Routledge.

Smart, Barry (1999) *Facing Modernity: Ambivalence, Reflexivity and Morality,* London: Sage.

Smircich, Linda (1983) 'Concepts of Culture and Organizational Analysis', *Administrative Science Quarterly*, 28: 339–358.

Smith, Dorothy (1990) *The Conceptual Practices of Power: A Feminist Sociology of Knowledge*, Boston: Northeastern University Press.

Spencer, Herbert [1850] (1972) *On Social Evolution*, Chicago IL: University of Chicago Press.

Spender, Dale (1982) *Women of Ideas – And What Men Have Done to Them*, London: Routledge and Kegan Paul.

Spivak, Gayatri Chakravorty (1990) *The Post-Colonial Critic: Interviews, Strategies, Dialogues*, ed. Sarah Harasym, London: Routledge.

Sturrock, John (ed.) (1979) *Structuralism and Since: From Lévi-Strauss to Derrida*, Oxford: Oxford University Press.

Sudnow, D. (1965) 'Normal Crimes: Sociological Features of the Penal Code in a Public Defenders Office', *Social Problems*, 12(3): 255–276.

Taylor, Charles (1989) *Sources of the Self: The Making of the Modern Identity*, Cambridge, MA: Harvard University Press.

Taylor, F.W. [1911] (1967) *The Principles of Scientific Management*, New York: W.W. Norton.

Thompson, Kenneth (1990) 'Secularization and Sacralization', in Alexander, J. and Sztompka, P. (eds), *Rethinking Progress: Movements, Forces, and Ideas at the End of the 20th Century*, Boston: Unwin Hyman.

Thompson, E.P. (1993) *Witness against the Beats*, Cambridge: Cambridge University Press.

Thompson, Paul (1983) *The Nature of Work: An Introduction to Debates on the Labour Process*, Basingstoke: Macmillan.

Toms, Justine Wills and Toms, Michael (1998) *True Work: The Sacred Dimensions of Earning a Living*, New York: Bell Tower.

Toulmin, Stephen (1972) *Human Understanding*, Oxford: Clarendon Press.

Toulmin, Stephen (1990) *Cosmopolis: The Hidden Agenda of Modernity*, Chicago: University of Chicago Press.

Touraine, Alain (1988) *Return of the Actor: Social Theory in Postindustrial Society*, Minneapolis: University of Minnesota Press.

Touraine, Alain (1995) *Critique of Modernity*, trans. David Macey, Oxford: Blackwell.

Touraine, Alain (1996) 'A Sociology of the Subject', in *Alain Touraine*, Clark, Jon and Diani, Marco (eds), London: Falmer Press.

Trist, E.L., Higgin, G.W., Murray, H. and Pollock, A.B. (1963) *Organizational Choice*, London: Tavistock.

Trotsky, Leon (1937) *The Revolution Betrayed*, New York: Doubleday.

Tucker, Robert (ed.) (1978) *The Marx-Engels Reader*, New York: W.W. Norton.

Waldo, Dwight (1948) *The Administrative State*, New York: Roland.

Wallerstein, Immanuel (1998) *Utopistics, or Historical Choices of the Twenty-first Century*, New York: New Press.

Warner, W.L. and Low, J.O. (1947) *The Social System of the Modern Factory*, New Haven, CT: Yale University Press.

Weber, Max [1904–05] (1958) *The Protestant Ethic and the Spirit of Capitalism*, New York: Charles Scribner.

Weber, Max [1915] (1946) 'Religious Rejections of the World and Their Directions', in Gerth, Hans and Mills, C. Wright (eds), *From Max Weber: Essays in Sociology*, New York: Oxford University Press.

Weber, Max [1918] (1989) 'Science as a Vocation', in Lassman, Peter and Velody, Irving (eds), *Max Weber's Science as a Vocation*, London: Unwin Hyman.

Weber, Max [1919] (1946) 'Politics as a Vocation', in Gerth, Hans and Mills, C. Wright (eds), *From Max Weber: Essays in Sociology*, New York: Oxford University Press.

Weber, Max [1922] (1946) 'Bureaucracy', in Gerth, Hans and Mills, C. Wright (eds), *From Max Weber: Essays in Sociology*, New York: Oxford University Press.

Weber, Max [1922] (1978) *Economy and Society*, ed. Guenther Roth and Claus Wittich, Berkeley, CA: University of California Press.

Weber, Max [1922] (1989) *Weber: Selections in Translations*, ed. W.G. Runciman, trans. Eric Matthews, New York: Cambridge University Press.

Weick, Karl (1995) *Sensemaking in Organizations*, Thousand Oaks, CA: Sage.

Wexler, Philip (1983) *Critical Social Psychology*, London: Routledge and Kegan Paul.

Wexler, Philip (1987) *Social Analysis of Education: After the New Sociology*, New York: Routledge.

Wexler, Philip (1996a) 'Alienation, New Age Sociology and the Jewish Way', in Geyer, Felix (ed.), *Alienation, Ethnicity and Postmodernism*, London: Greenwood.

Wexler, Philip (1996b) *Holy Sparks: Social Theory, Education and Religion*, New York: St Martin's Press.

Whyte, W.F. (ed.) (1946) *Industry and Society*, New York: McGraw Hill.

Whyte, W.F. (1951) *Patterns of Industrial Peace*, New York: Harper.

Whyte, William, H. (1956) *The Organization Man*, New York: Doubleday.

Willmott, Hugh (1993a) 'Breaking the Paradigm Mentality', *Organization Studies*, 14(5): 681–719.

Willmott, Hugh (1993b) 'Bringing Agency back in Organizational Analysis', in Hassard, John and Parker, Martin (eds), *Postmodernism and Organizations*, London: Sage.

Wood, Stephen (1982) *The Degradation of Work?* London: Hutchinson.

Wright, Barbara Drygulski (ed.) (1987) *Women, Work and Technology*, Michigan: University of Michigan Press.

Wuthnow, Robert (1998) *After Heaven: Spirituality in America since the 1950s*, Berkeley, CA: University of California Press.

Zeitlin, Irving (1973) *Rethinking Sociology: A Critique of Contemporary Theory*, Englewood Cliffs, NJ: Prentice-Hall.

Zeitlin, Irving M [1968] (1990) *Ideology and the Development of Sociological Theory*, Englewood Cliffs, NJ: Prentice-Hall.

Zey-Ferrell, M. and Aikin, Michael (eds) (1981) *Complex Organizations: Critical Perspectives*, Glenview, IL: Free Press.

Zohar, Danah (1990) *The Quantum Self*, New York: William Morrow.

Index